Aimé Césaire is the best known poet in the French Caribbean. His poetry and drama have established his formidable reputation as the leading francophone poet and elder statesman of the twentieth century. In this study Gregson Davis examines the evolution of Césaire's poetic career and his involvement with many of the most seminal political and aesthetic movements of the twentieth century. Davis relates Césaire's extraordinary dual career as writer and elected politician to the recurrent themes in his writings. As one of the most profound critics of colonialism, Césaire, the acknowledged inventor of the famous term "négritude," has been a hugely influential figure in shaping the contemporary discourse on the postcolonial predicament. Gregson Davis's account of Césaire's intellectual growth is grounded in a careful reading of the poetry, prose and drama that illustrates the full range and depth of his literary achievement.

CAMBRIDGE STUDIES IN AFRICAN AND
CARIBBEAN LITERATURE

AIME CESAIRE

CAMBRIDGE STUDIES IN AFRICAN AND CARIBBEAN LITERATURE

Series editor: Professor Abiola Irele, Ohio State University

Each volume in this unique series of critical studies offers a comprehensive and in-depth account of the whole *œuvre* of one individual writer from Africa or the Caribbean, in such a way that the book may be considered a complete coverage of the writer's expression up to the point the study is undertaken. Attention is devoted primarily to the works themselves – their significant themes, governing ideas and formal procedures; biographical and other background information is thus employed secondarily, to illuminate these aspects of the writer's work where necessary.

The emergence in the twentieth century of black literature in the United States, the Caribbean and Africa as a distinct corpus of imaginative work represents one of the most notable developments in world literature in modern times. This series has been established to meet the needs of this growing area of study. It is hoped that it will not only contribute to a wider understanding of the humanistic significance of modern literature from Africa and the Caribbean through the scholarly presentation of the work of major writers, but also offer a wider framework for the ongoing debates about the problems of interpretation within the disciplines concerned.

Already published

Chinua Achebe, by C. L. Innes
Nadine Gordimer, by Dominic Head
Edouard Glissant, by J. Michael Dash
V. S. Naipaul, by Fawzia Mustafa

AIME CESAIRE

GREGSON DAVIS

Andrew W. Mellon Distinguished Professor of Humanities
Duke University

CAMBRIDGE
UNIVERSITY PRESS

PUBLISHED BY THE PRESS SYNDICATE OF THE UNIVERSITY OF CAMBRIDGE
The Pitt Building, Trumpington Street, Cambridge CB2 1RP, United Kingdom

CAMBRIDGE UNIVERSITY PRESS
The Edinburgh Building, Cambridge CB2 2RU, United Kingdom
40 West 20th Street, New York, NY 10011–4211, USA
10 Stamford Road, Oakleigh, Melbourne 3166, Australia

First published 1997

Printed in the United Kingdom at the University Press, Cambridge

Typeset in Baskerville No. 2 11/12½ pt

*A catalogue record for this book is available from
the British Library*

Library of Congress cataloguing in publication data

Davis, Gregson.
Aimé Césaire / Gregson Davis.
p.   cm.
Includes bibliographical references and index.
ISBN 0 521 39072 9 (hardback)
1. Césaire, Aimé – Criticism and interpretation. 1. Title.
PQ3949.C44Z65   1997   96–51158 CIP
841 – dc21

ISBN 0 521 39072 9 hardback

WD

Contents

Preface   *page* ix
Acknowledgements   xii
Chronology   xiii

Introduction   1

1   From island to metropolis: the making of a poet   4

2   Exploring racial selves: "Journal of a Homecoming"   20

3   Inventing a lyric voice: the forging of "Miracle
    Weapons"   62

4   Lyric registers: from "Sun Cut Throat" to "Cadaster"   92

5   The turn to poetic drama   126

6   The return to lyric: "me, laminaria..."   163

Epilogue   178

Notes   185
Bibliography   194
Index   207

Preface

In this account of Aimé Césaire's dual career as verbal artist and statesman I have pursued a flexible chronological scheme. The order of publication of his major literary works (chiefly collections of poems and plays) has determined the sequence, no less than the rubrics, of the chapters. I have sought to present and describe these key compositions in their historical and biographical context. The term "biographical," however, requires stringent qualification: my focus is predominantly on the life of the mind – the intellectual and aesthetic evolution of the poet as I attempt to sketch it.[1] Literary texts are therefore very much in the foreground of my account, with the political and socio-cultural extensions providing a backdrop for the discussion of the art and ideology. As ultimate justification for this dominant focus, I can do no better than to quote Césaire's own words on the subject of a putative "biography":

> I am in the habit of saying that I have no biography. And in truth, in reading my poems, the reader will know about me all that is worth knowing, and certainly more than I know myself.[2]

In view of my concentration on the literary *œuvre* I have relied on frequent citation of the original French texts, accompanied, except in the case of prose excerpts, by English renditions. At stake in this bilingual mode of presentation is a principle I regard as paramount in any serious attempt to characterize the accomplishment and growth of a verbal artist: the obligation to make his actual words accessible to the reader. Citation, however, whether in bilingual format or solely in English translation, is by definition selective and reductive;

and in the case of a lyric poet whose language is by many
regarded as relatively obscure, I have considered it *de rigueur*
to let the reader see clearly how I have arrived at my own
interpretations of individual passages. In the case of the early
work that all critics agree is seminal to Césaire's development
as a writer and thinker–*Cahier d'un retour au pays natal* ("Journal
of a Homecoming") – I have deemed it crucial to devote an
entire chapter to a summary explication of the poem's central
themes. The narrative I have constructed of the poet's subsequent evolution (chapters 2–7) aims to be transparent both
in its approach to exegesis and in its grounds for the selection
of representative texts from the entire range of Césaire's
literary production.

Wherever pertinent, I have drawn extensively on the copious
interviews that Césaire has granted throughout his career to
scholars, critics and journalists. This fertile genre of publication has proven to be invaluable in relating fundamental
ideas expressed in the poetry to the author's evolving political
ideology, though even here it is important to be aware that
such interviews afford the writer, no less than the critic, a
privileged opportunity to legitimate, if not control, certain
lines of interpretation.

My debt to the vast and rapidly growing international community of scholars who have contributed to the understanding
of Césaire's work is, I hope, manifest and duly acknowledged in
the notes as well as in the bibliography. References to both
primary and secondary literature in the notes are given in the
summary form: author and year of publication (e.g. Delas
[1991]); more complete information on each item is located
in the bibliography on pages 194–206 under the appropriate
section. In addition, I have used the following abbreviations for
a few standard works and frequently cited journals:

E-S   Clayton Eshleman and Annette Smith, trans., *Aimé
        Césaire: The Collected Poetry* (Berkeley/Los Angeles/
        London: 1983).
Hale   Thomas Hale, *Les Ecrits d'Aimé Césaire: bibliographie
        commentée* (Montreal: 1978).[3]

M-C   Aimé Césaire, *La Poésie*, ed. Daniel Maximin and Gilles Carpentier, (Paris: 1994).

PA   *Présence Africaine*

T-H   Roger Toumson and Simonne Henry-Valmore, *Aimé Césaire: le nègre inconsolé* (Paris/Fort-de-France: 1993).

All references to the poetry are to the 1994 edition by Maximin and Carpentier cited above. I have also employed the following abbreviations for the French titles of some of Césaire's works:

Cahier   *Cahier d'un retour au pays natal*
Chiens   *Et les chiens se taisaient* (Paris 1956)
Christophe   *La Tragédie du roi Christophe* (2nd rev. edn. Paris 1970)
Saison   *Une Saison au Congo* (2nd edn. Paris 1967)

Acknowledgements

I am grateful to Abiola Irele, in the first instance, for having entrusted me with the task of contributing this study to the series of which he is editor-in-chief. In addition, his thorough scrutiny of the typescript led to significant improvements in the final product. Such infelicities that may remain are, of course, my unique responsibility.

I owe thanks to Stanford University Press for kind permission to quote, in whole and in part, from my previously published English versions of the following poems: "Incantation," "Blank to Fill in on the Visa of Pollen," "Raining Blues," Commonplace," "Word," "Spirals," "Fetters," "In Memoriam: Louis Delgrès," "Non-Vicious Circle." English versions of these poems are reprinted, with a few slight modifications, from *Non-Vicious Circle: Twenty Poems of Aimé Césaire*, translated, with an introduction and commentary by Gregson Davis, with the permission of the publishers, Stanford University Press, © 1984 by the Board of Trustees of the Leland Stanford Junior University. In a few places I have also revisited points of interpretation that I first broached in the annotations to that volume. [Permission to cite from the French text of Césaire's poems and plays has been granted by Editions du Seuil and by Présence Africaine.]

I would like to offer my special thanks to Jacqueline Leiner for her kindness in furnishing the photograph of Césaire that adorns the dust-jacket. Her long lasting engagement in Césaire scholarship has been exemplary for all scholars working in this subfield of francophone studies.

Chronology

1913   Aimé Césaire born on June 26th at Basse Pointe, Martinique, in the French Caribbean. Second of six children of Fernand and Eléonore Césaire.

1924   Enters Lycée Schoelcher in Fort-de-France, capital of Martinique.

1931   Leaves Martinique with scholarship for Paris to attend Lycée Louis-le-Grand. Meets Senegalese student, Léopold Senghor, of whom he becomes a close friend.

1932   The radical journal *Légitime Défense* is published in Paris.

1934   Co-founds (along with Senghor, Léon Damas and others) the student journal *Etudiant Noir*. Michel Leiris, ethnologist and writer, publishes *L'Afrique fantôme* (an account of an ethnological expedition to Africa).

1935   Enters Ecole Normale Supérieure (Rue d'Ulm).

1936   Spends summer vacation in Martinique. Begins work on *Cahier*. Leo Frobenius' *Histoire de la civilisation africaine* is published in France.

1937   Marries Suzanne Roussi, Martinican student. Writes a research paper (*mémoire*) on "Le thème du Sud dans la poésie négro-américaine des États-Unis." Léon Damas publishes lyric volume *Pigments*.

1938   Birth of the Césaires' first child, Jacques.

1939   First version of *Cahier* appears in the periodical *Volontés*. Césaire family leaves Paris for Martinique.

Outbreak of Second World War during their journey home.

1940   Teaches, as does Suzanne Césaire, at Lycée Schoelcher. Co-founds local periodical *Tropiques* (with Suzanne Césaire, Aristide Maugée, René Menil and others). Surrealist poet André Breton visits Martinique.

1942   Limited edition of *Cahier* in Spanish appears in Havana, Cuba, with illustrations by Wifredo Lam and introduction by surrealist poet, Benjamin Péret.

1944   New York edition of *Cahier* (with preface by André Breton). *Les Temps Modernes* founded in Paris (founders include Michel Leiris and Jean-Paul Sartre).

1945   Visits Haiti on lecture tour. Elected mayor of Fort-de-France and deputy in the Constituent Assembly on the French Communist Party ticket.

1946   Lyric collection *Les Armes miraculeuses* is published. Co-sponsors historic bill to convert Martinique and Guadeloupe into "Overseas Departments" ("Départements d'Outre-Mer"). Writes tribute to painter Wifredo Lam.

1947   Participates, along with Senghor, Damas and others, in the founding of the journal *Présence Africaine*, brainchild of the Senegalese Alioune Diop. Editions of *Cahier* appear in both New York and Paris (with preface by André Breton).

1948   Publishes the lyric collection *Soleil cou coupé*. Senghor's *Anthologie de la nouvelle poésie nègre et malgache de langue française* is published with laudatory preface ("Orphée noir") by Jean-Paul Sartre.

1950   The volume of verse *Corps perdu* is published in a deluxe, limited edition, with illustrations by Pablo Picasso. First version of the polemical essay *Discours sur le colonialisme*.

1952   Martinican writer and activist Frantz Fanon publishes *Peau noire, masques blancs*.

1954   Defeat of French forces by Vietnamese at Dien-Bien-Phu. End of the French war in Indochina.

1955   Bandung Conference convenes in Bandung, Indonesia. Along with Jean-Paul Sartre, François Mauriac and others, Césaire joins a committee of French intellectuals opposed to the Algerian war.

1956   Resigns from the French Communist Party. *Lettre à Maurice Thorez* appears in print. First "International Congress of Negro Writers and Artists" held in Paris. Composes the essays "La mort des colonies" and "Culture et colonisation." *Chiens* re-arranged for theater.

1958   Founds "Parti Progressiste Martiniquais" in Fort-de-France. Guinea (led by Sekou Touré) becomes first independent francophone African nation. André Malraux visits Martinique as a diplomatic envoy of Charles de Gaulle.

1959   Second "Congress of Negro Writers and Artists" held in Rome. Césaire delivers talk "L'homme de culture et ses responsabilités."

1960   Publishes historical monograph *Toussaint L'Ouverture: La Révolution Française et le problème colonial*. The volume of poems *Ferrements* appears; is awarded Prix René Laporte. Léopold Senghor becomes Senegalese head of state. *Les Damnés de la terre* by Frantz Fanon is published.

1961   Publication of poetic collection *Cadastre*. Assassination of visionary Congolese leader Patrice Lumumba.

1963   *La Tragédie du roi Christophe*, a play on the rule of the postrevolutionary Haitian monarch, is published.

1964   *Christophe* is performed in various European capitals. Charles de Gaulle visits the French Antilles.

1966   Appearance of *Une Saison au Congo*, a drama on the career of Patrice Lumumba. Attends first "Festival Mondial des Arts Nègres" held in Dakar, Senegal, where *Christophe* is performed. Death of Suzanne Césaire.

1968   Publishes first version of *Une Tempête*, a radical
        adaptation of Shakespeare's play *The Tempest*.
1972   Visits Université Laval (Quebec), where he delivers
        lectures and holds seminars.
1974   Death of the novelist Miguel Angel Asturias.
1976   Publication of *Œuvres complètes* in three volumes in
        Fort-de-France. Senghor visits Martinique.
1978   Death of Léon Damas.
1981   Martinican poet Edouard Glissant publishes *Le
        Discours antillais*.
1982   Publishes the lyric collection *moi, laminaire . . .*
        Awarded the "Grand Prix National de la Poésie."
        Under the regime of Socialist president François
        Mitterrand, a law of "decentralization" ("Loi
        Deferre") is passed, creating new "conseils
        régionaux" ("regional councils") in the various
        overseas departments.
1983   Assumes presidency of the local "conseil régional."
1988   François Mitterrand elected President for a second
        term.
1990   Death of Michel Leiris.
1991   *Christophe* is revived in Paris in a performance by the
        august Comédie-Française.
1993   Césaire retires from electoral politics.
1994   Publication in Paris (Editions du Seuil) of *Aimé
        Césaire, La Poésie*.

Introduction

Aimé Césaire is a major contemporary poet from the French
Antilles who is renowned throughout the francophone world.
Although he is perhaps best known to the English-speaking
public for his early book-length poetic masterpiece *Cahier d'un
retour au pays natal* ("Journal of a Homecoming"), he is the
author of seven volumes of lyric verse and four works for
the theater that have brought him international acclaim.
Three of his plays, which he has himself described as forming a
"triptych," were composed in the 1960s and explore problems
of political independence and cultural decolonization in major
areas of the black world (Africa, the Caribbean and North
America).

Césaire has been an eloquent and robust critic of colonialism throughout his career, and some of his polemical prose
essays on the subject, such as his *Discours sur le colonialisme*
(*Discourse on Colonialism*), are veritable classics of the genre. A
vivid idea of his stature in the French literary world may be
gleaned from a cursory glance at some of the formal and
informal honors he has garnered over the decades. These
include not only prestigious French literary prizes, such as the
Grand Prix National for poetry, but also the rare distinction of
having special editions of his poems illustrated by artists of the
caliber of Pablo Picasso and Wifredo Lam. In 1962, when he had
not yet attained the age of fifty, a volume in the series Poètes
d'Aujourd'hui was devoted to him – a step tantamount to his
canonization as a major modernist voice.

Césaire's well-deserved reputation in France and in what
used to be referred to commonly as the Third World is by no

means confined to his poetic œuvre: he has also pursued a parallel and highly visible career as a statesman. For close to half a century (from 1946 to 1993) he has been simultaneously engaged in electoral politics with conspicuous success. He has been consistently re-elected as deputy in the French parliament and mayor of Fort-de-France, the capital of Martinique. A direct result of his success in public office is that he has been in a position to exert considerable influence on the political evolution of the French Caribbean islands. Perhaps his most famous contribution in this sphere is his co-sponsorhip of the law that created "departmental" status for the former colonies of Martinique and Guadeloupe soon after the Second World War.

His substantive role as an intellectual force – a "sower of ideas," as he has recently characterized it – has been no less significant.[1] When he was active as a lycée teacher in Martinique in the immediate postwar years, he was an inspiring presence for a gifted younger generation that included the writer and activist Frantz Fanon, and the poet Edouard Glissant. With regard to his contributions to shaping a postcolonial ideology, his name is indelibly associated with the seminal concept of "négritude" – a word that he is reputed to have coined, and which was to become a rallying-point for several generations of black francophone youth both in Africa and in the Caribbean in their struggle to construct a positive racial identity.

The task of charting the course of this extraordinary dual career has been especially challenging. In my effort to describe, and at the same time to distill, Césaire's unique intellectual achievement, I have focussed predominantly on the literary artist, while seeking to place his creative writings within a broader political and historical context. In the nature of the enterprise, I have been obliged to be radically selective, since it would be impossible to offer close, integral readings of lyric poems and dramatic works in a general study of this kind. My sample of illustrative texts is not, however, arbitrary: it aims at being representative of Césaire's paramount preoccupations and recurrent themes. With the exception of *Cahier*, which, because of its centrality to his work as a whole, requires more extensive exegesis, I have generally striven to be succinct without being dogmatic.

In presenting my selections for discussion I have scrupulously juxtaposed the original French text to my translations. The latter are meant to be faithful to what I take to be the basic underlying patterns of ideas conveyed in the author's notoriously dense verses. Though I have endeavored to compose my translations in a style worthy of the original, I remain poignantly aware of the astute definition of poetry as "that which is lost in translation." With regard to Césaire's discursive prose, I have generally omitted the French text, except in the rare cases where I have judged that the quoted passage approximates the opaque, symbolic language of the lyric œuvre. In my discussions accompanying the selections, I have attempted to steer a middle course between the extremes of oversimplification, on the one hand, and "overinterpretation," on the other.

The poet of négritude has recently made the momentous decision to retire gracefully from the political arena and "pass the torch" on to a younger generation. His literary output, however, cannot be presumed to have come to a close. In the interim, his withdrawal from electoral politics in 1993 at the advanced age of 80 has furnished literary critics an ideal vantage-point from which to fashion a retrospective assessment of his signal achievements as poet, playwright, and above all "sower of ideas."

CHAPTER I

From island to metropolis: the making of a poet

I adore volcanoes

Aimé Césaire

Content conditions form

Aimé Césaire

The poet Aimé Césaire was born in 1913 in the French Caribbean island of Martinique. Like many ambitious post-emancipation blacks in the archipelago during the early decades of the twentieth century, his parents, Fernand and Eléonore, were passionately devoted to instilling in their children a deep respect for education, and they made extra-ordinary sacrifices to ensure that all six of their children took full advantage of the opportunities available on the island and in the metropolis. These sacrifices on the altar of education were by no means insignificant, considering the social stric-tures on members of an ex-slave population in a plantation economy. When, for instance, the eleven-year-old Aimé, who was already an intense, even voracious, reader, won a coveted scholarship to secondary school (*lycée*) in Fort-de-France, the family moved from Basse Pointe – the poet's birthplace – to the capital in order to facilitate the studies of their gifted offspring.

Many anecdotes relating to the poet's infancy and early childhood in Basse Pointe emphasize the intense parental focus on schooling and, in particular, on the mastery of the French language, which, of course, was one of the pillars of the entire colonial system and a virtual guarantee of upward mobility. Not content with the pace and rigor of the primary

4

school curriculum in Basse Pointe, Césaire's father, Fernand, conducted supplementary classes at home, awakening his children every day at 6 a.m. to give them instruction until 7:45. Obsessed with the goal of perfecting their French, he inculcated in them, by means of a highly disciplined regime, an admiration for the literary models of the traditional canon, such as Victor Hugo and Voltaire.[1] This early bonding that the children established with the French language, and the aura of mystique surrounding its acquisition in a colonial society, need to be taken into account in any serious discussion of Césaire's ingrained preference for French, in opposition to Martinican creole, as his prime medium of literary expression.

Unwavering scholastic ambition did not begin with Césaire's generation as far as the family history is concerned. The tradition of intellectual excellence within the clan goes back at least as far as his paternal grandfather, also named Fernand, who is credited with having been the first Martinican to be trained at a metropolitan *école normale* (St. Cloud); on his return to his native town of St. Pierre, then the vibrant capital of the island colony, he occupied the respected post of schoolteacher and principal (*directeur*). Césaire's father, Fernand Elphège, also received training as a schoolteacher, though eventually he shifted to a better-paying employment as manager (*économe*) of a sugar estate – a position he held at the time of the birth of his second and much "beloved" son, Aimé (the name fully presaging the emerging reality).

The female ancestors in the lineage were no less crucial in determining the intellectual orientation of the Césaire children. We hear especially of a paternal grandmother, Eugénie Macni (known affectionately within the family circle as "Mama Nini"), who, besides initiating the rudimentary instruction of her grandchildren, seems to have exerted a formidable moral authority as well. In view of the poet's later efforts to recuperate an African cultural matrix, it is highly significant that he came to regard "Mama Nini" as "a woman who was visibly African in origin [. . .] She had a phenotype that was African in a very distinct and precise way."[2] Her quasi-mythic status in the eyes of Aimé and his siblings may have played a subliminal role in shaping the idealized conception of Africa that lies behind Césaire's version of négritude. Without digressing into facile psychobiography, we may not be far off the mark if we seek to explain some of the poet's later representations of Africa as a numinous female with reference to his childhood veneration of this powerful grandmother.[3]

In view of a transmitted family ethos centered on educational achievement, Césaire's precocious success as a pupil appears almost overdetermined. Predictably he won a string of scholarships to secondary schools, the first enabling him to attend the Lycée Schoelcher in the capital, Fort-de-France. On the strength of his superlative performance on attaining the baccalaureate certificate, he was awarded a coveted scholarship to continue the next phase of his schooling in Paris at the Lycée Louis-le-Grand (1931). An enthusiastic student, who by all accounts also possessed uncommon discipline, he excelled under the superb teaching faculty of the Lycée, and proceeded in due course to gain entrance to the prestigious Ecole Normale Supérieure in the Rue d'Ulm, where he was enrolled until his return to his native island on the eve of the Second World War (1935–1939).

The French colonial system of secondary education in the prewar years was distinctly elitist, though based, in principle at least, on strictly academic performance. Advancement into and through the system depended at each stage on arduous competitive examinations. As a consequence of this rigorously centralized regime (which, incidentally, had its parallels in the anglophone Caribbean), the student population at the Ecole Normale consisted of the intellectual cream of the francophone world (as defined, of course, by performance on the notoriously difficult examinations). Césaire's eight-year Paris sojourn, then, brought him into daily contact, on an intellectually equal basis, with members of the privileged classes of the French intelligentsia, as well as those of humble origins from French colonies as far apart as West Africa and French Guyana. As it transpired, his spiritual and ideological horizons were expanded as much, if not more, by his fertile interaction with other francophone black students as from his exposure to some of the future intellectual leaders of France. Of the former group, the most pivotal association, in terms of the adolescent Martinican's embryonic quest for cultural identity, was his close bond of friendship with the Senegalese student Léopold Sédar Senghor – a bond that was to endure in undiminished strength through the years, despite geographical separation.

It would be misleading and reductive to depict the adolescent Césaire in his Paris lycée years as an uncomplicated model student, intent on the passive absorption of the European intellectual tradition. To be sure, he was rapidly assimilating – in the systematic way for which the French academy is famous – the various interlocking canons (philosophic, philological and literary) that structured the secondary school curriculum. At the same time, however, he was also experiencing the incipient cultural alienation that afflicted other Third World students thrown together on the metropolitan scene in the latter half of the prewar decade. Students of color, in particular, sooner or later found themselves drawn, if only in self-defense, into a radically critical stance towards European civilization and its arrogant claims to superiority. Thus cultural assimilation ironically engendered, in proportion to its very thoroughness, a form of resistance on the part of its youthful recipients that can usefully be labeled "counter-assimilationist." Since the stigmatization, or even erasure, of non-Western cultural traditions was a common subtext of the promotion of the canon both inside and outside the confines of the lycée, many students of African origin sought vigorously to repossess a degraded identity – the more so because their skin color marked them off as "other" in a manner both irreducible and pronounced.

For Aimé Césaire the relationship he struck up with Senghor was nothing short of a revelation as far as his received image of Africa and Africans was concerned, for in the colonial Martinique of his childhood, as in the rest of the Antilles, the African continent and its cultures were either virtually ignored or else branded with the mark of "primitive." The colonizing country arrogated to itself a "civilizing mission" ("mission civilisatrice"), while Africa was projected as the very paradigm

of the non-civilized world. In the face of such egregious
European ethnocentrism there emerged a solidarity among
francophone students of diverse cultural backgrounds that
became the point of departure for a robust self-education
about the extent and nature of the African heritage. In
regard to their cultural identity as "French" they inevitably
experienced a tension between assimilationist and counter-
assimilationist perspectives, a tension that each individual
strove to resolve in his or her own psyche by various means. It is
plausible to speculate that whereas Césaire the artist appears
to have succeeded in surmounting this tension through the
outlet of poetry, Césaire the statesman has not been fully able
to transcend a certain deep ambivalence towards France.[4]

The counter-current to the stream of assimilation is
manifest in Césaire's later efforts to re-educate himself concerning not only the African matrix, but also its derivatives in
the black diaspora in the Antilles and the Americas. With
regard to the original matrix, it is axiomatic that "Africa" is
not an unmediated given, but rather an idea that has to be
constantly re-invented, as V. Y. Mudimbé, among others,
has recently reminded us.[5] Césaire and Senghor were to construct, each with his own peculiar inflection, an "Africa" that
was essentially mediated through the writings of European
ethnographers. The most important influence from this
quarter was the German anthropologist Leo Frobenius (1873–
1938), whose enthusiastic account of the evolution of African
cultures was published in French translation under the title
Histoire de la civilisation africaine in 1936, during Césaire's second
year as a *normalien*.[6] Frobenius' reception among researchers
in the discipline of anthropology was, from the start, deeply
sceptical of his sweeping generalizations surrounding such
vague concepts as *Kultur* (culture). Today his theories are
prone to strike both specialists and non-specialists alike as
fanciful and so mystical as to be non-falsifiable. He is perhaps
best known for a notion he entertained about cultural essence
that he called the *paideuma*.[7] For the small group of adolescents
studying together in the metropolis, however, Leo Frobenius'
glowing appraisal of past black civilizations commanded

attention and admiration. Senghor, who went on to become the Senegalese head of state and a renowned man of letters, was later to recall that he and his close friend, Aimé Césaire, read and re-read the *Histoire* so frequently that they came to know whole sections of the text by heart. The impact of the German ethnologist on Césaire's ideas at a formative stage in his career may be seen in certain "purple" passages in *Cahier*, especially the oft-quoted section that talks of négritude and its discontents (see ch. 2 below).[8] In the case of the black diaspora in the New World, the cultural self-assertion that took place in the North American movement known as the Harlem Renaissance was also very instrumental for Césaire in his re-configuration of his racial identity. As he himself was later to explain:[9]

I remember quite well that we read the poems of Langston Hughes and Claude McKay. I knew who McKay was because an anthology of black North American poetry had appeared in France around 1939–1940. In 1930, McKay's novel *Banjo*, which described the life of the dockers of Marseilles, came out. This was indeed one of the first works in which one saw a writer speak of blacks and give them some kind of literary dignity.

This familiarity with black American literary expression was not exclusively confined to his extra-curricular reading and intense conversation with black student friends; for Césaire succeeded in incorporating his intellectual re-orientation into his formal education. Thus in his second year at the Ecole Normale the research paper he wrote for his diploma in English (*Diplôme d'Etudes Supérieures*) bore the title "The Theme of the South in the Negro-American Poetry of the United States" ("Le Thème du Sud dans la poésie négro-américaine des Etats-Unis"). Though the text of this thesis is no longer extant, we may gain an idea of its young author's admiration for the black muse of the Harlem Renaissance from the brief article that appeared a few years later in *Tropiques*, "Introduction to Negro-American Poetry."[10]

Césaire's new-found consciousness of the culture of race is perhaps nowhere more evident than in his brief but significant role as co-editor of the ephemeral student publication

L'Etudiant Noir ("The Black Student"), which had a two-year
life (1935–1936). To grasp the ideological impact of his role, we
need to glance at certain aspects of the chequered history of
black student journals in the metropolis. Césaire's arrival in
Paris had coincided with the founding of the equally ephemeral
journal *Revue du Monde Noir* ("Review of the Black World"),
which ran for six issues in the years 1931–1932.[11] Though the
scope of subjects it addressed included, in principle, the entire
black world, as its title implies, the majority of the contributors
represented an older generation of voices from the francophone New World (French Guyana, Haiti and the French
Antillean colonies), such as the eminent Haitian Jean-Price
Mars and the Martinican Gilbert Gratiant, a former teacher
of Césaire at the Lycée Schoelcher. In a spinoff from this
conglomeration, a more militant group of younger students led
by Etienne Léro established their own separate journal in 1932
called *Légitime Défense* (roughly translatable as "Justifiable Self-
defense"), which clearly showed its debt to radical modernist
theories (chiefly Freudian psychology, Marxism and above all
surrealism).[12] Neither of these two journals (*Revue du Monde
Noire* and *Légitime Défense*) focussed sufficiently on the singu-
larity, as Césaire came to perceive it, of the black historical
experience: the former tended to dissolve that experience in
the concept of cultural amalgamation or *métissage*, the latter to
subsume race into the dominant category of class. It is against
this backdrop of strenuous intergenerational debate on the
issue of Antillean racial and cultural identity that Césaire's
gesture of re-naming the student organ *L'Etudiant Noir* (as
opposed to its previous title, *L'Etudiant Martiniquais*) acquires a
certain symbolic importance. Although the epithet *noir* did not
carry a derogatory charge comparable to that inhering in the
French *nègre* or the American "nigger," the titular shift at once
signaled the new editors' desire to embrace a more inclusive,
transnational black identity.

One of Césaire's co-editors and close associates (along with
Senghor) was the French Guyanese student Léon Damas,
whose unclouded convictions on the nature of color prejudice
and the need to reclaim a lost black heritage were soon to take

poetic shape in the volume entitled, appropriately enough, *Pigments*, which made its memorable appearance in 1937. Damas had been a fellow-student of Césaire's in the Lycée Schoelcher days, and the two had happily resumed their deep-rooted friendship in Paris. The unswerving admiration and affection that Césaire felt for Léon Damas are splendidly registered in the poem he later composed in his memory and included in the 1982 lyric collection, *moi, laminaire* . . . : "Léon G. Damas: feu sombre toujours . . . " ("Léon G. Damas: flame dark always . . . "). This short encomium comes to a sonorous conclusion in lines that recall and memorialize their warm camaraderie as well as their spiritual bonds:

soleils
oiseaux d'enfance déserteurs de son hoquet
je vois les négritudes obstinées
les fidélités fraternelles
la nostalgie fertile
la réhabilitation de délires très anciens
je vois toutes les étoiles de jadis qui renaissent et sautent
de leur site ruiniforme
je vois toute une nuit de ragtime et de blues
traversée d'un pêle-mêle de rires
et de sanglots d'enfants abandonnés

et toi

qu'est-ce que tu peux bien faire là
noctambule à n'y pas croire de cette nuit vraie
salutaire ricanement forcené des confins
à l'horizon de mon salut

frère
feu sombre toujours

(suns
birds of childhood that relinquish its hiccup
I see tenacious négritudes
fraternal loyalties
fertile nostalgia
rehabilitation of very old deliriums
I see all the stars of former eras resurrect
rebounding from their site of seeming decay

I see an entire night of ragtime and blues
traversed by laughs that tumble pell-mell
and sobs of abandoned offspring

and you

what can you do there
nightwalker not to be believed in this true night
redeeming and delirious chuckle from the fringes
to the horizon of my salvation

brother
flame dark always)

The recapitulated image of "flame dark always" that the poet bestows on his former comrade-at-arms in the battle of négritudes closely echoes the language of an earlier tribute from the collection, *Cadastre*, to an unnamed freedom fighter: "homme sombre qu'habite la volonté du feu" ("dark man in whom the will of fire lives on").[13] It is during this period of interrogation and cross-fertilization among soulmates that the concept, as well as the vocable, "négritude" first saw the light of day. We shall be dissecting this famous concept in greater detail in the course of the succeeding chapter on *Cahier*. For the present purpose it is pertinent to unpack briefly some parts of the linguistic baggage of this loaded term. Césaire himself is generally credited with having made the coinage, though he has claimed in an interview that the word was to some extent a "collective creation" of his circle of friends. Be that as it may, the form of the new lexeme marvelously embodies what we have been calling the tension between assimilationist and counter-assimilationist worldviews. On the one hand, the final syllable of *négritude* is formed by analogy with Latin-derived abstract nouns ending in the suffix *-tudo*; on the other, the syllable *nègr-*, though ultimately derived from the Latin *niger* ("black," in a value-neutral sense) had come close to acquiring, in French, the semantic cargo of a racial slur. Thus the very form of the word is redolent both of its author's classroom instruction in Greek and Latin and of his subversive resistance to the process of unexamined cultural assimilation. From this standpoint the invented word is a perfect sign for its erudite author's double loyalty to European paradigms and black consciousness.

The birth of négritude was by no means painless. On the contrary, the casting of a new psycho-social identity plunged the young Antillean into an emotional vortex that can with some accuracy be described as a "crisis."[14] The late Erik Erikson has given us the classic account of that stage in late adolescence in which the drama of self-definition is played out in relation to the choice of vocation. To quote from *Identity, Youth and Crisis*: "We can study the identity crisis also in the lives of creative individuals who could resolve it for themselves only by offering to their contemporaries a new model of resolution such as that expressed in works of art or in original deeds . . . "[15] In the individual case of Césaire, the sublime resolution – the conversion from model student to poet – was gained at acute, though transient, cost to his ego. Distracted, as we have seen, from his strictly academic goals, and afflicted moreover with emotional and physical exhaustion and deteriorating health, he predictably failed the *agrégation*. With a biographer's hindsight we can now see that this outcome (unparalleled in his brilliant scholastic career) was a symptom of an emergent obsession that was to re-channel his mental energies: the private forging of a poetic voice. Towards the end of 1939 we find a Césaire who has passed through the crucible of a severe identity crisis with the external signs of adult commitment to a *métier* and fresh ambitions. In the personal sphere, his recent marriage to Suzanne Roussi, a younger, intellectually gifted student also from Martinique, had brought him a measure of emotional stability and fatherhood as well (his first child, Jacques, was born in 1938). After a prolonged gestation, the first edition of his famous poem *Cahier d'un retour au pays natal* saw the light of day in the pages of the Paris periodical *Volontés* (August 1939). Very soon thereafter, as the storm-clouds of war gathered on the horizon, Aimé Césaire and his family embarked on the vessel *La Bretagne* that took them back to his *pays natal*.

What were the main aesthetic foundations on which the young verbal artist was to construct a radical new poetics on the eve of his return to the island of his birth? The members of the French poetic canon that spoke most directly to him may be recovered in the robust programmatic piece he composed in 1944, *Poésie et connaissance* ("Poetry and Knowledge"),[16] where the line of succession of genuine poets includes, not surprisingly, some of the major precursors of surrealism: Baudelaire, Rimbaud, Mallarmé, Lautréamont and Apollinaire. In the chapters that follow we shall describe, with reference to specific poems, the peculiar form that Césairean surrealism was to assume in the years of exploration during and immediately after the war. In the interim – and at the risk of grossly schematizing a very complex bundle of "influences" – we may usefully locate his inchoate aesthetic agenda at the interface between artistic "modernism"[17] and black consciousness movements. The nature of this cultural and historical interface cannot be fully recuperated without reference to the visual arts. As we shall have occasion to demonstrate throughout this study, art and literature are closely intertwined in the aesthetic theory and practice of contemporary verbal artists, such as the surrealist poets André Breton, Robert Desnos and Benjamin Péret.

The anthropologist and cultural historian James Clifford has furnished us with the most insightful description to date of the intellectual collage that made the convergence between surrealist practice (both verbal and visual) and European ethnography both probable and fecund at this epoch. Black anti-colonial intellectuals and European avant-garde thinkers alike found common creative ground in the conjuncture that Clifford has astutely dubbed "ethnographic surrealism."[18] It is a truism that earlier twentieth-century visual artists, such as the founders of Cubism, had "discovered" the value, in terms of their own break with representational norms, of what was indiscriminately called *art nègre* – a catchall category that encompassed cultural products of such diverse provenance as Africa, Oceania and the Arctic of the Eskimo peoples. The vogue of the "primitive" was reflected in the African ritual masks that adorned the studios of a Picasso or a Braque. On the more strictly ethnographic side of the equation, a great

French expedition making collections for museums, the "Mission Dakar-Djibouti" of the early 1930s, served to enhance the profile of the artistic legacy of "phantom Africa" (to borrow the expression of the ethnologist and man of letters Michel Leiris, who accompanied the expedition and recorded his experiences in a published journal). An index of the heightened interest in global "primitive" art and artifacts is the reconfiguration of museum collections in European capitals devoted to their display.[19] Thus in Paris the older Musée Trocadéro, whose notorious jumble of art objects from around the world epitomized Clifford's "ethnographic surreal," was transformed into the more rationally organized Musée de l'Homme in 1938 – seven years after the mammoth "International Colonial Exhibition" (held in Paris) had advertised its motley array of artistic trophies. In fine, the wherewithal for a sensitive black artist to contribute to the rehabilitation of a non-Western aesthetic while continuing to assimilate the most progressive components of the West was abundantly present in the vibrant intercultural ambience of prewar Paris.

Césaire has remained fiercely loyal to his own verbal marriage of négritude and the surreal, even when it has brought him into open rupture with doctrinaire ideologues of the political left, like the Communist poet Louis Aragon. A graphic representation of his commitment to what he came to see as the liberating function of surrealism (his preferred brand of modernism) may be observed in the stance he took in a public dialogue with the Marxist Haitian poet René Depestre. A brief look at some key passages from the poem "The verb 'to maroon'" ("Le verbe marronner"), in which a part of that dialogue is immortalized, will function as a coda to this sketch of the *bildung* of the poet of négritude. Though written a decade and a half later than *Cahier* (it was first published by Présence Africaine in 1955 under a different title), it re-affirms an aesthetic that was already implicit in the form of the earlier groundbreaking poem. Its central importance as a polemical assertion of poetic tenets is underscored by the fact that Césaire was to alter not only the text, but the actual title, of the poem in its three successive editions.[20]

The title of the first published version bore the revealing parenthesis "elements of an *ars poetica*" – a clear signal to the reader that it contains a partial re-statement, in a vivid mode, of Césaire's artistic credo, which he had previously expressed in a highly abstract form in his essay "Poetry and Knowledge." Though the bracketted subtitle disappeared from the final revised version of the poem that appeared in the collection *Noria*, the prescriptive tone of the verses points to its self-referential, quasi-manifesto status.

As the poem opens the speaker is gently berating his fellow-Caribbean poet for having abandoned his cultural resources of creativity in order to conform to the current French Communist party line:

> C'est une nuit de Seine
> et moi je me souviens comme ivre
> du chant dément de Boukman accouchant ton pays
> aux forceps de l'orage
>
> DEPESTRE
>
> Vaillant cavalier du tam-tam
> est-il vrai que tu doutes de la forêt natale
> de nos voix rauques de nos cœurs qui nous remontent
> amers
> de nos yeux de rhum rouges de nos nuits incendiées
> se peut-il
> que les pluies de l'exil
> aient détendu la peau de tambour de ta voix
>
> (It is a night on the Seine
> and as for me: I remember as though drunk
> the mad song of Boukman delivering your homeland
> with the forceps of the thunderstorm
>
> DEPESTRE
>
> Intrepid horseman of the tom-tom
> is it true you no longer trust in the woods of your birth
> our hoarse voices, our hearts that hoist us upward
> to bitter heights
> our rum ruddy eyes, our night in flames
> can it be

> that the rains of exile
> have loosened the drumskin of your voice)

The speaker, who is situated in Paris, reminds the Haitian of his own historical roots: the violent insurrection led by Boukman that helped to set in motion the full-fledged slave revolution (popular accounts tell of a meeting organized by Boukman in the woods, the *Bois Caïman*, during a severe thunderstorm). In addition to the Haitian Revolution (which Césaire celebrated in *Cahier* as the first assertion of négritude in history), Depestre is reminded of yet another cultural resource he has betrayed: the Afro-Caribbean cult of Vodun that was instrumental in furthering the revolt in its formative stages and remains an integral part of the Haitian worldview. The drum (*tam-tam*) here serves as icon of the continuity between old and diaspora black cultures at their most assertive. In the following apostrophe the Césairean voice exhorts the Haitian poet to break ranks and join him in an artistic secession:

> marronerons-nous Depestre marronerons-nous?
>
> (Shall we turn maroon, Depestre, shall we turn maroon?)

In inventing a verb, "to maroon" (*marronner*), based on the noun denoting slaves who escaped from the New World plantation to live in autonomous communities, the speaker hoists aloft the banner of artistic freedom and resistance to cultural totalitarianism. What he especially denounces is the party's advocacy of conventional forms that many modernist poets had rejected as outmoded:

> C'est vrai ils arrondissent cette saison des sonnets
> pour nous à le faire cela me rappellerait par trop
> le jus sucré que bavent là-bas les distilleries des mornes
> quand les lents boeufs maigres font leur rond au zonzon
>   des moustiques
>
> Ouiche! Depestre le poème n'est pas un moulin à passer
>   de la canne à sucre ça non
> si les rimes sont mouches sur les mares
> sans rimes

toute une saison
loin des mares
moi te faisant raison
rions buvons et marronons

(It is true they are rounding off this season with sonnets
for us to do so would remind me too much
of the sweet cane-juice foaming in those hilltop
    distilleries
when the slow lean oxen turn round and round to the
    buzz-buzz of mosquitoes

Look! Depestre the poem is no sugar-mill
to grind the cane-stalk
and if rhymes are flies on the ponds
then without rhymes
for a whole season
far from ponds
with me your partner
let us laugh drink and be maroons together)

Césaire's own poetry, of course, has consistently eschewed rhyme, which in the poem's polemic is equated, via the metaphor of the sugar-mill, with the mechanical and the monotonous – not to mention the oppressive. In this view the authentic poet is necessarily liberated from the grind of inherited forms. Pursuing the question of form, Césaire's verse epistle modulates, a few lines later, into a friendly conversation between revolutionary comrades, though not without a certain ironic distance on the part of the author:

Camarade Depestre
C'est un problème assurément très grave
des rapports de la poésie et de la Révolution
le fond conditionne la forme
et si l'on s'avisait aussi du détour dialectique
par quoi la forme prenant sa revanche
comme un figuier maudit étouffe le poème
mais non
je ne me charge pas du rapport
j'aime mieux regarder le printemps.

(Comrade Depestre

> It's assuredly a very serious problem
> the relations between poetry and Revolution
> content conditions form
> and if one took thought also for the dialectical detour
> by which form exacting its revenge
> smothers the poem like a curséd figtree
> but no
> I do not burden myself with such relations
> I prefer to observe the spring)

The tenet "content conditions form," which is here enunciated like an axiom, is consonant with Césaire's practice throughout the entire trajectory of his poetic career. *Cahier*, for instance, conspicuously avoids either regular meter or rhyme (the rare examples of the former are exceptions that prove the rule). The groups of lines into which the poem is spatially organized vary in length and resemble paragaphs in a prose-poem. In its disjointed style and apocalyptic tone, Césaire's first poem seems to erupt onto the page with all the violence of a volcano, as layers of images are superimposed like so many successive flows of lava. The comparison would no doubt appeal to Césaire, who has described himself as "Péléean" after the famous Martinican volcano, Mt. Pélée, which arose from its slumber in 1902 to obliterate the former capital city of the island colony, St. Pierre. The volcanic trope, however appealing it may be to the poet and his critics alike, is potentially misleading in one crucial respect: it evokes a spontaneous "outpouring" from the depths that fits all too neatly into the Romantic view of poetic genesis – a view that the surrealists did much to foster with their ostensible espousal of "automatic writing." There is ample evidence that Césaire has always labored to polish his verse with a care that belies the neo-Romantic myth of pure spontaneity. With this caveat in mind, a short guided tour of the first site of a Césairean verbal "eruption" is in order.

CHAPTER 2

Exploring racial selves: "Journal of a Homecoming"

There is no predetermined négritude; there is no essence; there is only history – a living history

Aimé Césaire

The notion of a "definitive text" belongs to religion or perhaps merely to exhaustion.

Jorge Luis Borges

Césaire's first published poem, "Journal of a Homecoming" (*Cahier d'un retour au pays natal*), has also remained his best known. Several facets of this "greatest lyric monument of our time," as André Breton famously styled it, make it unique within the Césairean poetic corpus.[1] By virtue of its length alone (it occupies approximately 50 pages in the Maximin-Carpentier edition) it stands apart from the rest of the author's lyric output, which otherwise manifests a pronounced partiality for the short poem. Despite its length and broad thematic sweep, however, it is manifestly the poet's most accessible and, not surprisingly, most quoted, translated and anthologized opus. Its relative accessibility, as compared with most of Césaire's subsequent poetry, is due in part to the youthful author's explicit desire to play the role of major spokesman for the black world. So ambitious a role obviously requires a certain straightforwardness in the coding of the "message," and indeed Césaire, while forging the densely metaphorical style that is his signature, spectacularly succeeds, in the pages of *Cahier*, in creating a sustained lyric prose-poem whose basic "message" is fairly transparent to the careful reader.

Cahier is fundamental to Césaire's œuvre from more than one crucial vantage-point. Nothing symbolizes the poem's foundational status more strikingly than the story of its many metamorphoses in print. Thanks to the archival work of Thomas Hale and others[2] we have the benefit of a careful account of the text's evolution through the successive phases that culminated in the final so-called "definitive edition" put out under the auspices of Présence Africaine in 1956. Thus the poem existed in a virtually plastic state until it achieved a form of textual consummation over twenty years after its initial debut in print. In coming to terms with this plasticity, I am tempted to concur with Jorge Luis Borges's witty remark (which stands as one of the two epigraphs to this chapter) that "The notion of a 'definitive text' belongs to religion or perhaps merely to exhaustion."[3] Prior to the enshrinement of the "definitive" text (if we may go along with the first of Borges's playful alternatives), Césaire produced no less than four separate published versions of the poem – a long-term engagement in revision that testifies to his creative obsession. The first version (often inaccurately referred to as "fragments," as Hale was the first to remind us) appeared in Paris in the periodical *Volontés* in 1939. Between the *Volontés* version and the Présence Africaine "definitive" edition, the published text underwent two other incarnations, both of which took place in the year 1947: a New York edition, with a famous laudatory preface by André Breton, and a Paris edition, with an introduction by the author's Yugoslavian friend Petar Guberina.

It would take us far beyond the scope of this book to speculate on the details of these transformations.[4] With the hindsight of a literary historian writing nearly half a century after the poem achieved its final form, we can now clearly see that the text's continued evolution in print was already foreshadowed in its title. The word *Cahier* (literally "exercise book," "notebook") suggests a project that is incomplete, if not sketchy, and furnishes a clue to its experimental character, which is congruent with the history of its successive alterations. The "Journal," as I have elected to render it, purports to chronicle "a return" (*Cahier d'un retour*), but the singular form is deceptive, because the poem describes not a single return, but a series of abortive returns that are superimposed on each other. Like a musical rondo that returns repeatedly to its theme, *Cahier* portrays the homecoming of the poet as a recurrent event that is continually in the process of rehearsal.

A reader who is attuned to the Western literary canon may readily detect intertextual resonances in the idea of a deferred homecoming (*retour au pays natal*). The archetypal return in the Western tradition is, of course, that of the Homeric Odysseus, and far from downplaying the potential significance of the parallel, we would do well to pose, albeit briefly, the question of how *Cahier* subtly exploits the association. The thematic resonance may serve to mark a differentiation no less than a parallel: the poet of *Cahier* both is and is not cast as an epic hero returning to his homeland to reclaim his birthright. On the one hand, the distance from Greek epic is measured in generic terms, for Césaire's lyrical poem is far removed in style and tone from the measured cadences of Homeric verse; on the other hand, the heroic paradigm remains in the background of the poem as a kind of shadowy presence that occasionally traverses its surface. The Homeric shadow in the title portends the difficulties inherent in any homecoming. Hence, though the speaker may not be faithfully cast as a black Odysseus, the phantom in the title has sounded an alert that leads us to anticipate a central problematic of all literary homecomings: the indeterminate identity of the returning figure. The Odyssean subtext, in particular, alerts us to the dynamics of impersonation – the disguise that the returning hero is obliged to assume –and his painful social reintegration into a world whose horizons have been inevitably altered during the period of his absence. As I hope to illustrate below, this nexus of questions is centrally germane to the *Cahier* narrative.

In a brief overview such as this I cannot attempt to take the reader through the poem with any pretense to completeness. I shall instead be highly selective as I draw attention to major features of its macro-structure and its motival rhythms. As a point of departure, let us partly unpack the three opening "segments" of the poem, which constitute a dense, expository prologue:[5]

Au bout du petit matin . . .

Va-t'en, lui disais-je, gueule de flic, gueule de vache, va t'en je déteste les larbins de l'ordre et les hannetons de l'espérance. Va-t'en mauvais gris-gris, punaise de moinillon. Puis je me tournais vers des paradis pour lui et les siens perdus, plus calme que la face d'une femme qui ment, et là, bercé par les effluves d'une pensée jamais lasse je nourissais le vent, je délaçais les monstres et j'entendais monter de l'autre coté du désastre un fleuve de tourterelles et de trèfles de la savane que je porte toujours dans mes profondeurs à hauteur inverse du vingtième étage des maisons les plus insolentes et par précaution contre la force putréfiante des ambiances crépusculaires, arpentée nuit et jour d'un sacré soleil vénérien.

Au bout du petit matin bourgeonnant d'anses frêles les Antilles qui ont faim, les Antilles grêlées de petite vérole, les Antilles dynamitées d'alcool, échouées dans la boue de cette baie, dans la poussière de cette ville sinistrement échouées.

(At the end of early dawn . . .

Get lost, I told the man, pig-snout, honkie-snout, get lost, I despise law-and-order goons, maybugs of fond hope. Get lost, foul gri-gri, puny grub of a monk. Then, more composed than the face of a woman telling a lie, I turned towards paradises lost to him and his kin, and there, lulled by the ebb and flow of a tireless thought, I nurtured the wind, I unloosed the monsters and I heard rising from the other shore of the catastrophe, the river of turtle-doves and savannah clover that I always carry in my inmost being at a depth inverse to the height of the twentieth floor of the most supercilious edifices and as a talisman against the putrefying power of crepuscular settings, patrolled night and day by an accursed venereal sun.

At the end of early dawn, burgeoning with frail bays, the starved Antilles, the Antilles pockmarked with small-

pox, the Antilles dynamited with alcohol, run aground in
the mud of this bay, in the dust of this town inauspiciously
grounded.)

The phrase that opens the poem, "at the end of early dawn,"
returns to punctuate it again and again in the manner of a
fragmentary refrain. What are the predominant symbolic
implications of the "early dawn" ("petit-matin") that situates
the text in time? To begin with, the locution suggests a
"liminal" state, if I may use a spatial, rather than temporal,
metaphor (the word "liminal" is, of course, derived from Latin
limen = threshold). Speaker and audience are located on an
indeterminate time threshold that is "betwixt and between" –
neither day nor night. Often marked typographically in the
text with an ellipsis (. . .), the refrain periodically reminds
us that the speaker is between two worlds, positioned at the
margins where cultures intersect and, above all, where lines of
identity become blurred. As the phrase is repeated at key
points throughout the poem it acquires increasing depth and
complexity of meaning. Here at the very threshold of the
poem itself it clearly carries an additional programmatic
aura: the "early dawn" is also to be understood as the locus of
poetic creativity, because it straddles the borderline between
the oneiric and the real – an important crossroads for
the surrealist imagination. This liminal space occupied by the
poetic creator is precisely what Césaire emphasizes in his own
aesthetic manifesto, "Poetry and Knowledge" ("Poésie et
Connaissance"),[6] which locates the poet "at the lived borders
of dream and reality, of day and night, between absence and
presence" ("aux confins vécus du rêve et du réel, du jour et de
la nuit, entre absence et présence").

In the following segment we plunge *in medias res* into a
narrative in which the speaker first vehemently repudiates an
oppressive order (likened to a police state) and then makes a
"turn" towards a utopian place of the imagination. Excluded
from the envisioned utopias (*paradis*) are not only the petty
functionaries who maintain the rejected social order, but also
their affiliates (*les siens*), who represent a materialistic culture

of "supercilious edifices." To this culture that reaches upward in its hubris is opposed the speaker's, that extends inversely downwards into the depths (*profondeurs*). This framing cultural polarity later emerges, in various transformations, as central to the poem's thematic. The "savannah clover" orients us towards the grasslands of Africa as surely as the skyscrapers point us towards the daring artifacts of Western technological invention. A salient feature of the antithesis is that the world evoked as a counter to the technological is inner and spiritual. These inner resources, which function as a countervailing force against decay and putrefaction, do not, however, come into operation without strenuous action on the part of the speaker, who must "nurture the wind," and, like the Greek god Zeus in the cosmic struggle against his father's generation, must unloose and enlist monstrous allies before the "catastrophe" (*désastre*) can be surmounted. Readers familiar with Césaire's repertoire of emblems will have no difficulty in identifying the "catastrophe" as the imposition of slavery on the African people, and will have gleaned the scope of the speaker's utopian vision of transcending the worst consequences of that historical event. In sum, a program of cultural regeneration for the Antilles has been economically adumbrated in the sentence that concludes the second segment.

The extreme composure of the speaker as he is about to launch his project is suggested through an unexpected comparison: "more composed than the face of a woman telling a lie." In view of the preceding outburst directed at the "law-and-order goons," the terms of the comparison (poet and woman), no less than its point (a composed demeanor), are sudden and jarring, especially if one raises the question, compulsory for our time, of the representation of the female in the text. The function of the female figure in this context is consistent with the typical surrealist view of woman as "mediatrix between man and the surreal."[7] The rapprochement of poet-speaker and female figure also includes the no less unsettling conception of a "false" discourse ("telling a lie"). The implied notion of poetic discourse as capable of embodying the art of lying is, we may recall, a Western literary

topos that goes back as far as Hesiod's famous formulation in
the *Theogony* (lines 27–28): "We [sc. the Muses] know how to
tell many falsehoods as though they were the truth, but we
know, when we wish, how to utter the truth." Césaire's brusque
redeployment of the topos is oblique (it is purveyed by means of
the comparison between poet and "lying" mediatrix), yet it has
the effect of insinuating a subversive undercurrent at the very
outset. How, we may be provoked into pondering, is the poem's
evolving utopian myth to be comprehended in terms of its
relation to "truth?" Or to re-phrase the query in surrealist
terms, where does the "truth" of dream end and the "false-
hood" of reality begin?

The speaker's dramatic "turn" has also brought him into
imaginary contact with a paradise that excludes the colonizer,
but that paradise proves to be shortlived and elusive, for it is
abruptly shattered in the next segment by the intrusion of a
harsh reality. The archipelago of the Antilles makes its first of
many entries onto the stage of *Cahier* as a site of misery (here in
the form of hunger, disease, alcoholism and despair) – in sum,
as site of a culture "run aground" (*échoué*) and floundering in
the mud. It is this rude irruption of a depressing reality that
dominates, by its continual "return," the early scenes of the
unfolding narrative. The prelude of *Cahier*, then, describes a
motival loop that will come to typify the poem's circular structure. Succinctly put, the speaker first portrays a liminal state of
being, which is then surmounted by a euphoric vision, only to
be abruptly re-installed in a move of violent deflation. The
instrument of the deflation is the image of a Caribbean that is
prostrate and moribund, as in this early passage:

> Au bout du petit matin, cette ville plate – étalée,
> trébuchée de son bon sens, inerte, essoufflée sous son
> fardeau géométrique de croix éternellement recom-
> mençante, indocile à son sort, muette, contrariée de
> toutes façons, incapable de croître selon le suc de cette
> terre, embarrassée, rognée, réduite, en rupture de faune
> et de flore.
>
> (At the end of early dawn ... This town spread-out flat,
> tottered from its commonsense, inert, out of breath

under its geometric load of a cross eternally to be picked
up, refractory to its lot, without a voice, cross and crossed
in every way, unable to grow with the juice of this earth,
out of sorts, cut short, reduced, ruptured from its flora
and fauna.)

This picture of an abject and inert populace is later transformed into its opposite as the poem approaches its dynamic
close.

The narrator of *Cahier* is an "I" (*je*) who, like the *Journal*
itself, is plastic and subject to successive re-makings and
transformations. The construction of a lyric self (or, to be
more accurate, a plurality of selves) is the central leitmotif
of the poem. The progress of the construction is, however,
spasmodic, as the speaker makes and unmakes, constructs and
decomposes, a series of images of the self that are variously
compatible and incompatible. Thus the identity of the speaker
is continually interrogated as the text, moving by thematic fits
and starts, insists on taking stock, at strategic points, of its own
itinerary.

To convey a sense of the poem's recursive movement I
shall have recourse to theatrical metaphors. It is, I believe,
consonant with the poem's figurative texture to conceive it as
a drama of self-exploration in which the speaker typically
impersonates differing versions of the self and holds them up to
merciless scrutiny. It will be useful to think of these discrete
identities as masks (in the ritual-dramatic sense) that the poet
assumes and discards at the dictates of his plot. From this
perspective, négritude, which many readers rightly regard as
the defining theme of *Cahier*, can be interpreted not as static
datum or essence, but as a plastic concept in the process of
construction. If we may cite Césaire's own later clarification
of the concept: "There is no predetermined négritude; there is
no essence; there is only history – a living history."[8] In a word,
the poem undogmatically explores the "fit" of various racial
selves (masks of négritude, so to speak) from contingent
vantage-points. With this as a working hypothesis, let us
now examine some of the more important masks that the text
displays for our inspection.

The first grand impersonation we confront occurs early in the poem:

> Partir.
> Comme il y a des hommes-hyènes et des hommes-panthères, je serais un homme-juif
> un homme-cafre
> un homme-hindou-de-Calcutta
> un homme-de-Harlem-qui-ne-vote-pas
>
> l'homme-famine, l'homme-insulte, l'homme-torture on pouvait à n'importe quel moment le saisir le rouer de coups, le tuer – parfaitement le tuer – sans avoir de compte a rendre à personne sans avoir d'excuses à présenter à personne
> un homme-juif
> un homme-pogrom
> un chiot
> un mendigot
>
> mais est-ce qu'on tue le Remords, beau comme la face de stupeur d'une dame anglaise qui trouverait dans sa soupière un crâne de Hottentot ?
>
> (To leave.
> As there are hyena-men and panther-men, I would be a Jew-man
> a Kaffir-man
> a Hindu-man-from-Calcutta,
> a Harlem-man-who-does-not-vote
>
> a famine-man, an insult-man, a torture-man, one could at any moment lay hold of him, pummel him with blows, kill him – actually kill him – without having to account to anyone, without having to make excuses to anyone
> a Jew-man,
> a pogrom-man
> a puppy dog
> a beggar-bum
>
> but does one ever kill Remorse, as fair as the startled face of an English lady as she uncovers in her soup tureen a Hottentot skull?)

The speaker here confidently takes on the identity of a racial pariah who functions as a universal scapegoat. He is treated as subhuman and is the victim of random violence. An important aspect of this mask is its inclusiveness: whatever the particular oppressed race may be (black, Hindu or Jew), it is subsumed under a global underclass. In introducing the role, the narrator alludes to the tradition, common in African cultures, of donning animal masks for ritual performances ("hyena-man," "panther-man"). Having assumed the mask of the pariah, he proceeds to proclaim an ambitious program of empowerment:

> Je retrouverais le secret des grandes communications et des grandes combustions. Je dirais orage. Je dirais fleuve. Je dirais tornade. Je dirais feuille. Je dirais arbre. Je serais mouillé de toutes les pluies, humecté de toutes les rosées. Je roulerais comme du sang frénétique sur le courant lent de l'œil des mots en chevaux fous en enfants frais en caillots en couvre-feu en vestiges de temple en pierres précieuses assez loin pour décourager les mineurs. Qui ne me comprendrait pas ne comprendrait pas davantage le rugissement du tigre.

> (I would rediscover the secret of grand communications and of grand conflagrations. I would say hurricane. I would say river. I would say tornado. I would say leaf. I would say tree. I would be soaked with all the rains, moistened with all the dews. I would circulate like frenetic blood on the slow current of the eye of words, becoming mad horses, or fresh children, or clots, or curfew, or traces of a temple or precious stones remote enough to discourage miners. He who failed to grasp my meaning would no more grasp the roaring of a tiger.)

Each of the principal masks (and there are principal as well as subsidiary ones in the course of the poem's evolution) endows the wearer with a distinctive voice. What is chiefly conferred in this instance is a mysterious power of potent speech (note the fivefold anaphora, "I would *say*"). The poet imagines himself as articulating powerful utterances. On closer examination, these take the grammatical form of five nouns denoting natural forces that fall into two groups: the first refers to forces of wind and water (hurricane, river, tornado), the second to vegetation (leaf, tree). The combined forces of wind, water and tree are reclaimed by the poet *qua* pariah and reflected in his newly acquired voice. The first stage of the scenario, then, involves the vocal empowerment of the speaker, who proceeds to conjure up and address phantasmagoric cosmic forces and find "words vast enough to contain" such presences. In this elated frame of mind he describes one of several hypothetical returns to his country and the grandiose pronouncements he would make on these occasions. One such pronouncement sets the poet up as spokesperson for all the oppressed:

> "Ma bouche sera la bouche des malheurs qui n'ont point de bouche, ma voix, la liberté de celles qui s'affaissent au cachot du désespoir."

> ("My mouth shall be the mouth of adversities that have no mouth, my voice, the freedom of those voices that languish in the dungeon of despair.")

The emboldened speaker even goes so far as warn himself against becoming a spectator of life's drama as he turns to soliloquy:

> Et venant je me dirais à moi-même:
> "Et surtout mon corps aussi bien que mon âme, gardez-vous de vous croiser les bras en l'attitude stérile du spectateur, car la vie n'est pas un spectacle, car une mer de douleurs n'est pas un proscenium, car un homme qui crie n'est pas un ours qui danse ... "

> (And as I come I would say to myself:
> "This above all, my body and my soul: beware of crossing your arms in the sterile pose of a spectator, for life is not a show on stage, for a sea of troubles is not a proscenium, for a screaming human being is not a dancing bear ... ")

Is the poet here repudiating the dramaturgical trope as such ("life is not a show on stage" versus Shakespeare's "All the world's a stage")? It would be more typical of Césaire's subtle rhetoric to say that he is rather warning himself against confounding the figurative stage with the real world stage. Hamlet's "sea of troubles" (my translation retains what I take to be a Shakespearean tag) is to be a token of the lived reality envisaged by the narrator, who intends to participate fully in his society's transformation rather than observe it from a safe distance. The speaker is artfully "staging" his arrival so as to reduce the distance between performer and audience.

The moment of arrival, we soon learn, is also the moment of acute disillusionment, as the real abruptly supplants the imaginary:

> De nouveau cette vie clopinante devant moi, non pas cette vie, cette mort, cette mort sans sens ni piété, cette mort où la grandeur piteusement échoue

> (Once more this life limping in front of me, no not this life, this death without meaning or devoutness, this death where greatness pitifully runs aground)

Disillusionment, in turn, entails the abandonment of the mask as well as the optimistic voice that accompanied it, and the self beneath (*moi*) is starkly exposed on the stage:

> et moi seul, brusque scène de ce petit matin
> où fait le beau l'apocalypse des monstres puis, chavirée,
>   se tait
> chaude élection de cendres, de ruines et d'affaissements

> (and I alone, brusque stage of this early dawn,
> where the apocalypse of monsters first vaunts, then,
>   subverted, lapses into silence
> hot settlement of ashes, of ruins, of downfalls)

In a typical moment of insecurity and self-doubt, the disillusioned speaker clings for just a while longer to the mask that has promised so much and allows himself a final plea for indulgence in a last-ditch effort to stave off the inevitable self-reduction:

> – Encore une objection! une seule, mais de grâce une seule: je n'ai pas le droit de calculer la vie à mon empan fuligineux; de me réduire à ce petit rien ellipsoïdal qui tremble à quatre doigts au-dessus de la ligne, moi homme, d'ainsi bouleverser la création, que je me comprenne entre latitude et longitude!

> (One last objection! One only, but grant me just this one: I do not have the right to measure human life by

my sooty span; to reduce myself to this tiny ellipsoidal
nothing trembling at four fingers above the parallel, I, a
human being, to overturn creation to such an extent that
I circumscribe myself between latitude and longitude!)

Self-reduction, however, is the ineluctable price the speaker
must pay if he is to relinquish the grandiose mask of global
spokesperson – if, in short, the insights of the "reality
principle," as Freud would term it, are to be acted upon. The
move to avoid it proves futile and ineffectual, and the poetic
persona sets aside the fantasy in which he has fulsomely
indulged:

> me voici divisé des oasis fraîches de la fraternité
> ce rien pudique frise d'échardes dures
> cet horizon trop sûr tressaille comme un geôlier.

> (Here I am separated from the cool oases of fraternity
> this modest nothing curls into tough bristles
> this too smug horizon quakes like a gaoler)

What has the chastened speaker relinquished (and what
accepted) in the course of his roller-coaster quest for identity?
Gone are the "oases of fraternity" where he might have been
able to preen himself as the grand mouthpiece of all oppressed
races and ethnicities (Jews, Kaffirs, etc.). Reluctantly he
begins to come to terms with his narrower Caribbean self (the
first formulation is geographic: the "ellipsoidal nothing"
alludes to the schematic shape of the island of Martinique).
Included in the speaker's reduced state is the element of
membership in a black fraternity which, in my reading, is
obliquely present in the imagery of curly hair ("this modest
nothing curls into tough bristles"). As the loop is completed, we
hear the poet dismissing his own brief flirtation with a more
inflated identity ("your last triumph, obstinate crow of
Betrayal"). Refusing to be seduced into a facile disavowal
of race, he is now fully able to re-position himself as a black
West Indian and acknowledge his country's peculiar history.
Central to that acknowledgement is the reclaiming of independent Haiti, cradle of négritude in the Antilles:

Ce qui est à moi, ces quelques milliers de mortiférés
qui tournent en rond dans la calebasse d'une île [...] Et
mon île non-clôture, sa claire audace debout à l'arrière de
cette polynésie, devant elle, la Guadeloupe fendue en
deux de sa raie dorsale et de même misère que nous, Haïti
où la négritude se mit debout pour la première fois et dit
qu'elle croyait à son humanité

(What is mine: these few thousand mortally wounded
who go round and round in the calabash of an island [...]
and my non-closure island, its open brashness right at the
back of this polynesia; in front: Guadeloupe severed into
two halves at the dorsal bone and no less wretched than
ourselves, Haiti where for the first time négritude stood
up tall and straight and declared that it believed in its
humanity)

The divestment of the mask, then, has a positive outcome. The
speaking subject is able to reconnect with his historical roots
(here represented by the Haitian revolution and its historic
self-assertion) just at the moment when he has been
disconnected from the oasis of an ecumenical pariah solidarity.
As a symbol of that reconnection he effusively honors the
memory of the great Haitian general and leader, Toussaint
L'Ouverture, whose imprisonment and death are the subject of
a poignant vignette.

I have described a structural rhythm of emotional inflation
and deflation, followed by insight: a threefold process, corresponding, in terms of the mask trope, with adoption and
removal, followed by sober disclosure. Not all of the scenarios
to follow in *Cahier* are as clearly articulated as this initial
example. Nonetheless a brief account of some chief variations
on the pattern may help to guide the reader through the
vertiginous course of the poem.

One of the more hallucinatory sequences features the
persona of the madman (*le fou*) so dear to the surrealist
universe. In this go-around we hear the change of voice before
we are given a definition of the concomitant new role:

Au bout du petit matin ces pays sans stèle,
ces chemins sans mémoire, ces vents sans tablette.
Qu'importe?

Nous dirions. Chanterions. Hurlerions.
Voix pleine, voix large, tu serais notre bien, notre pointe
  en avant.
Des mots?
Ah oui, des mots !

(At the end of early dawn these countries without
  monuments,
these pathways without memory, these winds without
  inscribed tablets.
What does it matter?
We would say. Sing. Howl.
Full-blown voice, ample voice, you would be our boon, our
  advancing spearhead.
Words?
Ah yes, words!)

The voice is at the outset booming and militant: loud enough,
it seems, to compensate for the silence that has hitherto
prevailed in the cultural pathways. With the discovery of
the voice, words of strange power leap forth from the lips. The
liberating words are from a hybrid lexicon that combines
the surrealist shibboleth of "madness" with the myth of the
primitive cannibal:

Raison, je te sacre vent du soir.
Bouche de l'ordre ton nom?
Il m'est corolle du fouet.
Beauté je t'appelle pétition de la pierre.
Mais ah! la rauque contrebande
de mon rire
Ah ! mon trésor de salpêtre!
Parce que nous vous haïssons vous et votre raison,
nous nous réclamons de la démence précoce de la folie
flambante du cannibalisme tenace

Trésor, comptons:
la folie qui se souvient
la folie qui hurle
la folie qui voit
la folie qui se déchaîne

(Reason, I consecrate you wind of evening.
Your name you claim is mouth of order?

For me you are corolla of the lash.
Beauty I re-name you pursuance of stone.
But ah! the raucous contraband
of my laughter
Ah my treasure of saltpeter!
Because we detest you, yes you and your reason
we repossess ourselves in the name of dementia praecox,
of blazing madness, of inveterate cannibalism.

Treasure, let us take the tally:
the madness that remembers
the madness that howls
the madness that sees
the madness that bursts its chains)

The speaker's utterances here acquire the force of "speech acts." The re-naming is enacted in the text: reason and order, often employed by colonialist regimes as euphemisms or alibis of oppression, are summarily re-christened with their "true" names that disclose slavery ("corolla of the lash"). In his tally of an opposing "madness" capable of subverting the order of reason, the speaker proceeds to reckon up the explosive forces ("treasure of salpeter") at his disposal. There is more at stake in the speech act of re-naming, however, than a desire to overthrow the Cartesian world of reason and replace it with a surrealist utopia reinstating madness (*la folie*). The vindication of madness is also an act of repossession in which Césaire consciously re-valorizes images of the self that were formerly pejorative. It is a truism that all major social revolutions, in this century at least, have sought to re-possess the terminology of vilification. Consider, for instance, the recuperation of the word "black" by the sixties generation of African-Americans, which paralleled the reclaiming of the derogatory "nègre" by an earlier generation of francophone blacks in the Caribbean (hence the force of Césaire's famous coinage, "négritude"). Through the mask of the madman the poet seeks to re-vitalize his compatriots by restoring historic memory ("madness that remembers"), voice ("madness that howls"), and vision ("madness that sees") – all in the service of liberation ("madness that bursts its chains"). After further rehabilitating a

madness that rejects mathematical logic in favor of what
earlier ethnographers called "animism" ("and you know the
rest: / that 2 plus 2 make 5 / that the forest miaows . . . "),
Césaire's speaking "I" ("je") becomes a plural "we" ("nous")
which then foregrounds the pivotal question of the poem:

> Qui et quels nous sommes?
> Admirable question!
>
> (Who and what are we?
> Excellent question!)

No other passage in *Cahier* is more explicit than this in its stark
formulation of the problem of identity.

The mad persona who has become a representative of the
black man in search of a viable identity merges in the next
segment with the no less puissant persona of the African witchdoctor and his New World congener, the Vodun priest. In a
giddy sequence that is surely one of the most hauntingly
beautiful in the entire poem, Césaire's shamanistic avatar
displays his awesome power to transform the self:

> A force de regarder les arbres je suis
> devenu un arbre et mes longs pieds
> d'arbre ont creusé dans le sol de larges
> sacs à venin de hautes villes d'ossements
> à force de penser au Congo
> je suis devenu un Congo bruissant de
> forêts et de fleuves
> où le fouet claque comme un grand étendard
> l'étendard du prophète
> où l'eau fait
> likouala-likouala
> où l'éclair de la colère lance sa hache
> verdâtre et force les sangliers de la
> putréfaction dans la belle orée violente
> des narines.
>
> (By dint of gazing upon trees I have
> become a tree and my long rooted feet
> have dug into the ground huge
> pouches of toxin, cities of bones piled high
> by dint of meditating on the Congo

I have become a Congo rustling with
jungles and rivers
where the lash cracks like a large banner
the banner of the prophet
where the water sounds
likwala-likwala
where the lightning-flash of anger hurls its
grass-green axe and flushes the wild boars of
putrefaction into the lovely violent clearing
of the nostrils.)

The tree, as commonly in Césaire's poetry, is not a static, but a dynamic image of robust empowerment, of aggressive "racination" – the act of re-rooting black culture in its originary African soil. Self-conscious meditation upon his forgotten roots has brought him to a point of identification with the "Congo," an obvious synecdoche for the African continent. By a clever sleight of hand, which is congruent with this evolving identification, the Martinican subject slips into the related role of Vodun officiant. All of a sudden the punctuation of the refrain transports the reader into the sacred space of a Vodun ceremony:

Au bout du petit matin
un petit train de sable
un petit train de mousseline
un petit train de grains de maïs
Au bout du petit matin
un grand galop de pollen
un grand galop d'un petit train de
petites filles
un grand galop de colibris
un grand galop de dagues pour défoncer
la poitrine de la terre

(at the end of early dawn
a little trail of sand
a little trail of muslin
a little trail of grains of corn
At the end of early dawn
a great gallop of pollen
a great gallop of a little trail of
little girls

a great gallop of humming-birds
a great gallop of daggers to stave in the bosom of the earth)

A reader familiar with Haitian Vodun ritual will no doubt have picked up the echoes of lustral sprinkling of "vévé" symbols strewn on the ground and elsewhere in the precinct to mark the sacred enclosure for the ensuing devotions. The presence of "pollen" among these items is an apt transposition of a major, recurrent Césairean symbol for the transplantation of African peoples to the Antilles. Similarly, the equestrian image to which it is linked ("a gallop of pollen") conjures up the central event in Vodun modes of worship: the ritual possession of the celebrant by a divinity who "rides" him or her like a horseman. The passage culminates in a reference to a sacrificial ritual which is *de rigueur* in Vodun ceremonial and is here augmented to a cosmic scale ("daggers staving in the bosom of the earth").

In terms of the poem's leading ideas, the actor's ongoing recognition of the African component of his Caribbean identity is an important stage in his maturation, and he proceeds to pull all the stops in proclaiming (and reclaiming) his "Congolese" self, which has been portrayed by the European colonizer as primitive and ugly. With caustic irony he next admits his "relapse" into pagan backwardness and he defiantly embraces the role of transplanted witchdoctor:

> je déclare mes crimes et qu'il n'y a rien à
> dire pour ma défense.
> Danses. Idoles. Relaps. Moi aussi
>
> J'ai assassiné Dieu de ma paresse de
> mes paroles de mes gestes
> de mes chansons obscènes
>
> J'ai porté des plumes de perroquet des
> dépouilles de chat musqué
> J'ai lassé la patience des missionnaires
> insulté les bienfaiteurs de l'humanité.
> Défié Tyr. Défié Sidon.
> Adoré le Zambèze.
> L'étendue de ma perversité me confond!

Mais pourquoi brousse impénétrable encore cacher le vif
zéro de ma mendicité et par un souci de noblesse apprise
ne pas entonner l'horrible bond de ma
laideur pahouine ?

voum rooh oh
voum rooh oh
à charmer les serpents a conjurer
les morts

(I confess my crimes and aver there is nothing
to plead in my defence.
Dances. Idols. Relapse. Me too

I have assassinated God with my laziness with
my words with my gestures
with my obscene songs

I have worn parrot feathers
musk-cat skins
I have worn down the patience of missionaries
insulted the benefactors of humanity
Defied Tyre. Defied Sidon.
Prayed to the Zambezi.
The immensity of my perversity confounds me!

But why, impenetrable jungle bush, do you continue to
conceal the sheer nonentity of my mendicancy and by a
yearning for acquired pedigree fail to drum up the horrible leap of my Bantu ugliness?

voom roo o!
voom roo o!
to charm snakes to summon up
the dead)

The self-interrogation of the persona is shaded with inter-
cultural nuances. The rhetorical question is posed in such an
ironic mode that the "confession" of an adherence to "Bantu
ugliness" (as seen, of course, through the eyes of a European)
acquires the positive value that has historically been denied
it. The "mendicancy" (*mendicité*) of the narrator refers
primarily to the socio-economic degradation of the enslaved
African; at the same time, the state of mendicancy may

subliminally evoke the famous impersonation of a beggar by the returned hero Odysseus. By insisting on playing out the imposed role of unregenerate primitive, rather than simply arrogating to himself a noble African lineage ("a yearning for acquired pedigree"), the poet makes it clear that he will not be taking an easy route to a restored self-esteem, but will fearlessly pursue his quest for an authentic self. Eventually, however, even this recovered Bantu "voice" will be brutally suppressed in the text, and by a typical twist that gives this poem its vigorous rhythm, the speaker dramatizes the sorcerer's moment of truth:

> Mais qui tourne ma voix? qui écorche
> ma voix ? Me fourrant dans la
> gorge mille crocs de bambou. Mille
> pieux d'oursin. C'est toi sale bout
> de monde. Sale bout de petit matin.
> C'est toi sale haine. C'est toi poids
> de l'insulte et cent ans de coups
> de fouet. C'est toi cent ans de ma
> patience, cent ans de mes soins
> juste à ne pas mourir.
> rooh oh

> (But who is twisting my voice? who is flaying
> my voice? Shoving into my
> throat a thousand bamboo hooks. A thousand
> sea-urchin spines. It is you foul world's
> end. Foul early dawn.
> It is you foul hate. You weight
> of insult and a hundred years of lashings
> with the whip. It is you a hundred years of my
> patience, a hundred years of my taking pains
> just in order not to die
> roo o)

With this downward turn we complete another spiral of elevation/depression. The black voice, we recall, had derived its seemingly elemental force from its determination to re-connect with historical experience, and it proclaimed this ambitious agenda with exuberance and expansiveness. What now dampens it, ironically, is the very content of that historical reality. In concrete terms, the harrowing experience of New World plantation slavery is what undermines the exuberant speaker, as he feels his black skin – his incarnated "voice" – being flayed by the slave-driver's whip. For the first time in the poem the "liminal" condition of the homecoming poet is explicitly connected with the consequences of enslavement. The silencing, or rather the severe diminution, of the voice is marked in the text by the truncation of the sorcerer's onomatopoeic vocables – "voum rooh oh" loses its first booming syllable to become an echoing "rooh oh." The reduction leaves us wondering what tonal inflection the next voice (and its concomitant mask) will convey.

The answer is not far to seek. The very next spiral, which we shall refrain from analyzing in detail, parades a speaking subject who takes on cosmic proportions. The voice is apocalyptic in scope, and its articulated project is nothing less than "the End of the world" ("La Fin du monde"). As with previous impersonations, the prophetic voice of doom needs appropriate language, and the poem foregrounds this imperative:

> Des mots? quand nous manions
> des quartiers de monde, quand nous épousons
> des continents en délire, quand
> nous forçons de fumantes portes,
> des mots, ah oui, des mots! mais
> des mots de sang frais

> (Words? when we handle
> whole sections of the world, when we marry
> continents in delirium, when
> we force open smoking doors
> words, ah yes, words! but
> fresh-blooded words)

Though grandiose and ambitious, the staying power of this voice is, in turn, eventually compromised by forces both internal and external. In fine, it takes its place alongside the larger parade of voices that rise and fade in succession, attesting to the plurality of constructed selves that the poet subjects to scorching examination.

Not all of the speaker's impersonations are as elaborate as

the ones I have chosen to describe. A few are simply adumbrated in a kind of rapid stretto. Of special note in this regard are the many evocations of racial stereotypes, such as the black's propensity for rhythm:

> Ou bien tout simplement comme on nous aime!
> Obscènes gaiement, tres doudous de jazz sur leur excès
> d' ennui.
> Je sais le tracking, le Lindy-hop et les claquettes.
>
> (Or else quite simply as they love to see us!
> Joyfully obscene, very sexy with our jazz upon their
> overdose of boredom.
> I can do boogie-woogie, the Lindy-hop and tap-dancing)

The stereotypes, which are images of the self projected by the other, are also brought into the evanescent limelight, only to be discarded in their turn along with the others. Throughout Césaire seems to be cataloguing the various forms or guises that the black identity has assumed in its interaction with the European colonizer. In subjecting them to uncompromising scrutiny he is not so much concerned with repudiating them outright (though exorcism is certainly part of his plan) as with exploring the nature of racial identity, which is always constructed in relation to the other; for it soon becomes painfully clear, as the poem progresses, that certain negative self-images are, or have been at one time, internalized by the first-person narrator.

We have so far been focussing on a strategy of impersonation that appears central to the structure of *Cahier*. Let us now shift attention to an important motif sequence that has contributed greatly to the poem's authority in the universe of letters. This central sequence takes the form of a confessional, in which the narrator, in an attitude of unrelenting candor, bares his soul to the reader and recounts an episode that exposes him in a weak moment of unconscious self-hatred. To appreciate fully its pivotal significance for the poem as a whole, it will be useful to digress briefly on the literary affinities of the motif within the narrative framework of a "return."

In dissecting the poem's title above, we suggested that the

"returning hero" of ancient Greco-Roman epic may at times operate as a kind of subtext to the "retour" of the Martinican student to his island home. If our suggestion is apposite, then the poet's narration of a shameful episode in his past gains a certain rhetorical force from comparison with the epic motif of the "descent into the underworld" (*katabasis*). In the Odyssean variant of the motif, the warrior-hero summons up the shades of various dead comrades and kin and enters into dialogue with them. In Vergil's later epic poem, the descent of Aeneas into Hades enables him to come to terms with his past and includes his well-known poignant confrontation with the silent shade of his lover, Queen Dido. In both these mythical accounts the hero is made to undergo a "descent" before he can achieve a truly representative status for humankind. Césaire's text, as we have seen, portrays a narrator who intermittently assumes an heroic role and undergoes many emotional ups and downs in his efforts to understand the meaning of a "homecoming." Before he can achieve success in his venture he must first enact a descent: in this case, a descent into the psychological depths that brings him face to face with ghosts of his former self.

The descent of the Césairean hero-figure is announced with a measured gravity of tone that underscores its importance:

> Par une inattendue et bienfaisante révolution intérieure, j'honore maintenant mes laideurs repoussantes.

> (By a surprising and salutary internal conversion I now pay homage to my ugly, repellent aspects.)

What follows this solemn declaration is an anecdote that situates the speaker, by way of a virtually allegorical passage, in a ghostly underworld ambience:

> A la Saint-Jean-Baptiste, dès que tombent les premières ombres sur le bourg du Gros-Morne, des centaines de maquignons se réunissent dans la rue "De profundis," dont le nom a du moins la franchise d'avertir d'une ruée des bas-fonds de la Mort. Et c'est de la Mort véritablement, de ses mille mesquines formes locales [. . .] que surgit vers la grand'vie déclose l'étonnante cavalerie des rosses impétueuses.

(At the feast of St. John the Baptist, as soon as the first
shadows fall on the hamlet of Gros-Morne, hundreds of
horse-dealers assemble on "De PROFUNDIS" street, a
name that at least gives clear notice of an influx from the
shallows of Death. And it is from Death in very truth,
death in its thousand ignoble local forms [. . .] that there
surges forth from the barriers towards the great race of
life the staggering cavalry of intrepid nags.)

The narrative setting has explicit eschatological color that
points the reader to the threshold of death. Before making
his foray into the world of the dead, the hero of *Cahier* must
first shed, like his ancient Mesopotamian and Greco-Roman
archetypes, his pretensions to grandeur:

Non, nous n'avons jamais été amazones du Dahomey,
ni princes de Ghana avec huit cents chameaux, ni
docteurs à Tombouctou Askia le Grand étant roi,
ni architectes de Djenné, ni Madhis, ni guerriers.

(No, we have never been Amazons of the king of
Dahomey, nor princes of Ghana with eight hundred
camels, nor scholars at Timbuctu under the reign of Askia
the Great, nor architects of Djenné, nor Madhis, nor
warriors.)

Sardonically denying all claims to a glorious civilized past, the
hero tactically concedes his "ignoble" status. Thus ostensibly
humbled, he is now represented as hearing sounds emanating
from the hold of a slave-ship:

J'entends de la cale monter les malédictions
enchaînées, les hoquettements des mourants, le bruit
d'un qu'on jette à la mer. . . les abois d'une femme en
gésine. . . des raclements d'ongles cherchant des gorges
. . . des ricanements de fouet . . . des farfouillis de vermine
parmi des lassitudes. . .

(I hear rising from the hold the curses in chains, the
hiccuping of the dying, the sound of a person being
thrown overboard . . . the baying of a woman in labor . . .
the scrapings of fingernails groping for throats . . . the
tauntings of the whip . . . the rummaging of vermin amid
bouts of exhaustion . . .)

The phrase "I hear rising from the hold" recalls the poem's opening lines alluding to the "catastrophe" of slavery ("I heard rising from the other shore of the catastrophe"). The tone of the "confessional," therefore, turns out to be quite subtle; for the speaker's sarcasm is directed with uncompromising candor at both the oppressor and the oppressed. As a spokesman for the latter, the current self (*moi*) noisily disavows a noble pedigree and, having stripped away all pretense, proceeds to narrate an incident from his earlier metropolitan life in which he behaved in an unflattering, cowardly manner. The incident occurred on a streetcar and involved a decrepit black man whose hideous appearance evoked ridicule and disdain on the part of the other passengers – among them the narrator himself, who inadvertently slipped into a negative perception of a member of the black underclass:

> Un nègre comique et laid et des femmes derrière
> moi ricanaient en le regardant.
>   Il était COMIQUE ET LAID,
>   COMIQUE ET LAID pour sûr.
> J'arborai un grand sourire complice...
> Ma lâcheté retrouvée!

> (A black man comical and ugly and the women behind me
> sniggered as they looked at him.
>   He was COMICAL AND UGLY
>   COMICAL AND UGLY for sure
> I planted a smile of complicity
> My cowardly self rediscovered!)

The depths of cowardice the narrator confesses to have uncovered are none other than those suppressed feelings of self-hatred that allowed him to share, however briefly, the disdain and ridicule directed against a member of his own race. Spiritually, this moment of antipathy that he dredges up from his past represents a nadir of being, which, however, is a prerequisite of his later recovery of a healed and integrated self-image. At this low point in the re-enactment of his "cowardice," his unrelenting introspection leads him to a moment of illumination:

Mon héroisme, quelle farce!
Cette ville est à ma taille.
Et mon âme est couchée. Comme cette ville dans la crasse
et dans la boue couchée.
Cette ville, ma face de boue.

(My heroism, what a farce!
This town is my measure
And my spirit is prostrate. Like this town prostrate
in filth and mud.
This town, my face of mud)

In this moving self-revelation, the distance the speaker had
earlier maintained between himself and his prostrate country
is made to collapse abruptly, and the abject condition of the
latter becomes one with the moral abjection of the former. Put
another way, the narrator has hitherto in the poem been
representing Martinique as alien to his own project of self-
renewal. The alienation reaches an extreme in the episode on
the tram, which, paradoxically, enables him to come to terms
with the repressed facets of his psyche. Thus the descent of the
poet is pivotal to the poem's macro-structure, because it causes
the reader to revise his or her perspective on the speaker's
relationship to his subject up to this juncture. All the prior
reiterations regarding the dejected state of the island and its
populace are now fully acknowledged to be aspects of the poet's
self. There is no glossing over, no convenient self-serving
elisions of the embarrassing or unsightly. Above all, the
narrator-hero ("my heroism, what a farce!") will be capable of
achieving empathy with his race only by uncompromising self-
searching ("this town, my face of mud"). The ever-present
temptation of all "assimilated" blacks to "identify with the
oppressor" is here both faced and transcended. The means to
that transcendence, we have come to learn in the course of
the poem, is a fearless interior journey into one's subliminal
consciousness.

   It is against the background of a painfully gained insight
that we can best understand the positive affirmation of
négritude we hear resounding through the later portions
of *Cahier*. This is particularly so in regard to those purple

passages, often cited without reference to context, in which the speaker appears to supply a definition of négritude. These passages offer a golden opportunity to anthologizers in search of a simple message, and as such have played a formidable, though misleading, role in the international reception of *Cahier*. Let us take a fresh look at some of these famous lines within the framework of our theme of the exploration of multiple selves:

> Tiède petit matin de chaleur et de peur ancestrales je tremble maintenant du commun tremblement que notre sang docile chante dans le madrépore.

Et ces têtards en moi éclos de mon ascendance
    prodigieuse!
Ceux qui n'ont inventé ni la poudre ni la boussole
ceux qui n'ont jamais su dompter la vapeur ni
    l'électricité
ceux qui n'ont exploré ni les mers ni le ciel
mais ils savent en ses moindres recoins le pays de
    souffrance
ceux qui n'ont connu de voyages que de déracinements
ceux qui se sont assouplis aux agenouillements
ceux qu'on domestiqua et christianisa
ceux qu'on inocula d'abâtardissement
tam-tams de mains vides
tam-tams inanes de plaies sonores
tam-tams burlesques de trahison tabide

> Tiède petit matin de chaleurs et de peurs ancestrales
> par-dessus bord mes richesses pérégrines
> par-dessus bord mes faussetés authentiques
> Mais quel étrange orgueil tout soudain m'illumine?

(Warm early dawn of our forefathers' heat and fears I am trembling now with the communal trembling that our compliant blood sings in the madrepore

And these tadpoles within me hatched from my
    prodigious lineage!
Those who have invented neither gunpowder nor
    compass
those who have never tamed steam or electricity
those who have explored neither oceans nor sky,

but know in its innermost recesses the country of
   suffering
those whose only journeys have been uprootings
those who have become pliant with kneelings
those who have been domesticated and christianized
those who have been inoculated with debasement
tom-toms of empty hands
jejune tom-toms of resonant sores
burlesque tom-toms of a wasting betrayal

   Warm early dawn of my forefathers' heat and fears
Overboard with my alien wealth
overboard with my authentic deceptions
But what strange pride illumines me all of a sudden?)

The timing of this affirmation of pride, and of its attendant
illumination, is as important as its form and content. The note
of assertiveness in the voice is the gauge of the new insight
the narrator has gained from the ordeal of the *katabasis*.
Figuratively, the note is registered as an emerging warmth
that suffuses the ambience of dawn ("*warm* early dawn . . . ").
The gradual access of ancestral heat causes the speaker to
tremble in a rapture of rediscovered empathy with his African
self. The lyric context, then, of Césaire's assertions about
African civilization ("those who . . . ") discourages us from
misconstruing them as straightforward declarations of an
"essential" blackness; rather, they are presented in the poem
as the proud utterances of a speaking subject who has been
experimenting with various forms of self-characterization
and who has now emerged from the crucible with new
insight.

   It is important to note that the grammatical formulation of
the series of assertions is, at first, in the negative: the African
achievement ("négritude") is basically introduced by a
declaration of what it is *not*. Moreover, as we already pointed
out above, there is undeniable irony in the speaker's outright
denial of technological inventiveness to Africans. At the same
time, the "definition" of négritude in this passage reconnects
with the poem's opening vision in which the inner (spiritual)
resources of the black protagonist ("turtledoves and savannah

clover") were seen as antipodal to the hubristic skyscrapers of the dominant culture.

The sense of a deep cultural difference between Europe and Africa is part and parcel of the poet's embryonic self-understanding, which he expresses in zoological metaphor as "tadpoles within me hatched from my prodigious lineage." The tadpole metaphor, despite its biological cast, has "African" cultural origins of a sort: the creation of the world is pictured in at least one prestigious Ancient Egyptian cosmogonic myth as taking place in a watery primal mud from which life emerges in the form of amphibious, frog-like creatures. Thus the trembling self (*moi*) who intones the encomium of négritude is warmed by the renascence of a black identity that is fundamentally cultural and historical. This broader identity is not reducible to a simplistic notion of a strictly biological essence, but is specially qualified in terms of historical experience ("the country of suffering"). In fine, the "country" to which the poet is attempting to return has once again been re-defined according to the ever-shifting contours of the poet's imagination. This re-defined country, moreover, is not presented as a separate, pristine entity, but rather is intimately entangled with that of the European "other." In erecting his famous antitheses, then, Césaire is not positing two divorced civilizations (Black Africa and Europe); instead, with a sophistication that often escapes both his admirers and his critics, he perceives négritude as a dynamic, historically rooted locus of cultural interaction between the two (while, of course, recognizing the often violent nature of such interaction).

As he progressively articulates his vision of black civilization, the poet returns to sweeping characterizations that serve to refine the concept of négritude:

> ô lumière amicale
> ô fraîche source de la lumière
> ceux qui n'ont inventé ni la poudre ni la boussole
> ceux qui n'ont jamais su dompter la vapeur ni
>   l'électricité
> ceux qui n'ont exploré ni les mers ni le ciel mais ceux
> sans qui la terre ne serait pas la terre

gibbosité d'autant plus bienfaisante que la terre déserte
davantage la terre
silo où se préserve et mûrit ce que la terre a de plus terre
ma négritude n'est pas une pierre, sa surdité ruée contre
la clameur du jour
ma négritude n'est pas une taie d'eau morte sur l'œil
mort de la terre
ma négritude n'est ni une tour ni une cathédrale
elle plonge dans la chair rouge du sol
elle plonge dans la chair ardente du ciel
elle troue l'accablement opaque de sa droite patience.

(O friendly light
O pristine source of light
those who invented neither gunpowder nor compass
those who have never tamed steam or electricity
those who have explored neither oceans nor sky
but without whom the earth would not be the earth
excrescence all the more benign as the earth more and
more deserts the earth
grain silo where germinates and ripens what is most
earth upon the earth
my négritude is not a stone, its deafness heaved against
the clamor of day
my négritude is not a film of dead water on the dead eye
of earth
my négritude is neither a tower nor a cathedral
it delves into the red flesh of the soil
it delves into the burning flesh of the sky
it penetrates the dark debasement of its righteous
patience)

Whereas the earlier pseudo-definition concentrated on what
négritude was *not*, the reprise gives us a more elaborate statement of what it presumably *is*. Here again the predications
need to be understood in the context of an evolving concept of a
valorized self. Syntax, as usual, provides a salient clue to the
underlying ideas: négritude is positively defined not by
predicate nouns (like its opposite number) but by verbs (*plonge*,
troue: delves, penetrates). The shift to verbs strongly indicates
that négritude is not to be regarded as a state, but an activity –
an activity of self-exploration, of "delving" into the psycho-

social unconscious. Négritude is nothing less than the ongoing process itself, the subterranean interior journey. The "hole" dug (*troué*) by négritude in this process is a key figure to which we shall be reverting when we come to discuss the poem's enigmatic closing lines that speak of "the great black hole."

We shall from time to time revisit the question of what négritude signifies for the poet of *Cahier*. So far we have adduced enough textual support for the view that the definition is elastic and cannot therefore be encompassed by a simple predicate of the form "négritude is X." Let us continue our guided tour through the poem's main ideas by focussing on the last two grand sequences, which we may label "Prayer" and "Transfiguration."

"Prayer" is, in fact, the actual term the speaker employs to initiate the penultimate sequence:

> et voici au bout de ce petit matin ma prière virile
> que je n'entende ni les rires ni les cris, les yeux fixés
> sur cette ville que je prophétise, belle

> (and here at the end of this early dawn is my virile prayer
> that I may hear neither mockery nor howling, my eyes
> focussed on this town that I presage beautiful)

The prayer becomes a self-fulfilling prophecy, for the new-found beauty of the town (in contrast to its former ugliness) is actually celebrated, by implication, in the remainder of the poem.[9] Students of liturgical style have long been aware that a basic strategy of hymns is to request a favor from a divine agent in such a way that the granting of the favor appears to be a foregone conclusion. In a famous hymn to Aphrodite by the poet Sappho, for example, the composer calls on the goddess to appear and proceeds to represent her in the text as actually appearing in answer to her prayer. It is consonant with such a covert strategy that the prayer sequence in *Cahier* should culminate in what I have called a Transfiguration. Before looking more closely at the scope of the latter, it will be useful to analyze certain features of the "virile prayer" itself.

In terms of our broader framework of successive masks, it is significant that the prayer sequence is uttered by a hierophant who also has prophetic powers. The tone of the utterance is conciliatory, even reverent. The voice of the speaker has modulated to a new key, in which opposites are reconciled, as the liturgist simultaneously solicits and affirms the need for both creation and destruction, sowing and reaping:

> faites de moi un homme de terminaison
> faites de moi un homme d'initiation
> faites de moi un homme de recueillement
> mais faites aussi de moi un homme d'ensemencement
>
> faites de moi l'exécuteur de ces œuvres hautes
> voici le temps de se ceindre les reins comme un vaillant
>   homme –
>
> (make of me a man of closure
> make of me a man of initiation
> make of me a man of reaping
> but also make of me a man of sowing
>
> make of me one who implements these grand projects
> now is the time to gird one's loins like a valiant man –)

In the contrasted pairs, closure/initiation and reaping/sowing, we may detect undertones of the biblical text of Ecclesiastes ("a time to sow and a time to reap"), especially since the speaker has just renounced all vanity ("make me repudiate all vanity," "faites-moi rebelle à toute vanité"). The subject of human vanity, is, of course, a major leitmotif of the "preacher" who composed the book of Ecclesiastes ("Vanity of vanities, saith the preacher; all is vanity and vexation of spirit"). Césaire's humbled persona, who has thereby acquired inner strength, now launches into a dialogue with his own no longer divided self ("heart of mine", "mon cœur"):

> Mais les faisant, mon cœur, préservez-moi de toute haine
> ne faites point de moi cet homme de haine
> pour qui je n'ai que haine
> car pour me cantonner en cette unique race
> vous savez pourtant mon amour tyrannique
> vous savez que ce n'est point par haine des autres races
> que je m'exige bêcheur de cette unique race
> que ce que je veux

c'est pour la faim universelle
pour la soif universelle

la sommer libre enfin
de produire de son intimité close
la succulence des fruits

(But in so doing, heart of mine, preserve me from all hate
Do not make of me that man of hate
for whom I have only hate
for to enclose myself in this unique race
you know nonetheless my despotic love
you know that it is not from hatred of other races
that I make myself the husbandman of this unique race
that what I most desire
is for the universal hunger
the universal thirst

is to commit my race, free at last,
to producing from its closed intimacy
the succulence of fruits.)

In this renowned disavowal of racial hatred, the mature persona is able to come to terms with his own particular racial identity ("enclose myself in this unique race"), while envisioning a world in which diverse cultures flourish side by side. *Cahier* thus contains its own correction to the mistaken notion that négritude is a form of "racism in reverse," or even "anti-racist racism," as Jean-Paul Sartre famously styled it in his influential essay "Black Orpheus." Although careful readers of *Cahier* have grasped its universalist values, Césaire has been obliged in later years to clarify this aspect of the concept of black identity:

The question has been raised whether this notion of négritude is not a form of racism. I believe that the texts speak for themselves [*les textes sont là*]. One has only to read them and any reader of good faith will perceive that if négritude involves taking root in a particular soil [*un enracinement particulier*], négritude is also transcendence and expansion into the universal.[10]

An image that comes to assume a central role in the climax of the prayer is that of the poet on a sea-voyage. In our first

encounter with the image, the speaker is praying for a partial
metamorphosis into a proud vessel:

> Faites de ma tête une tête de proue
>
> (make of my head a figure-head)

The part is extended to the whole a few lines later where the
poet represents himself as a proud canoe (*pirogue*) that braves
the open sea:

> donnez-moi sur cet océan divers
> l'obstination de la fière pirogue
> et sa vigueur marine.
>
> La voici avancer par escalades et retombées sur le flot
>   pulverisé [...]
> et voici par vingt fois d'un labour vigoureux la pagaie
> forcer l'eau
> la pirogue se cabre sous l'assaut de la lame,
> dévie un instant,
> tente de fuir,
> mais la caresse rude de la pagaie la vire,
> alors elle fonce, un frémissement parcourt l'échine
>   de la vague,
> la mer bave et gronde
> la pirogue comme un traîneau file sur le sable.
>
>
> (grant me on this changing ocean
> the tenacity of the proud canoe
> and its marine robustness
>
> Here it comes forward rising and falling on the
>   pulverized wave [...]
> Now look: twenty times over with strenuous labor the
>   paddle
> shoves the water
> the canoe rears under the assault of the surge
> wavers a while
> tries to escape
> but the rough caress of the paddle makes it veer,
> then it surges forward, a shudder runs down the spine of
>   the wave,
> the sea slavers and growls
> the canoe like a sled slips onto the sand)

The epic journey of the vessel over the tumultuous sea becomes a metaphor for the poem's course of self-discovery with its uneven, spasmodic, progress, temporary setbacks, twists and turns, divagations.

The marine voyage eventually culminates in a spectacular Transfiguration. Here the humble canoe is supplanted by a slave-ship. In the final lap of the journey the slave-ship itself goes through a dramatic mutation: the poet imagines a reversal of history whereby the abject, enchained slaves in the hold break their bonds, stand upright and, in effect, become masters of their destiny. Though the conceit is too elaborate and extensive to be fully reproduced here, the following excerpt will serve to convey the riveting impact of the passage as a whole:

> Je dis hurrah! La vieille négritude
> progressivement se cadavérise
> l'horizon se défait, recule et s'élargit
> et voici parmi des déchirements de nuages la fulgurance
>   d'un signe
> le négrier craque de toute part . . . Son ventre se convulse
> et résonne. . . L'affreux ténia de sa cargaison ronge les
> boyaux fétides de l'étrange nourrisson des mers! [. . .]
>
> La négraille aux senteurs d'oignon frit retrouve dans son
> sang répandu le goût amer de la liberté
>
> Et elle est debout la négraille
>
> la négraille assise
> inattendument debout
> debout dans la cale
> debout dans les cabines
> debout sur le pont
> debout dans le vent
> debout sous le soleil
> debout dans le sang
>   debout
>   et
>   libre
> debout et non point pauvre folle dans sa liberté et son
> dénuement maritimes girant en la dérive parfaite
> et la voici:

plus inattendument debout
debout dans les cordages
debout à la barre
debout à la boussole
debout à la carte
debout sous les étoiles
   debout
     et
       libre
et le navire lustral s'avancer impavide sur les eaux
   écroulées

(I say "hurray!" The old négritude
is gradually becoming a corpse
the horizon falls apart, retreats and expands
and behold the lightning-flash of a sign as it tears
   asunder the clouds
the slave-ship cracks in every part . . . its belly goes into
spasms . . . The gruesome tapeworm of its cargo gnaws at
the foul bowels of the seas' grotesque nursling [. . .]

The black cargo with its fried onion smell rediscovers in
its spilled blood the bitter taste of freedom

And the black cargo stands upright

The black cargo that was sitting down
is unexpectedly standing upright
upright in the hold
upright in the cabins
upright on the bridge
upright in the wind
upright under the sun
upright in the blood
   upright
     and
       free
upright and by no means pauperized or mad in its
seaborne freedom and destitution, turning and turning in
a perfect drift
and here it is:
most unexpectedly upright
upright in the rigging
upright at the helm

upright at the compass
upright at the map
upright beneath the stars
  upright
    and
      free
and the lustral vessel advances without fear over the
  whelming flood)

Césaire's vision of a transfiguration is presented not as a prescription for the future, but as a radical reversal of history. The emblem of past affliction – the vessel carrying its black human cargo across the Atlantic – is converted into a site of imagined revolution. In the new topsy-turvy order the slaves take command of the ship and usurp control of the helm. Some of the vivid images used to describe the transfiguration of the slave cargo hark back, like so many others in the closing portion of *Cahier*, to the beginning of the poem. Thus the stasis and horizontal posture of the present-day Martinican populace is now systematically reversed in this projection into the past, and they are restored to an upright stance (the word "upright", "debout," is reiterated in a powerful crescendo).

The epithet "lustral" as applied to the ship tells us that we are witnessing an act of cleansing and exorcism (compare the Latin *lustrum* in its primary sense of ritual purification). The empowerment of the subjugated black race is represented figuratively as a kind of redemptive mutiny in the course of the infamous Middle Passage, whereby the crew is displaced on shipboard by its cargo, the slaves. As we reflect on the controlling image of the sea-voyage and its permutations, we avail ourselves of the hindsight afforded by this Atlantic takeover to interlink Prayer and Transfiguration. Self-knowledge pursued mercilessly and aggressively has led to both psychic liberation and empowerment.

The finale of *Cahier* is grand and heavily orchestrated. The speaker now assumes the mask of a triumphant apostle of freedom who is envisaged as ascending to a paradise in which racism is finally left far behind. Enlisting in his aid his reclaimed cultural inheritance (including his "bad nigger

dances," "Mes danses de mauvais nègre") he summons up the
wind and, in a ritual gesture of riddance, he delivers himself of
oppressive icons of the slave-trade, such as the chain-gang and
"the visa for the triangular circuit." Once the cathartic gesture
is complete, the speaker enjoins the same wind, which has both
apotropaic and regenerative powers, to embrace him and
ultimately to "bind" him. This "binding," paradoxically, is
purely positive. Having relinquished the bonds of slavery, he
voluntarily acquires new "bonds":

> mais alors embrasse
> comme un champ de justes filaos
> le soir
> nos multicolores puretés
> et lie, lie-moi sans remords
> lie-moi de tes vastes bras à l'argile lumineuse
> lie ma noire vibration au nombril même du monde
> lie, lie-moi, fraternité âpre
> puis, m'étranglant de ton lasso d'étoiles
> monte,
> Colombe
> monte
> monte
> monte
> Je te suis, imprimée en mon ancestrale cornée blanche
> monte lécheur de ciel
> et le grand trou noir où je voulais me noyer l'autre
> lune c'est là que je veux pêcher maintenant la langue
> maléfique de la nuit en son immobile verrition!

> (therefore embrace
> like a stand of equable casuarinas
> at eventide
> our pure multicolored selves
> and bind, bind me without chagrin
> bind me with your vast arms to the luminous clay
> bind my black vibration to the very navel of the world
> bind, o bind me, bitter fraternity,
> then strangling me with your lasso of stars
> ascend
> Dove
> ascend
> ascend

ascend
I follow you, who are inscribed in my ancestral white
    cornea
ascend to lick the sky
and the great black hole wherein I longed to drown myself
the other moon – that's where I now long to fish out the
baleful tongue of night in its lustral stillness!)

The instrumentality of the "wind" (*vent*) in the speaker's closing ascension is rigorously predetermined: it recapitulates the expository section of the poem in which the poet is said to have "nurtured the wind" and "unloosed the monsters." The end is thus closely tied to the beginning in its dominant imagery.

The last three lines of the poem, which I have here translated into English in terms less opaque than the original, are an interpretive crux. The very final phrase "lustral stillness" ("immobile verrition") contains a neologism that remains cryptic despite efforts on the part of translators and exegetes to conjecture a plausible Latin etymological base.[11] "Still" (*immobile*) when conjoined with the act of "sweeping" (*verrition*) constitutes an oxymoron that creates an aura of mystery and epiphany. Without attempting to dissolve Césaire's complexity into a reassuring unity, we would do well to focus our attention on the imagistic structure of the passage as a whole.

A salient aspect of the imagery in the finale is the conjunction of opposites, chief among them earth and heaven. Thus a terrestrial "luminous clay," for instance, is brought into contact with a celestial "lasso of stars" (the intermediary being the bound poet). In short, the paradise to which the poet/narrator ascends in his transfigured state is not a realm detached from mundane historical and social realities. On the contrary, it is precisely because he has been re-connected, in his visionary ascension, to his cultural umbilicus ("the very navel of the earth") that he is able to transcend the slough of oppression and racism. This ultimate re-connection is the fulfillment of what the poet foreshadowed in the poem's overture, where he spoke of reaching downwards into the depths of his cultural (notionally "African") subconscious: "savannah clover that I always carry in my inmost being at a depth inverse to the height of the twentieth floor of the most supercilious edifices." His spectacular "ascension," then, is predicated on a prior "descent" into the depths of self-knowledge – the journey accomplished by speaker and reader in the course of *Cahier*.

Despite the intimation of apotheosis implied in the motif of a ritual ascension, the poem's finale re-focusses our perception of négritude as a *process* of self-exploration and recuperation. This re-focussing is mainly facilitated by the mention of "the great black hole" (*grand trou noir*) in which the speaker previously wished to drown, but from which he now wishes to "fish out the baleful tongue of night." For partial illumination of the "black hole" figure the reader may recall one of the earlier pseudo-definitions of négritude offered in the poem, where it was described as an *activity* of excavation ("it penetrates [*troue*] the dark debasement of its righteous patience"). The black hole (*trou*), then, may be read as an internal cross-reference, signifying, among other things, the spiritual space uncovered by the poet's persistent probing of the depths of a plural black identity. In this account, the figure of "fishing" in the black hole points to the never-quite-concluded quest for an authentic self – a search that is not without the danger of "drowning" in a vast sea of racial consciousness. The poem's closure, then, is intimately bound up with the complex thematic trajectory it has followed throughout. The liberation that *Cahier* envisions is ultimately the freedom to examine ready-made identities – fragmentary models of the self – and to re-make them into an integrated whole with the connivance of an engaged reader.

Our account of négritude as it is obliquely articulated on the pages of *Cahier* sees it as multivocal. The history of the poem's reception, however, is replete with accounts that read it as largely univocal. More often that not, one of the many voices in the poem that utters confident pronouncements about blackness is assumed to be the authentic voice of Césaire himself. As a consequence of this reductionism, the poem has often acquired an almost scriptural authority for writers who tend to rely upon appeals to an authoritative text in justification of their particular ideological positions. As there are many socialisms and many feminisms, however, so there are many négritudes that have taken Césaire's famous text as their point of departure. Even Césaire's close friend Léopold Senghor has developed his own elaborate version that differs from the Martinican's in its adherence to an essentialist view of racial identity. Césaire himself has come to regard his own verbal invention (no less than the elusive premisses that underlie it) as something of an intellectual albatross, and has gone so far as to disavow any notion of a biological dimension inhering in the controversial concept. In my view, the very cloudiness that has come to envelop the term and the contentious discourse it has generated is due, in large part, to the medium in which it was first articulated. Poetry constructs its own myths. The Césairean myth of négritude has proved to be potent precisely because it strikes sensitive readers as true to the density and opacity of social identity-formation. More abstract formulations are best left to pseudo-science, as Césaire himself suggested when, in the course of an interview with the Haitian writer, René Depestre, he insisted on the concrete, lived reality of négritude as he envisions it:[12]

There has been a great deal of theorizing about négritude. I have avoided doing so, due to my personal involvement with it. But if I am asked how I conceive of négritude, I would say that négritude is above all the achievement of a concrete, as against an abstract, awareness of a situation [...] I always thought that the black man was in search of an identity. And it seemed to me that the first thing one had to do to affirm this identity was to achieve a concrete consciousness of one's situation, of the primary fact: that one is a Negro, that we are blacks who had a past, that this offered cultural elements which had been valid, that the blacks [...] had not fallen out of the blue, that there had been black civilizations which were important and beautiful.

The concrete articulation of négritude in the verses of *Cahier* is the conceptual embryo from which all of Césaire's subsequent lyric œuvre has grown and ramified.

CHAPTER 3

Inventing a lyric voice: the forging of "Miracle Weapons"

> I do not often have occasion to re-read my poems. They
> have traced the pathway of my life, have circumscribed
> and defined my life.
>
> Aimé Césaire[1]

Césaire's actual return to his native island (as distinct from his
fictional "return" enacted in the pages of *Cahier*) plunged him
at once into a maelstrom of intense political and intellectual
activity. The monsters of the Second World War had already
been unleashed (hostilities broke out, in fact, as he was making
the homeward journey by ship), and the Martinique to which
he came home fell temporarily under the sway of the infamous
Vichy regime, which was in open collaboration with the Nazi
government. The society to which he now sought to commit his
passion and energy was thus subject to the double oppression
of colonialism and fascism. Not content to be an inspired
teacher at the Lycée Schoelcher, where he himself had
previously been a prize pupil, he soon took his place at the fore-
front of the local artistic and political scene. His emergent
lyric voice, then, was forged in the heat of a traumatic global
convulsion and its aftermath, when the educated elite of the
colonies was both reacting to the apparent debacle of
European culture and intent on supplanting, if not destroying
once and for all, the colonial order. Before attempting to
illustrate these developments, it may be useful to sketch very
briefly the political and social circumstances in which Césaire
invented his distinctive lyric voice.

Now that the war was in full career Martinique was, of

course, plagued by acute economic hardships such as food shortages, and the entire archipelago, though geographically peripheral to the main conflict, became an arena of sporadic military (mainly naval submarine) activity. The military conflagration (which came, it must be remembered, on the heels of the Great Depression) effectively ruled out any immediate prospect of improving the harsh conditions of the black population of the island. No less painful than the subsequent material deprivation was the grim realization that a black working-class population whose emancipation from slavery was less than a century old would be obliged to endure further postponement of its complete liberation. For a young poet who was also deeply committed to radical social change (the author of *Cahier* was 28 years old in 1941) the incubus of the war must have occasioned a great deal of frustration. Social progress, which entailed, at bottom, the success of decolonization, had to be deferred while the Martinicans, like other subject peoples at the margins of the global conflict, experienced the repercussions of a major crisis of Western civilization. In words that seem, in retrospect, to have foreshadowed the debacle, Césaire had written in *Cahier*:

> Listen, all, to the white world
> grimly exhausted from its bloated striving
> its protesting joints cracking under rigid stars
> its blue steel stiffness piercing through mystic flesh
> listen, each, to its pyrrhic victories trumpeting its defeats
> listen, each, to its grandiose alibis, its dismal stumbling

It was during this historical moment of "dismal stumbling" on the part of the European colonial powers that Césaire and his intellectual comrades (who included his wife, Suzanne Césaire, and his friends, René Menil, Aristide Maugée and Georges Gratiant), co-founded the remarkable literary journal *Tropiques*, which ran, except for a year's hiatus, from 1941 to 1945, and became the standard-bearer of a new orientation for francophone Caribbean poetics. The journal gave the editors and contributors a unique forum for articulating a new Caribbean aesthetic and, more broadly, for valorizing the non-European – primarily African – element in the cultures of the New World. The socio-political impact of the war is partly registered in the precarious life of the journal itself, which, in its five-year span, barely survived official censorship, not to mention material threats such as lack of paper (at one point the authorities actually refused to allow delivery of a shipment of paper to the local printers). Publication of the journal was actually interrupted during the turbulent events of 1943, when there were popular demonstrations against the colonial administration in the person of its local representative, Admiral Robert. Because of official harassment, the *Tropiques* circle resorted, like many artists working within the orbit of totalitarian regimes, to oblique means of political critique. Poetry was one such means, a "miracle weapon," to borrow from the title Césaire would give to his next collection of lyric poems, that enabled the writers to register their dissent from the official propaganda of German-occupied France.

In its deceptively modest way, therefore, the group associated with the journal may be said to have played its part in the resistance to Vichy through its constant promulgation of an ethos of freedom, both cultural and political. In more concrete terms, Césaire himself spoke out against collaboration, most conspicuously in an "open letter" to a local Catholic prelate who had attempted, in a pastoral communication, to exculpate the Catholic church from complicity in the racialist policies of the Third Reich. What sparked the confrontation between the bishop and the poet was a courageous public lecture (delivered in Martinique at Césaire's invitation) by René Etiemble with the pointed title "The opposition between Vichy ideology and French thought" ("L'idéologie de Vichy contre la pensée française"). Like the rest of Césaire's prose, the defense of his friend Etiemble – a devastating critique of the connivance of the church in negro slavery, among other oppressions – is laced with apt historical documentation and well-chosen citations, and written in a vivid, arresting style that employs pungent irony. As an exposé of Western hypocrisy it anticipates the fulgurance of the author's later masterpiece, *Discourse on Colonialism* (*Discours sur le colonialisme*). Césaire's willingness to confront publicly a figure of considerable regional stature proves that his opposition to fascism was by no means confined to cryptic utterances in poetic texts.

The years during and immediately after the global cataclysm were therefore pivotal in the shaping of Césaire both as literary artist and as future political leader. The culmination of this formative period was marked by two events of equal importance in his dual identity: his election as mayor of Fort-de-France (Martinique's capital) in May 1945, and the publication, a year later, of his first collection of poems in book form, *Les Armes miraculeuses* ("Miracle Weapons"). The chronology of these two landmark events is not due to mere coincidence: they precisely mirror Césaire's profound conception of the poet as socially committed (*engagé*). Poetic activity, in his way of thinking no less than in his practice, goes hand in hand with a program of social transformation. In this regard, Césaire's attitude is in tension with the famous dictum of W. H. Auden in his tribute to the poet W. B. Yeats: "For poetry makes nothing happen." Césaire clearly has considerable faith in the magical power of words, as passages in *Cahier* so eloquently testify. At the same time, however, he has always been prepared, like so many intellectuals and artists in the French tradition, to act on his convictions, rather than to fold his arms in the guise of a spectator ("for life is not a stage," as he says in *Cahier*). To his great credit, while espousing the notion that poetry can and does make things happen, he has always taken the further step of involvement in electoral politics at the highest levels of leadership of his community. Thus the seeds of a fecund integration of art and life, of poetry and politics, which was to become a constant of Césaire's extraordinary career had already been sown in the fervid intellectual climate of wartime Martinique.

The hybrid subtropical plant that sprouted in the mayoral elections of 1945 bore an aura of the miraculous: here was a tireless, optimistic intellectual who did not shrink from playing a decisive role in the events that determined the constitutional status of postcolonial Martinique. To this end he courageously met the challenge of helping to bring about a social transformation by working within the framework of the French Communist Party. His prominent activities as a delegate to the first National Constituent Assembly led naturally to his being elected deputy in the inaugural legislative body of the Fourth Republic in November 1947. Césaire was henceforth in a position to be an effective spokesman for his people – to enact, that is, one of the many exalted roles he had imagined for the speaker of *Cahier*. It was in this parliamentary capacity that he became a prime supporter of the controversial law that led to the creation of "departmental" status for the former French Caribbean colonies (Martinique, Guadeloupe, French Guiana and their dependencies). Since the consequences, social and economic, of "departmentalization" cannot properly be evaluated without reference to an ongoing postcolonial debate about the true meaning of decolonization and nationhood, let us defer our discussion of this vexed issue until we come to consider Césaire's interrelated activities as poet and politician in the 1950s (see ch. 4). For the moment, let us return to the ambience of a moribund colonial order in an impoverished island where Césaire, as writer and activist, composed the poems that were to be gathered into his armoury of "Miracle Weapons."

At the very same time that his political destiny as mayor and deputy began to take definitive shape, Césaire also went to work fabricating a poetics that can be reconstructed, in part, by a visit to the workshop – the journal *Tropiques*. One of the main instruments utilized in that literary workshop is the aesthetic movement that came to be called "surrealism." The explicit use of surrealist ideas as well as techniques is attested by a significant number of articles by Césaire himself and his wife and important collaborator, Suzanne, extolling the achievements of surrealism's major progenitors, such as Lautréamont, Rimbaud and, above all, André Breton himself. Without a clear grasp of the peculiar Caribbean inflexion that Césaire and his circle imparted to the grander surrealist project, the reader who tries to penetrate the often opaque world of "Miracle Weapons" is at a distinct disadvantage.

As we remarked above in chapter 1, it was during his student days in the metropolis that Césaire, under the stimulus of contact with other francophone blacks, first seriously confronted the question of cultural "assimilation" as it affected colonials of African descent. Prewar Paris was also, of course, the matrix of major European (and *ipso facto* "white") avant-garde movements in art and literature, and these currents indisputably made a deep impression on a young, black, ambivalently "assimilated" poet. Chief among these movements was arguably surrealism, which had a very ambitious agenda for a wholesale spiritual revolution and did not shrink from allying itself, albeit shakily, with radical politics – especially with the French Communist Party. Such a combination of the socially progressive with the artistically iconoclastic could not but appeal to a sensitive black intellectual who was being drawn, by education and temperament, into the struggle against colonialism and racism. As the dedications of several of his poems indicate, Césaire was personally acquainted with, as well as intellectually attracted to, leading members, poets as well as visual artists, of the surrealist group, such as Paul Eluard, Benjamin Péret, André Breton and Pablo Picasso – to name a few of the more renowned practitioners. As A. J. Arnold and others have amply documented, Césaire's work cannot be dissociated, in its artistic kernel, from a fundamental modernist agenda, however culturally inflected it came to be in the immediate context of postcolonial Martinique. In this regard it is essential to realize that his familiarity with some of the prominent architects of modernism was in no way superficial, or confined to a study of their work. Actual historical contacts between surrealist artists and Césaire's circle should not be minimized or glossed over. André Breton, the self-anointed leader of the movement, actually visited the island of Martinique in 1941 on his way to America – a visit that both he and Césaire separately declared to have been mutually inspiring. Other artists, like the painter André Masson and the poet Benjamin Péret, made their presence felt among, and were themselves affected by, their New World artistic counterparts (Péret spent the war years in Mexico, along with other surrealist comrades).

It is by no means fortuitous, therefore, that the symbolic induction of Césaire into the surrealist "canon" was marked in spectacular ways. First and foremost in these acts of canonization was Breton's well-known accolade in the preface to the 1947 editions of *Cahier*. Breton's encomium has to be appreciated in the context of his own account of his meeting with Césaire, which we shall be discussing below in connection with our presentation of Caribbean surrealism. For the overall history of the movement, it is of prime significance that Césaire contributed to the International Exhibition of Surrealism that took place in Paris, also in the year 1947. Finally, and perhaps no less conspicuously in terms of international prestige, a volume of Césaire's poetry, *Corps perdu* ("Break Neck"),[2] was published in Paris three years later (1950) in a deluxe, limited edition, with illustrative drawings by none other than Pablo Picasso himself.

It is a truism that surrealism, which began as a literary movement in Paris of the 1920s, came to embrace a somewhat diverse and fluid grouping of artists and writers, especially during its heyday in the interwar decades. Despite the quixotic efforts of its acknowledged leader, André Breton, to prescribe what he saw as authentic surrealism (the 1947 International Exhibition was one such gesture), the painters, poets and cinematographers who aligned themselves with the movement at various times proved uncontainable within strict doctrinal bounds. At the risk of over-simplification, it will be useful to summarize briefly the main features of the common ground shared by most of its devotees.

Absolutely fundamental to the creed was the elevation of the unconscious (in Freud's sense) as the source of a liberated art, and a corresponding denigration of the conscious and the rational. As Breton himself made crystal clear in an important speech, "The Situation of Surrealism between the Two Wars":[3]

One must grant to Freud that the exploration of the unconscious life furnishes the only worthwhile basis for appreciation of the motives which make the human being act. The so-called conscious justifications which pretend to dismiss these motives easily only cover over the dirt with polish. Starting from these premises, surrealism has continuously emphasized "automatism," not only as a method of expression on the literary and artistic level, but, moreover, as a first-step toward a general revision of the modes of knowledge.

Breton and his followers thus strove to valorize those psychic activities that appeared to register the unconscious in its purest, unmediated form, e.g. dreams (including nightmares), hallucinations, psychoses ("madness") and the play of the libido. They were also driven by a desire to recapture and reveal the "sur-real" world of the "marvelous" (*le merveilleux*) – a world that intersects randomly with the real, but is normally veiled, except to privileged persons such as true poets, madmen, children, primitives and, predictably, women. From these fundamental beliefs and desires may be derived all the familiar shibboleths of surrealist rhetoric, e.g. the vogue of so-called "automatic writing" (realized more in the breach than the observance), the obsession with shocking images that juxtapose objects from disparate spheres of life, the alleged subversion of Cartesian logic, the worship of magic and mystic revelation, the idealization of Woman as embodiment of Nature. Above all, the surrealist project was conceived in the most grandiose terms: it envisaged no less than a total transformation of the human spirit as a result of the widespread adoption of its central tenets. At bottom, then, life and art are fused in the surrealist vision. Though originating in the realm of the surreal, the work of art affects, and even helps to re-define, the real. Running through the entire enterprise is a strong millenarian streak that is perhaps most clearly visible in the published "manifestos" for which the movement is famous. As the poet Octavio Paz says in his illuminating and sympathetic essay on the chief surrealist guru:

In the case of Breton, moreover, there is the vision of time not as a succession but as the constant, though invisible, presence of an innocent present. The future struck him as fascinating because it was the territory of the unexpected: not what will be according to reason, but what might be according to imagination. The destruction of the actual world would permit the appearance of real time, not historical but natural, not ruled by progress but by desire [. . .] He never thought that there was an essential contradiction between myths and utopias, poetry and revolutionary programs.[4]

As far as the historical, as well as philosophical, intersection between Césaire and surrealism is concerned, we have already twice alluded to Breton's verbal "canonization" of the Martinican bard in his preface to the first book editions of the *Cahier*. To recuperate for the reader some of the intense excitement, akin to a revelation, that Breton experienced when he accidentally came across Césaire's verse during his stopover in Martinique on his way to America, we can do no better than to quote his own vivid account of the episode:

It was under these circumstances that I chanced, in the course of purchasing a ribbon for my daughter, to browse through a publication on display in a haberdasher's shop. There in the most unpretentious of formats was the first issue of a journal entitled *Tropiques*, that had just appeared in Fort-de-France. It goes without saying that, knowing to what depths the debasement of ideas had reached over the past year, and having experienced the total lack of consideration that characterized the knee-jerk response of the Martinican police, I opened the issue with extreme diffidence . . . I simply could not believe my eyes! What was said in those pages was precisely what needed to be said, not only at the best, but at the highest level at which it could be said. All those menacing shadows were annihilated, dissipated; all the lies, the mockeries, were torn to shreds. So the voice of humanity had not been extinguished after all, nor buried: it stood upright here once again in a pristine shaft of light. *Aimé Césaire* was the name of the person who spoke.[5]

As a direct consequence of this serendipitous encounter, Breton was introduced to Aimé and Suzanne Césaire as well as to René Menil. A leading Césaire scholar, Lilyan Kesteloot, has correctly cautioned us against the anachronistic view that the Césaires' adherence to surrealism at this era was merely the result of their island encounter with Breton.[6] What Breton's own impassioned account of his visit discloses, in no uncertain terms, is that like Columbus, he had "discovered" his own New World: a native poet whose "surrealist" affiliation was in a sense prior to, and independent of, his own famous discovery of the Martinican. Breton was initiated into the text of *Cahier* by "objective chance" ("le hasard objectif"), as the surrealists were fond of saying, and the rest is history. The French poet went on to sponsor both the Caribbean poet and his major poem with the fervor of an evangelist.

What did adherence to a surrealist creed mean to the Martinican circle in the context both of Occupied France and of French colonialism? Suzanne Césaire has furnished us with an insider's perspective on the topic in a *Tropiques* article called "1943: Le Surréalisme et nous" ("1943: Surrealism and us").[7] Using as her epigraph a few lines from Césaire's long poem "Batouque," she intersperses her praise of the movement with apt excerpts from the pen of its main exponent, André Breton. She does not hesitate to invest the Frenchman with an aura of heroic leadership of a spiritual adventure: "What does Breton ask of the most clairvoyant spirits of the age? Nothing less than the courage to embark on an adventure of which one cannot yet know whether the outcome will be fatal, but from which one can hope – and therein lies the essential point – for the complete conquest of the mind [*esprit*]." In her role as co-articulator of the group's aspirations, she advocates surrealism in art and life as the weapon of liberation: "But when in 1943 liberty itself is seen to be threatened in the entire world, surrealism, which has never ceased even for one instant to serve the total emancipation of man, may readily be summed up in the single magic word: liberty." Later on she makes a more precise, less tautological correlation between liberation and the surrealist dream of demystification through access to the truths hidden in the unconscious: "Such is the surrealist activity, a total activity: the only one that can liberate man in revealing to him his unconscious; one of the means that contribute to the liberation of the world's peoples by illuminating the blind myths that have led them to this juncture."

I have focussed on Suzanne Césaire's views because they are transparently representative of the group as a whole, though they have not, in my judgment, yet received the critical attention that they merit as testimony to the enthusiasm with which the surrealist program was embraced by young Martinican intellectuals. Suzanne Césaire, it is true to say, has been a relatively neglected source of literary history and of the seminal ideas that inspired the activities of the writers around *Tropiques*.[8] Her zeal in praising the adventure of Breton is mirrored in her husband's glowing tribute, the poem "Annunciation" (in "Miracle Weapons"), which annexes an episode of Christian mythology in the service of a surrealist epiphany of the marvelous, all imbued with local color.

What were some of the special inflections that marked off the Caribbean brand of the surrealist agenda from that of the metropolitan avant-garde? In regard to the overarching role of the Unconscious, Césaire eventually came to conceive it in terms that were culture-specific: to be precise, he sought to identify "Africa" as the fountainhead from which his own repertory of surreal images was ultimately derived. In seeking to describe accurately the nuances of Césaire's adaptation of the surrealist ethos, we can do no better than to pay attention to his own words on the subject. In a key interview that he gave to the Haitian writer René Depestre, we are allowed to recuperate the artist's own sense of what the surrealist project meant to him at a crucial stage of his poetic development:

R.D. Has surrealism been the instrument which helped you in the effort to find a new French expression?

A.C. I was receptive to surrealism because I had progressed through an interest in the same writers as the surrealist poets. Surrealism offered me what I sought in a confused sort of way. I welcomed its influence less as a revelation than as an aid to mutual intent. It was like dynamite to the French language. It was shaking everything up to the roots [*sic*]. This was very important because the traditional weighty, overused forms were holding me down . . .

R.D. You were therefore very sensitive to the notion of liberation inherent in Surrealism. Surrealism invoked the deep powers of the unconscious.

A.C. Exactly. And I reasoned in the following fashion: I said to myself, "If I apply the surrealist approach to my particular situation, I can call up the forces of the unconscious." For me this was the call to Africa. I told myself: "It is true that superficially we are French, we are marked by French customs. We are marked by Cartesianism, by French rhetoric, but if one breaks through this, if one descends to the depths, one can discover the fundamental African."⁹

If Césaire's surrealism functioned as a magical instrument in his quest for his submerged cultural roots, the central concept of the "marvelous" (*le merveilleux*) is equally securely linked to his recognition of an Afro-Caribbean social reality. The New World blacks' continuing, lived connection with a marvelous Africa was to be given new value. The connection was most obvious in the domain of religious belief and cult, folk customs and forms of musical expression (e.g. Haitian Vodun and its congeners, such as Cuban *santería* and Brazilian *cadomblé*; Antillean folktales and verbal art). From this perspective, the "marvelous" in its concrete, Caribbean incarnation was not, as it presumably became for the modern European, an artificially fabricated, escapist world of make-believe; rather it was present in the lived experience of people of African ancestry in their New World diaspora. In the way it perceives magic as built into the real, Césaire's version of surrealism came to resemble, in certain basic respects, the literary movement that has come to be known, chiefly in the hispanophone Caribbean, as "magic realism" (*lo real maravilloso*) and which is currently associated primarily with Latin American novelists such as Alejo Carpentier, Miguel Angel Asturias and Gabriel García Márquez. We can best discern this underlying resemblance in a pioneer text of magic realism: the prologue to Alejo Carpentier's novel *The Kingdom of This World* (*El reino de este mundo*),¹⁰ where the Cuban author expatiates on the magic that he saw as intrinsic to Haitian history and its famous slave revolt:

I began to reflect, moreover, that this presence of magic realism [*lo real maravilloso*] was not a unique privilege of Haiti but was rather the heritage of the entire New World, where the inventory of cosmogonic myths, for instance, still has not finished taking shape. Magic realism is encountered at every step in the lives of the men who inscribed dates in the history of the continent ...

Carpentier's seminal text goes on to privilege Haiti, the island that most richly preserves African cultural forms, as the site of marvelous revelation not only for himself but also for his chief European foil, the surrealist painter André Masson. In seeking to differentiate between an authentic Caribbean "marvelous" and that of the European surrealists, Carpentier privileges the New World writer/artist, who has only to transcribe the "real" of his experience and history into art (novel, poem, canvas) in order to represent the magical order (here a synonym for the "surreal"). For the Martinican poet, for whom, as we have seen, art and life are likewise conflated, the magical source of his "miracle weapons" turns out to be the cultural reserves of transplanted Africans. Slightly more than a decade after the publication of "Miracle Weapons," we find the Haitian writer, Jacques Alexis, explicitly appropriating the term "magic realism" in an effort to develop a homegrown aesthetic for his compatriots.[11]

Setting aside the abstract question of the approximation of Césaire's brand of surrealism (or more accurately, post-surrealism) to magic realism, we may observe that he took a crucial step in his rediscovery of Africa when he paid a visit of several months to the island of Haiti in 1944. There he not only delivered a series of invited lectures, but also participated in an international professional meeting of philosophers (Congrès International de Philosophie), at which he presented a paper, "Poetry and Knowledge" ("Poésie et connaissance"). We shall be re-visiting the substance of this paper when we turn, in the following chapter, to an analysis of the poem "Magique." For the moment it is important to be aware that Césaire's extended stay in Haiti at the height of the war undoubtedly brought him into vibrant contact with a flourishing site of Afro-Caribbean culture – in the widespread Vodun religious cult, for instance, as well as in Haitian drum music and visual folk art. His keen and lasting interest in Haiti, as we know in abundance from his writings, was far from academic in the narrow sense. Already in *Cahier* he had spoken with praise of Haiti as the cradle of négritude:

Haiti where for the first time
négritude stood up tall and straight and declared that
it believed in its humanity...

His sense of pride in the miraculous achievements of the black
slaves in a neighboring French colony during their successful
revolution is only partly reflected in his brilliant historical
sketch of the general Toussaint L'Ouverture, published in
1960. To get a more graphic impression of what Haiti meant to
Césaire at a crucial period of his formation, we need only listen
once again to what he told René Depestre on this subject in the
course of the interview cited above:[12]

A.C. Well, from the moment I discovered the black Northamerican
world, that I discovered Africa, I ended up exploring the whole
of the black world, and so it was that I hit on the history of Haiti.
I adore Martinique, but it is an alienated land, while Haiti stood
in my mind for the heroic Caribbean, and also the African
Caribbean. I connect the Caribbean with Africa; and Haiti, the
most African island in the Caribbean, is at the same time a
country with a remarkable history. The first black epic of the
New World was written by Haitians, by people like Toussaint
Louverture, Christophe, Dessalines, etc. In Martinique, little is
known about Haiti. I am one of the few Martiniquans who know
and love Haiti.

For our Martinican postsurrealist, then, the presence of Africa
in the Caribbean is the essential point of reference for his art
and the authentic source (both internal and external) of the
"marvelous." Internally, the poet delves into his own psychic
unconscious; externally, he recognizes his close kinship with
the totality of Afro-Caribbean culture. As a cosmopolitan who
was striving to surmount the artificial political divisions
imposed by colonialism, he came to appreciate the horizontal
resemblance between all those Caribbean societies created by
the New World sugar-plantation economy. Africa, he soon
grasped, was not the distant, dimly conceived continent of
nostalgic dreams, but a vital part of his own environment, the
common denominator between the ex-slave masses of Cuba,
Haiti, Martinique, etc. This re-discovery of Africanity at home,
so to speak, marked a turning-point in Césaire's artistic

identity. If the visit to Haiti was a major impetus to this re-discovery, it is also true that his antennae for things African responded to signals from other Caribbean shores, notably the vast neighboring island of Cuba, where writers like Alejo Carpentier were being drawn to manifestations of the African stratum in music and religious cult. Thus in an introduction he wrote to a story of Yoruba origin which had been edited by the Cuban writer Lydia Cabrera, we find Césaire enthusiastically lauding her ability to "make us feel, with an intensity rarely achieved, the will-to-live, the fluidity, animism [. . .] of this strange people robed in saltpeter and dawn that fringes the Caribbean shores with the cryptic shards of its laughter."[13] The artistic solidarity expressed in this text was mutual: it was Lydia Cabrera who, two years earlier, had published in Cuba a landmark Spanish-language translation of *Cahier*. The main point of spiritual contact between the French-speaking Martinican and the Spanish-speaking Cuban writer was, precisely, the vindication of neo-African creativity.

Césaire's drive to recognize and reclaim the African presence was not, however, confined to "Caribbean shores" ("le rivage caraïbe"): it extended to the entire span of the black diaspora in the New World. Afro-Brazilian culture, for instance, figures prominently in "Miracle Weapons," which includes a long lyric effusion entitled "Batouque." The poem's title signifies a Brazilian dance rhythm of African origin and is merely the first of several lyrics, scattered throughout Césaire's œuvre, that refer us to Afro-Brazilian musical art forms.[14] What is at stake here is nothing less than a campaign on the poet's part to re-possess his birthright. If the European nations had aggressively sought to acculturate the blacks to their norms, the liberated poet was determined to recoup the devalued black element in all its popular varieties in the diaspora. What was considered "low" culture in the Western-imposed heirarchy (e.g. Vodun rites, the drum, verbal art) was to be inverted and become the elevated platform for a new aesthetic fusion. On this platform a revised modernist perspective would join forces with a no longer subterranean, but openly celebrated, black cultural renaissance.

It is now time to take a closer look at some actual examples of what Césaire was producing at this time in the form of "miracle weapons." [15] We begin with the compact ten-line poem "Tam-tam II."

> à petits pas de pluie de chenilles
> à petits pas de gorgée de lait
> à petits pas de roulements à billes
> à petits pas de secousse sismique
> les ignames dans le sol marchent à grands pas de trouées
>   d'étoiles
> de trouée de nuit de trouée de Sainte
> Mère de Dieu
> à grands pas de trouée de parole dans un gosier de bègue
> orgasme des pollutions saintes
> alleluiah
>
> (with small steps: shower of caterpillars
> with small steps: gulp of milk
> with small steps: ball-bearing rolls
> with small steps: earthquake tremor
> the yams in the ground stride with giant steps: a
>   breakthrough of stars
> a breakthrough of night a breakthrough of Holy Mother
>   of God
> with giant steps: a breakthrough of speech in the throat
>   of a stammerer
> orgasm of holy miasmas
> allelujah)

Since the poem's dedication to Wifredo Lam affectionately employs the latter's first name, the fascinating story of the relationship between poet and painter is worth a brief preliminary digression.

Born in Cuba of mixed African and Chinese ancestry, Wifredo Lam had "returned," two years before this tribute was first published in the surrealist journal *VVV*,[16] to his native island, following an intense European apprenticeship that took him to Spain and, in the wake of the Spanish Civil War, to France. In Paris he had become a very close friend and protégé of Pablo Picasso and subsequently joined the surrealist group. It seems virtually preordained that he would thereafter be a refugee from German-occupied France and end up, quite literally, in the same boat that conveyed André Breton, Benjamin Péret and many other dissenting artists and intellectuals from the port of Marseille to Fort-de-France, Martinique, in the year 1941.[17] During his month-long layover in Martinique en route to Havana, he was detained along with other passengers in quasi-house-arrest conditions, but, unlike Breton, was not allowed to circulate freely on the island. His eventual return to Cuba re-opened his eyes to the vibrancy of the Afro-Cuban religion that he had been exposed to in his childhood. He spent the years 1942–1943 producing what most critics regard as his masterpiece, a large painting called "The Jungle" which occasioned much critical stir when it was exhibited in New York.

It is interesting to observe how the trajectory of his aesthetic development shows a certain convergence with Césaire's. Like the latter, he succumbed, while honing his talents in Paris, to the spell of the surrealist project and its promise of wholescale revolution. His maturation, likewise, took giant strides at the moment when he re-discovered the magic of the Cuban landscape – not simply the physical profusion of a subtropical flora, but the spiritual ebullience of the black population to which he was related by blood on his mother's side.

Césaire's affinity with Lam is marvelously captured in a glowing appreciation he wrote as a prelude to a selection of reproductions of the artist's canvases in the periodical *Cahiers d'Art*, at the end of the war. Entitled simply "Wifredo Lam," this succinct text is far more than a straightforward encomium of a fellow-Caribbean artist: it is remarkable for what it also reveals about the writer's own cognate vision. "Painting," he affirms, "is one of the rare weapons [*armes*] that remain available to us against the sordidness of history." In the context of the debasement of his people in the Antilles, Lam is portrayed as a heroic, mythic figure who speaks out, by means of his art, "in the name of these refugees from the greatest shipwreck [*naufrage*] of history." No less earth-shattering in its scope is the poet's ringing climax celebrating Lam's herculean labors:[18]

Through the efforts of Lam, the ludicrous, ready made, rock-hard, and uninspired forms that blocked the route explode in enormous blasts of solar dynamite. Through the labors of Lam, the primal spirit, by which I mean feeling, dream, heredity, is projected outward and hallucinates [se projette et hallucine].

Wifredo Lam is the first in the Antilles to have learnt how to salute freedom. And it is as a free spirit, free from all aesthetic scruple, free from all realism, free from all urge to document, that Wifredo Lam keeps, in magnificent fashion, the great and awesome rendezvous: with forest, swamp, monster, night, flying pollen grains, rain, liana, epiphyte, serpent, fear, leap, life.

Césaire here effusively presents the painter as a kind of post-surrealist demiurge. Most salient of all is the list of emblems that culminate the quoted paragraph – a list that reads like a selection of some of Césaire's own major, recurrent images. It is a plausible inference that, in attributing to the painter items from his own repertory of symbols, the Martinican poet was openly avowing his deep affinity with the Cuban's artistic agenda. As we saw in the case of Lydia Cabrera, however, there is a documentable symmetry in the admiration of the two artists; for Wifredo Lam, in his turn, had honored Césaire by creating illustrations for a Cuban edition of *Cahier* (the very same edition, in fact, for which Cabrera had provided the Spanish translation); and a Lam picture also adorns the Bordas edition of the poem (Paris 1947). Conversely, we find that Wifredo Lam re-appears later as the dedicatee of an important Césaire poem called "To Africa," in the volume "Sun Cut Throat."

Given the extraordinary rapport that existed between the two Caribbean artists (one verbal, the other visual), it is not surprising that "Tom-Tom II" celebrates their shared re-discovery of the African heritage. The poem registers this re-discovery as a profound transformation of the will to live, which is marked in the text by the jump from "small" to "giant" steps. The progress in question is figuratively achieved by the staple peasant cultigen that the slaves brought with them from the African continent – the yam. Fed by the rhythm of the drum (the "Tom-Tom" of the title), the people make a

momentous breakthrough in their journey to liberation, which
for a long time has taken place in slow, minuscule steps ("à
petits pas"). It is noteworthy that the breakthrough is not a
product of a pristine Africa *rediviva*, but rather of an ongoing
cultural synthesis. Afro-Cuban religion, as is well known, fuses
Christian beliefs and symbols with West African (primarily
Yoruba) iconology. The "holy pollution" of such powerful
syncretism readily allows for the assimilation of the figure of
the "Holy Mother of God," just as the Catholic saints are
conflated, in Vodun ritual, with powerful *loas* (spirits) of
African origin. No less significant, in terms of pagan/Christian
intermixture, is the unabashed erotic imagery that precedes
the final "allelujah!" Like Breton and the surrealists, Césaire
and Lam both celebrate an unfettered sexuality; or rather, an
unrepressed Eros is, for them, an emblem of a utopian future.
Finally, the miraculous transformation envisaged in the text is
amplified by the instrument of language: speech (*parole*) is a
spectacular dimension of the breakthrough "in the throat of
the stammerer" and a crucial weapon in the poet's aesthetic
of revolt.

As is appropriate in a tribute, Césaire's pregnant lines
mimic something of the dynamism and rampant metamorphoses that typically take place in Lam's canvasses; at the
same time, they reflect the poet's own obsession with sudden
mutation and revelation. In illustration of the latter point, we
need only compare the passage from *Cahier* that is echoed in
"Tom-Tom ii:"

> at the end of early dawn
> a little trail of sand
> a little trail of muslin
> a little trail of grains of corn
> At the end of early dawn
> a great gallop of pollen
> a great gallop of a little trail of
> little girls
> a great gallop of humming-birds
> a great gallop of daggers to stave in
> the bosom of the earth

Whereas the earlier *Cahier* passage represents the multiple epiphany, if we may so term it, as a magically efficacious Vodun ritual, the poem to Wifredo attributes to the visual artist the power to transform society. In form and syntax, however, the intertextual echoes are quite audible: the double use of anaphora in "little trail" and "great gallop" resembles that in "small step" and "giant step" (the French adjectives *petit* and *grand* are contrapuntally used in both). Underpinning the two texts is the idea that the seeds of dynamic social change ("gallop of pollen" or "breakthrough of stars") reside in the African cultural ground farmed by the Antillean peasant. "Peasant, strike the ground with your daba," exhorts Césaire in the more extended kindred poem, "To Africa / for Wifredo Lam", mentioned above. The drum and the hoe ("daba") are puissant West African instruments that precipitate a figurative uprising of the "yams" – a vision akin to the religious epiphany of an entire race.

In another praise-poem to Lam published in a much later collection, under the title "Wifredo Lam . . . ," Césaire was to renew his affirmation of solidarity with the painter's source of inspiration. At one point in the poem he actually apostrophizes the artist as "my brother," and towards the end of the eulogy he even goes so far as to make what appears to be an allusion back to his own "Miracle Weapons" when he names the "magic weapons" (*armes enchantées*) of his hero:[19]

> j'ai reconnu aux combats de justice
> le rare rire de tes armes enchantées
> le vertige de ton sang
>   et la loi de ton nom
> (I recognized in the contests of justice
> the unfamiliar laughter of your magic weapons
> the vertigo of your blood
>   and the law of your name.)

These verses come to a close with a cryptic etymological word-play that forms a perfect cadence to the earlier tributes we have been discussing. According to Fouchet the name "Lam Yam" borne by the artist's father signifies "the-man-from-the-rugged-mountain-looking-at-the-sky."[20] In an apparent

allusion to the denotation of the artist's name, Césaire seems
to be inscribing the artist's quasi-divine affinities ("the vertigo
of your blood") with the natural forces of earth, mountain and
sky.

The catalogue of symbols that Césaire includes in his
laudatory preface to Lam's work contains, as its second item,
the salt swamp (*le marais*). Unlike the forest (*la forêt*), which
leads off the catalogue, the salt swamp is a standard feature of
Antillean topography on the Leeward (as opposed to the
Atlantic) littoral. In the Césairean system of imagery, swamps
(*marais*; *marécages*) constitute a pervasive metaphor. A useful
step, therefore, in our brief inspection of "Miracle Weapons"
would be to focus on the short poem that elaborates the trope,
"N'ayez point pitié "("Do not have pity"), and the ideas that
cluster around it:[21]

> Fumez marais
>
> les images rupestres de l'inconnu
> vers moi détournent le silencieux crépuscule
> de leur rire
>
> Fumez ô marais coeur d'oursin
> les étoiles mortes apaisées par des mains merveilleuses
>   jaillissent
> de la pulpe de mes yeux
> Fumez fumez
> l'obscurité fragile de ma voix craque de cités
> flamboyantes
> et la pureté irrésistible de ma main appelle
> de loin de très loin du patrimoine héréditaire
> le zèle victorieux de l'acide dans la chair
> de la vie – marais –
>
> telle une vipère née de la force blonde de l'éblouissement.
>
>
> (Smoke on, salt swamp
>
> rock-painted icons of the unknown
> deflect towards me the muted nightfall
> of their laughter
>
> smoke on, salt marsh, sea-needle heart
> dead stars placated by marvelous hands dart forth

from the pulp of my eyes
Smoke on smoke on
the thin penumbra of my voice cracks with
flaming red cities
and my pure hand irresistibly calls forth
at a very far remove from the ancestral heritage
the undefeated zeal of acid in the flesh of
life – sea swamp –

like a viper sprung from the blond force of a blinding
     light.)

Taking our cue from the title, we note the speaker's peremptory exclusion of all feelings of compassion ("Do *not* have pity", "N'ayez point pitié"). To what audience, we wonder, is the strong negative command directed? Does it include the reader, and is it continuous with the "salt swamp" apostrophized in the opening line? The reader is left with a lingering ambiguity that is corroborated by a cursory glance at the history of the text. As we saw with *Cahier*, Césaire has a tendency to keep editing his poems with successive published versions; hence a serious critic needs to compare, meticulously, the variants against the particular text he chooses as his base. In the case at hand, the poem formerly appeared in the periodicals *Tropiques* and *Hémisphères* under the title "N'ayez point pitié *de moi*" ("Do not have pity *on me*" [my emphasis]), whereas the later editions show only the truncated title. The amputation of the reference to the object of compassion, the lyric self (*moi*), suggests that the original addressee may well have been imagined as an audience separate from the *swamp* – an audience that is being cautioned not to be condescending towards the speaker. Be that as it may, it is the personified swamp who dominates the rest of the poem as the target of the extended apostrophe. If pity is precluded from the emotional responses of the poem, it is because the persons incarnated in the swamp will find their own triumphant redemption in due course.

The proscription of pity in the poem's title also carries, in my view, an interesting programmatic nuance that has a clear intertextual basis. In the poem called "La jolie rousse," which closes his important collection *Calligrammes*, Guillaume

Apollinaire, whose role in promulgating a modernist aesthetic is indisputably crucial, looks back with some pathos at the plight of the artistic pioneer and pleads for the reader's compassion:[22]

> Pitié pour nous qui combattons toujours aux frontières
> De l'illimité et de l'avenir
> Pitié pour nos erreurs pitié pour nos péchés
>
> (Pity for those of us who do battle always at the frontiers
> Of the unbounded and of the future
> Pity for our errors pity for our sins)

The very last line of the Apollinaire text, which, as a sort of "personal testament," occupied an important place in the surrealist canon, reads:

> Ayez pitié de moi
>
> (Have pity on me)

The verbal connection between this famous *cri de cœur*, that signs off a modernist apologia, and Césaire's original, unabridged formulation, "Do not have pity on me ("N'ayez point pitié de moi") is too salient to require tendentious pleading. The Césairean speaker who stridently eschews the response of pity is striking a deliberately self-confident note, in blatant opposition to the almost penitential tone of the *Calligrammes* text. By contesting the latter's posture, the youthful Césaire seems to be differentiating his own brand of modernism from that of the European precursor who is responsible for having coined the term "surrealism." The colonized poet situated in the "swamp" (which can be seen as another kind of frontier) is also poised at the edge of an undefined future, but, in contradistinction to Apollinaire's apologetic persona, he is determined to influence that future – to contribute to the apocalypse that is its precondition. Such a pioneering role in the context of a colonial "combat" requires the kind of courage and self-reliance that is independent of the "other's" compassion. "Do not have pity" is the Martinican poet's counter-assertion of a special identity within the unbounded space opened up by modernism.

If we take the trouble to do a horizontal ("synchronic") comparison of swamp metaphors in Césaire's œuvre, it emerges that they almost always invoke the idea of post-colonial stagnation – a state of suspended animation on the part of the submerged ex-slaves who are not yet genuinely "free." The swamp in our short poem, however, is only deceptively stagnant. The poet, in the role of animator, enjoins it repeatedly to "smoke on," thereby insinuating an imminent change. "Where there is smoke," says the proverb, "there is fire." A huge, destructive conflagration ("flaming red cities") is precisely what bursts forth at the poem's turning-point, where the epithet *flamboyantes* ("flaming") highlights a sound-play dear to the author ("flamboyant," as noun, is the name for a spectacular, red-blossomed tree common in the Antilles). Apocalyptic destruction by fire, then, is the prelude to the desired re-birth of the swamp denizens. The midwife of this fiery event is, once again, the poet as manipulator of words ("the thin penumbra of my voice cracks") and we are reminded that the efficacy of speech (compare *parole* in the poem to Lam) is seminal to his worldview. Out of the fire ("blond force") springs a viper, symbol not only of aggression, but of the power of self-regeneration.

What is the ultimate source of this dormant, re-kindled force, as the poem imagines it? The second strophe hints at a remote, even perhaps prehistoric, heritage ("rock-painted icons of the unknown") that deflects its joyous energy towards the poet/speaker. That this limned rupestral patrimony is to be thought of as African is highly probable in view of the poet's deep admiration for the rock-paintings documented and interpreted by the German ethnographer Frobenius. Later in the poem, this heritage is no longer presented as remote, but rendered immanent in "the flesh of life." As the word of the poet becomes flesh, the personified swamp erupts into life, like the resilient Osiris of the ancient Egyptian myths, who, though murdered by his adversary Seth, is resurrected in the marshes of the Nile delta.

A certain surrealist color adheres to the images that begin the third strophe, where "dead stars" spurt forth from the poet's eyes. Magical re-births, in the universe of the poems, frequently occur in association with stars. In the text under scrutiny the stars, which were thought to be dead, suddenly blaze forth, but they do so under the placating of the poet's "marvelous hands" (*mains merveilleuses*). The re-kindling of stars thought to be dead is coherent with the repeated "smoke" of the refrain, since they are made to blaze not in the remote sky, but in the microcosm of the poet's body. The climactic interchange between sky and earth, stars and swamp, may be paralleled from the finale of the long poem from the same collection, *Le grand midi*, where the speaker asserts his indestructible identity:

> Les étoiles pourrissent dans les marais du ciel
> mais j'avance plus sûr et plus secret et plus terrible que
>   l'étoile pourrissante
>
> (The stars rot in the swamps of the sky
> but I advance more secure more secret and more
>   harrowing than
>   the rotting star)

In this example, however, the swamp trope is transposed into the sky, and the speaker's progress on earth eludes the process of putrefaction that goes on in the celestial marshes.

In addition to "Tom-Tom II," "Miracle Weapons" contains two other poems dedicated to prominent members of the surrealist circle, "Tom-Tom I" (to Benjamin Péret) and "Annonciation" ("to André Breton"). A brief glance at the former in the context of the stature of its addressee will complement our discussion of the Martinican poet's local adaptation of surrealism.

> à même le fleuve de sang de terre
> à même le sang de soleil brisé
> à même le sang d'un cent de clous de soleil
> à même le sang du suicide des bêtes à feu
> à même le sang de cendre le sang de sel le sang des sangs
>   d'amour
> à même le sang incendié d'oiseau feu
> hérons et faucons
> montez et brûlez

(on cue: the river of earth blood
on cue: the blood of ruptured sun
on cue: the blood of a hundred of nails of sun
on cue: the blood of the suicide fire-beasts
on cue: the blood of ashes blood of salt blood
    of bloods of love
on cue: the ignited blood of fire bird
herons and falcons
rise and burn)

Some illumination of this cryptic text may be gleaned from the historical circumstances that bonded the two poets. Like Wifredo Lam, the honorand of "Tom-Tom II" (which follows immediately on its namesake "Tom-Tom I"), Benjamin Péret was also a passenger on board the vessel that brought the group of refugee artists and others from the port of Marseille to the New World at the outbreak of the war. The anthropologist Claude Lévi-Strauss has written a lively first-hand account of the transatlantic voyage (which he too experienced) in his book *Tristes Tropiques*, while the enforced sojourn of the refugees in Fort-de-France is memorialized in the pages of André Breton's piece *Martinique charmeuse de serpents* ("Martinique Charmer of Snakes").[23]

Péret's status within the inner sanctum of the surrealist movement was very high: he was greatly admired by his fellow-practitioners for his poetic craft and his ideological consistency. Space precludes our recounting anecdotes from his intriguing biography, which includes participation in the Dada movement, a turbulent stay in Brazil and incarceration by the Vichy government on the eve of his departure from France, via Martinique, to Mexico. It was in Mexico City that he spent the remaining years of the war in the company of other European and Latin American surrealists, such as Yves Tanguy and Octavio Paz. As far as his convergence with Césaire is concerned, his physical presence on the Caribbean island was perhaps not as significant as his subsequent activities as a writer in the context of his promotion of a "magical" New World aesthetic which he saw as kindred to his own. It was Péret, in fact, who composed the brief, incandescent introduction to the Cabrera translation of *Cahier* – the same edition for which Lam provided a set of illustrations.[24] After saluting Césaire, in words that closely parallel Breton's, as "the only great poet of the French language that has appeared in twenty years," he proceeds to characterize the poet of *Cahier* in terms of the notion of a "natural," and hence "authentic," surreal voice: "For the first time there resounds a tropical voice in our idiom, not one to flaunt an exotic poetry [. . .] but to make resplendent an authentic poetry [*una poesía auténtica*]." In the very next paragraph of his ecstatic foreword, Péret makes the link between the magic of the natural order (the tropical landscape) and the Afro-Caribbean cultural heritage of sorcery: "Césaire is more than the interpreter of the natural tropical habitat [*naturaleza tropical*] of Martinique, he is a part of it."

The solidarity that Césaire himself expresses, through the medium of "Tom-Tom I," for the Parisian poet famous for his fidelity to "our idiom" (read "surrealism") is partly conveyed in the floating, repeated adverbial phrase *à même* (which I have rendered extremely freely above as "on cue," followed by a colon). If imitation, as has been said, is indeed the sincerest form of flattery, then surely it is relevant to the text's praise strategy that the profusion of blood in the anaphora may owe something of its resonance to an early poem of Péret called "Le sang répandu" ("Blood shed"). The blood that flows repeatedly through the first six lines of the Césaire poem appears to attest to a shared, apocalyptic vision, in which a Dionysian life-force is made to burst forth in an over-whelming flood. In the final injunction, "herons and falcons, rise and burn," the image of a sacrificial immolation, which has been interfused with that of blood (compare *sang de cendre*, line 5), forms a nexus with that of the ascending herons and falcons. The ascension of the apostrophized bird-figure(s) reminds us that the bird is a central icon of myth and cult in Aztec Mexico (Péret had moved to Mexico from Paris) as well as in ancient Egypt (compare the falcon divinity). At the same time, it unmistakably recalls the final "assumption" that consummates *Cahier*, which is also splendidly immortalized in a Lam drawing accompanying the Cabrera translation.

The violent image of the "ruptured sun" ("soleil brisé") was destined to resonate with the gruesome title "Sun cut throat" (*Soleil cou coupé*), that Césaire adopted for his next volume of poems which appeared in 1948. The intertextual mold of the title (and hence its programmatic implications) provides us with a perfect cadence to our suite of observations on Césaire's subscription to the surrealist adventure. The gory image is a deliberate "tag" – a citation from the final verse of Guillaume Apollinaire's iconoclastic poem "Zone." Apollinaire, as we mentioned above in connection with the poem "Do not have pity," was an acknowledged precursor of the surrealist poets and his collection *Alcools*, of which "Zone" is the opening shot, is a key text in the definition of a modernist stance. The poem actually commences with an outright disavowal of the traditional canon as embodied in the works of Classical Antiquity:

> A la fin tu es las de ce monde ancien
> Bergère ô tour Eiffel le troupeau des ponts bêle ce matin

> (In the end you are tired of this ancient world
> Shepherdess O Eiffel Tower your flock of bridges is
>   bleating this morning)

The celebration of the modern metropolis, which is a new version of the pastoral (compare the lines: "Now you walk in Paris alone amidst the throng / Herds of mooing buses roll by next to you"), closes eventually with the valedictory:

> Tu marches vers Auteuil tu veux aller chez toi à pied
> Dormir parmi tes fétiches d'Océanie et de Guinée
> Ils sont des Christ d'une autre forme et d'une autre
>   croyance
> Ce sont les Christ inférieurs des obscures espérances

> Adieu Adieu

> Soleil cou coupé

> (You walk toward Auteuil you want to go home on foot
> To sleep among your fetishes from Oceania and Guinea

> They are Christs of another form and another faith
> They are lesser Christs of obscure hopes
>
> Farewell farewell
>
> Sun cut throat)

Apollinaire's murdered sun is readily transposed into the
sanguinary world evoked by Césaire's recurrent imagery of
violent death and resurrection. An earlier manuscript draft of
the closing lines of "Zone" suggests an even closer link with the
Martinican's themes, since it connects the sun to random
violence directed against the poor and the outcast:[25]

> Le soleil est là c'est un cou tranché
> Comme l'auront peut-être un jour quelques-uns des
>   pauvres que j'ai rencontrés
> Le soleil me fait peur, il répand son sang sur Paris
>
> (The sun lies yonder it's a sliced throat
> As perhaps one day some of the poor whom I have met
>   the sun scares me, it sheds its blood all over Paris)

Whether or not Césaire was acquainted with the text of this
earlier draft, it is clear that the "sun cut throat" trope spoke
to the gratuitous violence he saw as endemic to the colonial
situation of blacks in the subtropical Caribbean. The appropriation, in so conspicuous a fashion, of the solar image of "Zone"
amounts to much more than a proclamation of Césaire's
adhesion to the surrealist project: the black poet takes up
precisely where his French precursor leaves off. Apollinaire
was one of the earliest European modernists to appreciate
African and "primitive" art – an aspect of avant-garde aesthetics
that became even more pronounced in seminal works by
leading European painters such as Picasso, Klee, Matisse and
Braque. Yet it must be admitted that his deliberate exoticism
(sleeping with his "fetishes") is to be carefully distinguished
from Césaire's complex annexation of African "Guinea"
and the murdered sun as sources of identity and cultural
restoration.

As a token of that crucial distinction, it is salient that
the very first poem of "Sun Cut Throat," which is entitled

"Incantation" ("Magique"), focusses on the revivification of the prostrate island corpse. The incantatory lines end in a vision of rebirth in which a black African god of thunder (distinctly unlike the "lesser Christ" of Apollinaire's imagination) is called back to life:

> lorsque les étoiles chancelières de cinq branches
> trèfles au ciel comme des gouttes de lait chu
> réajustent un dieu noir mal né de son tonnerre

> (when the five-branched chieftain stars
> clovers in the sky like drops of fallen milk
> restore a black god misbegotten of his thunder).

"Sun Cut Throat," then, signals the postwar emergence of a black poet who has sharpened his weapons with exquisite skill on the whetstone of surrealism and stands poised to use them in the service of liberation.

CHAPTER 4

Lyric registers: from "Sun Cut Throat" to "Cadaster"

> My conception of the universal is of a universal rich with
> the particular, rich with all particulars, the deepening
> and coexistence of all particulars.
>
> Aimé Césaire[1]

Although it was the long prose-poem "Journal of a Homecoming" that inaugurated Césaire's poetic career, its
magnitude proved to be unrepresentative of his subsequent
lyric production as a whole. If we exclude the lyric dramas, the
collection of discrete, relatively short poems of which "Miracle
Weapons" was the harbinger has been his preferred genre of
publication up to the present. The appearance of these
compact volumes of poetry has been intermittent, but it is of
capital importance to note that there have been no less than
seven to date (the tally includes *Cadastre*, which is essentially a
re-edition and partial revision of previously published poems).
The preponderance of short lyric collections in his overall
output spanning approximately half a century tells its own
tale: it is on these brief, highly polished gems that Césaire the
poet has chiefly staked his reputation. In this chapter I hope to
illustrate, by means of concrete examples, the poet's increased
mastery of his favorite genre in its major registers.

The postwar literary activity of Césaire in the 1950s is rather
neatly framed by two clusters of published lyric verse. The
beginning of the decade saw the appearance of *Corps perdu*
("Break Neck"), which came virtually on the heels of *Soleil cou
coupé* ("Sun Cut Throat"), published two years previously. At
the end of this period of experimentation and refinement

stands the mature achievement of *Ferrements* ("Irons"), which earned its author the prestigious Prix René Laporte in 1960 and was closely followed by a landmark volume, *Cadastre* ("Cadaster"), that is essentially a consolidated, revised, edition of both "Sun Cut Throat" and "Break Neck."

If I have chosen to bracket a crucial phase in Césaire's life with publications of poetic works, I have not done so out of a desire to downgrade his parallel activities as an elected politician. Those activities had far-reaching repercussions (economic, social, political) on the ex-colony of Martinique – repercussions that are still very much in evidence more than fifty years after Césaire assumed the double portfolio of mayor and deputy to the French National Assembly. A brief overview of his political evolution during the period of constitutional change and its aftermath may help to sharpen our perception of his maturation as a lyrist, from the ardent effusions of "Miracle Weapons" to the more mellow, parsimonious and, at times, meditative creations of "Irons."

In the immediate postwar years Césaire found himself propelled into a position of major responsibility just at a time when a truly momentous decision had to be made: the conversion of the French Antilles (along with other territories such as Réunion and French Guiana) from colonial to "departmental" status. The conversion meant that the former colonies would henceforth be administered as an integral part of France: in a word, "assimilated" bureaucratically and politically to the metropolis. Islands like Guadeloupe and Martinique would become centrally administered "Overseas Departments," ("Départements d'Outre-Mer"). This dramatic constitutional change occurred exactly one hundred years after the emancipation of the slaves in the French colonies. As Michel Leiris trenchantly encapsulates it: "1848: abolition of slavery, under the impetus of a White metropolitan, Victor Schoelcher; 1948: implementation of the law of departmentalization, of which in 1946 the Black Martinican Aimé Césaire had been the sponsor."[2] Taking the bull fearlessly by the horns, the fledgling Communist deputy did not flinch from mobilizing his new constituents in support of the legislation that enabled

Martinique to be formally incorporated into the French nation. Since his stance on the issue has provoked strictures from uncompromising proponents of political independence, it is important to place it in its historical context before yielding to the seduction of facile moral and ideological judgments.

In her brief analysis of *Cahier*, the eminent Guadeloupean novelist Maryse Condé has formulated the issue with her usual lucidity:

> On the one hand, Césaire in *Cahier*, and throughout the journal *Tropiques*, is seen as a champion in the cause of denouncing the colonial situation and rejecting cultural assimilation. He castigates alienation. On the other hand, he plays an active role in sponsoring the vote in favor of the law of assimilation.[3]

In coming to terms with this apparent contradiction, we need to remind ourselves, in the first instance, of the desperate economic straits of the Caribbean archipelago in the years following the Second World War. Uppermost in the new deputy's agenda was the alleviation of grinding poverty, disease, unemployment and inadequate social and educational services that characterized the island society of the 1940s. From the limited perspective of economic welfare, therefore, a push for autonomy, not to mention outright independence, coming from the French Antilles would have been premature under the circumstances. What chance did a small island colony like Martinique have of becoming economically viable on its own in the parlous conditions prevailing in the year 1946? With hindsight we can now point to the mini-states of the anglophone West Indies, whose history of colonial exploitation closely parallels that of Martinique and Guadeloupe. Their continuing stagnation testifies to the shallowness of the notion of an "independence" uncoupled from deep structural economic transformation. Neo-colonialism has not been effectively eliminated by political sovereignty as such, and despite the famous slogan adopted by Ghana's great founder Kwame Nkrumah, "Seek ye first the political kingdom," the economic dependence of ex-colonies on their former masters was, and still largely remains, the order of the day.

The impetus to champion the law of "departmentalization" is by no means reducible to mundane economic considerations on Césaire's part. A very important factor in his enthusiasm was the political euphoria that swept over liberated France in the wake of the Allied victory. This general euphoria had benefited the political left and contributed to the presence in the immediate postwar parliament of a large number of Communist deputies.[4] With the critical support of the latter and their Socialist colleagues, Césaire and a bloc of African deputies (including Senghor) spearheaded the campaign to pass the historic bill – a campaign that required two years of unflagging advocacy in the face of opposition from the Right before it was eventually successful. As Césaire himself was to characterize it in retrospect:

It was I who sowed [*semé*] the idea of departmentalization. I was even the sponsor [*rapporteur*] of the bill in 1946. Don't forget that it was once known as the "Césaire-Bissol law." I do not disavow it in the least. It has constituted a serious point of departure for the Martinique of today. We were not granted it: we had to fight for it. In fact we seized it. There had been all manner of subterfuge [*réticences*] on the part of the French government. It [the passage of the bill] was a victory of the Martinican people.[5]

What Aimé Césaire had the foresight to grasp with astonishing clarity was that by acquiescing in Martinique's elevation, in principle at least, to an equal administrative footing with the rest of France, he would be in a strong position, as deputy and mayor, to exercise moral, political and economic leverage over his former colonial masters. Once departmentalization became law, he pursued the role of gadfly to the French conscience with zeal, oratorical skill and, when all is said and done, comparative success. By insisting with legendary eloquence and fervor in the forum of the French chamber of deputies that France respect its legal obligations to its black overseas citizens, he has over all the years that he has been continually re-elected (from 1948 to 1993, when at age 80 he retired from politics) proved himself to be a skilfull negotiator for the Martinican people. It is a delicate irony of his political evolution that in vote after vote over the years, the vast majority of the people in Martinique and Guadeloupe have supported the departmental status quo, in preference to some form of autonomy – the alternative that Césaire himself had sought unsuccessfully to promote on more than one occasion since the late 1950s.

From the perspective of his political affiliations (and their wider philosophical significance), the middle of the decade marked a pivotal moment in the life of Aimé Césaire. What Maryse Condé has called a period of "intense political reflexion" came to a dramatic climax in his resignation from the French Communist Party (PCF) in the year 1956. His apostasy was accompanied with a certain fanfare: in one of his most celebrated tracts, "Letter to Maurice Thorez" (*Lettre à Maurice Thorez*), he made public his disappointment with the party's indifference to the colonial question. Under the leadership of Thorez, the PCF had gradually become notorious for its rigid conformity to Stalinist dogma. As with his stance on the departmental statute, the youthful deputy displayed uncommon prescience in his awareness of the discrepancy between Communist utopian ideology and actual Soviet practice.

Before pinpointing some of the reasons for his acute disillusionment with the metropolitan leadership, it may prove instructive to recall his stated motives for joining the Communist cause in the first place. In a party publication of 1946 in which several Parisian luminaries, such as the painter Pablo Picasso and the poet Paul Eluard, explained their adhesion to the party ("Why I am a Communist"), Césaire had tersely written:[6]

I have belonged to the Communist Party because, in a world not yet cured of racism, in which there persists the ferocious exploitation of colored peoples, the Communist Party embodies the will to work effectively for the advent of the only social and political order that we can accept – one founded on the right to dignity of all men without distinction of origin, religion or color.

Ten years after this unequivocal declaration, we find a Césaire whose optimism in regard to the European will to eliminate racism has been dampened by events both within France and on the international scene. Many factors converged to bring about his alienation from the central party bureaucracy as well as from the policies of the French government. Not only were the authorities in the metropolis reluctant to deliver on their constitutional responsibilities vis-à-vis the overseas departments, but with respect to other parts of the moribund empire – Madagascar, Ivory Coast, Algeria (to name a few conspicuous cases) – they did not shrink from employing brutally repressive measures in order to prop up the old colonial order. It was becoming transparent, in short, that the route to decolonization would be arduous and contested. At the same time, the French Communist party, in which many progressive intellectuals, European and non-European, had rested their hopes for the liberation of the oppressed, had become so subordinated to Moscow that it was incapable of taking a principled stand on such issues as the Soviet invasion of Hungary in 1956, or the crimes of Joseph Stalin as exposed in the same year by Nikita Krushchev. As an appointed spokesperson for his people, Césaire regarded as equally reprehensible the failure of the party hierarchy to address the disease of racism – the very disease, we may note, whose persistence had driven him to adherence to Communism in the first place.

It would be a fundamental mistake to imagine Césaire's motives in breaking with the PCF as circumscribed to internecine party politics. Alioune Diop has underscored this point in his foreword to the Présence Africaine edition of the "Letter": "One cannot grasp the full significance of this Césaire piece if one confines the explanation of its content to a banal struggle between communist factions in the bosom of the so-called French Union . . . He disqualifies the West from its hegemonic role in raising consciousness and making history."[7] The disqualification does not represent a sudden new moment of enlightenment, however, for even during the earlier student days in Paris Césaire had insisted on the need to complement Marx by advocating the full emancipation of blacks, as he later reported to the Marxist Haitian poet, René Depestre:[8]

R.D. You have tried to particularize Communism . . .

A.C. Yes, it is a very old tendency of mine. Even then Communists would reproach me for speaking of the Negro problem – they called it my racism. But I would answer: Marx is all right, but we need to complete Marx. I felt that the emancipation of the Negro consisted of more than just a political emancipation.

The celebrated "Letter," then, coheres with Césaire's self-styled "old tendency." In that sense, it did not so much mark a new intellectual tangent as bring memorably into the open the author's fidelity to the prior cause of négritude and its corollary, the struggle to eradicate racism, which he saw as a deeply rooted problem. The decisive turn, for him, was from Europe to black Africa ("the mother of our culture" in the language of the "Letter") from which the poet-politician had come to feel "cut off" by the interposition of the Stalinist apparatus. His defense of his "particularist" re-orientation strikes a chord that resonates remarkably well with the contemporary "multiculturalist" movement:

I do not bury myself in a narrow particularism; I do not wish, however, to lose myself in a disembodied universalism. There are two ways to lose oneself: by an immured segregation within the particular or by dilution in the "universal." My conception of the universal is that of a universal rich with the particular, rich with all particulars, the deepening and coexistence of all particulars.[9]

A mere two years after his dramatic disengagement from the PCF, Césaire reconfirmed what was to be a life-long commitment to electoral politics by founding his own local party, the "Parti Progressiste Martiniquais" (PPM), which he continued to lead down to his official retirement in 1993. The centrifugal shift on Césaire's part was no isolated gesture; rather it was a sign of the embryonic "Third World" consciousness that was coming to the fore in many ex-colonies. It certainly went hand in hand with an emerging sense of solidarity among black leaders – what Césaire referred to as "the great breath of unity [*le grand souffle d'unité*] passing over all black countries."[10]

The first of these was the birth of the journal *Présence*

Africaine (PA), which from its very inception in Paris in 1947 has provided an influential forum for cultural and political expression on the part of black intellectuals on various continents. The principal inspirer (and first director) of *PA* was the far-sighted Senegalese intellectual Alioune Diop, a friend of Léopold Senghor and a classical philologist, who was also the chief organizational brain behind the publishing house of the same name that was founded very soon thereafter. Included in the list of distinguished cofounders was the old triad of Senghor, Césaire and Damas, as well as Birago Diop, also from Senegal, and the Malagasy poet Jacques Rabemananjara. Présence Africaine had the critical support of members of the white French liberal intelligentsia, such as Michel Leiris and Jean-Paul Sartre, but its main cultural significance was that it was supranational in its conception of "African," the black diaspora in the New World being unequivocally part of the "presence" it sought to celebrate. The publishing arm of *Présence Africaine* immediately became an important source of dissemination of black creative writing, including Césaire's: witness the "definitive edition" of *Cahier* and the publication in book form of the *Lettre à Maurice Thorez* (both, incidentally, in the same year, 1956).[11]

The second emblematic event was a direct outgrowth of the first. It is again Alioune Diop who is credited with the key role in convening the "First International Congress of Negro Writers and Artists," which was held in Paris at the Sorbonne (September 1956). In this conference, as well as the second (held in Rome three years later), Aimé Césaire was a major voice whose opinions carried an authority comparable perhaps only to that of Senghor. The speeches he composed for both of these occasions constitute important statements and re-statements of his views on culture, politics and society, and we shall be turning to them for illumination of some features of his poetic output.

Yet a third event that had wide international repercussions was the famous Bandung Conference of non-European nations that took place in 1955. Though often thought of strictly in its political implications, Bandung also carried an underlying

cultural message of enduring validity, even though the super-
power confrontation that helped to give it impetus – the Cold
War – has recently come to a dramatic close. The Indonesian
venue was, of course, part of the message. This historic Afro-
Asian conference, the precursor of what in later years came to
be called the "Non-Aligned Movement," served conspicuous
notice that the West was not going to be allowed to call all the
shots in the relations between nations. Scarcely a year prior to
the conference, we may recall, the French had suffered a
memorably humiliating defeat in Indochina at the battle of
Dien-Bien-Phu (1954). In its cultural, no less than its military,
ramifications Bandung also sounded a warning note against
the dominance of Eurocentric paradigms of achievement.
Though the Afro-Asian compass of the Bandung Conference
was obviously more inclusive than the pan-Africanist network
of writers and artists who gathered in Paris the following year,
the two convocations helped to promote an unprecedented
sense of solidarity among peoples historically exploited by
the West for its own geopolitical and economic purposes. The
synergistic connection between the two was not lost on the
participants of the Paris congress: in the inaugural welcoming
speech Alioune Diop himself alluded prominently to Bandung
and drew attention to its significance for the black world and its
cultural aspirations – a significance that Césaire, in his turn at
the podium, was to echo in the context of a wider argument
that colonialism, as a political system, is lethal to the culture of
the colonized. Césaire's conviction that Bandung was an omen
of the demise of colonialism is most clearly recorded, however,
in a speech he delivered (also in Paris, in January 1956) at a
meeting of an "Action committee of intellectuals opposed to
the conduct of war in North Africa:"[12]

What happened at Bandung that was memorable? It is this:
thousands of millions of people convened in a town of Asia to
proclaim solemnly that Europe no longer had the task of unilaterally
ruling the world, to proclaim that European domination over the
non-European portions of the globe had led the world to an impasse
from which it had to escape. And Bandung was not, as one might
suppose, a banal manifestation of Asiatic or African xenophobia. It

was not a hate-filled and blind denunciation of Europe. On the contrary, not one of the persons meeting at Bandung was unaware of the immense importance of Europe in the history of humanity . . . What was condemned at Bandung was not European civilization: it was the intolerable form that, in the name of Europe, certain persons thought it imperative to impose on the relations that ought normally to have been established between Europe and non-European peoples.

The political backdrop I have been adumbrating is meant to suggest a broader ideological context for that phase of Césaire's poetic activity that extends from the first edition of "Sun Cut Throat" to the revised edition included in 'Cadaster." Let us now consider a brief selection of texts from the latter collection as well as from the volume "Irons," which was published in 1960. Our compact expositions are intended to exemplify some of the poet's major "obsessions" with regard to theme and rhetorical organization.

The very first poem of "Sun Cut Throat," "Incantation" ("Magique"), foregrounds, in majestic tones, the all-important socio-political program of the poet who employs the magic weapon of words: that of bringing about the resurrection of a culture destroyed by colonialism:

> avec une lèche de ciel sur un quignon de terre
> vous bêtes qui sifflez sur le visage de cette morte
> vous libres fougères parmi les roches assassines
> à l'extrême de l'île parmi les conques trop vastes pour
>   leur destin
> lorsque midi colle ses mauvais timbres sur les plis
> tempétueux de la louve
> hors cadre de science nulle
> et la bouche aux parois du nid suffète des iles
> engloutis comme un sou
>
> avec une lèche de ciel sur un quignon de terre
> prophète des îles oubliées comme un sou
> sans sommeil sans veille sans doigts sans palancre
> quand la tornade passe rongeur du pain des cases
> vous bêtes qui sifflez sur le visage de cette morte
> la belle once de la luxure et la coquille operculée
> mol glissement des grains de l'été que nous fûmes

belles chairs à transpercer du trident des aras
lorsque les étoiles chancelières de cinq branches
trèfles au ciel comme des gouttes de lait chu
reajustent un dieu noir mal né de son tonnerre

(with a sliver of sky on a hunk of earth
you brutes sniffling on this dead woman's face
you free ferns among the cutthroat rocks
at the margins of an island among conches too large
    for their lot
when noontide glues its worthless stamps to the
    storming ripples of the she-wolf
beyond the pale of null science
and its maw at the walls of the nest shophet of islands
engulfed like small coin

with a sliver of sky on a hunk of earth
prophet of islands overlooked like small coin
without sleep or wake without fingers or tackle
when the tornado comes gnawing at the bread of the
    hovels
you brutes sniffling on this dead woman's face
chic leopard of lust and operculate shell
soft gliding of summer grains we once were
sleek flesh to be pierced by the beak of the macaw
when the five-branched chieftain stars
clovers in the sky like drops of fallen milk
restore a black god misbegotten of his thunder)

In the recapitulated figure of the island as a murdered female
("this dead woman's face") the speaker graphically presents
the idea of the violent death of a culture ("Mother Africa" in
Caribbean folk mythology). The idea is paralleled, though
in more prosaic terms, in Césaire's speech "Culture and
Colonization," which he delivered in Paris at the First
Congress of Negro Writers and Artists. There he argues that
colonization is, historically if not by necessity, lethal to the
indigenous cultures that it exploits, and he supports his
argument with an impressive array of references to the anthropological literature in English no less than French (e.g.
Kroeber, Mead, Malinowski and Mauss all come under
contribution):

The mechanics of the death of culture and of civilizations under the colonial regime is becoming familiar. In order to flourish, every culture must have a framework, a structure. Now it is certain that the elements that structured the cultural life of a colonized people disappear or become debased as a result of the colonial regime.[13]

The demise of a cohesive (African) culture for the Antilles is not, however, portrayed in "Magique" as irreversible. On the contrary, one of the multiple restorative roles that the speaker assumes is that of a magician-seer, who, at the poem's close, utters words that are efficacious in resurrecting the ill-omened offspring: "restore a black god misbegotten of his thunder." Like the Greek Zeus rescuing the infant Dionysus from the womb of his mother blasted by lightning, the "clovers in the sky" bring timely aid to the almost still-born anonymous African deity. The poet's function is conceived as mantic as well as necromantic: as "prophet of islands" the speaker is fore-telling the cultural resurrection, but he represents his forecast as self-fulfilling – as taking place, that is, as the poem unfolds. By the deliberate echo *prophet/shophet* he also contrives to bring together the poetic and the political programs he envisages for himself (the rare word of Hebrew origin, "suffète," that I have rendered as "shophet," designates an ancient Carthaginian magistrate). As elected official ("shophet"), then, no less than poet-seer ("prophet"), the incantatory voice will become involved in the challenge of restoring islands "engulfed" and "forgotten." It is tempting to relate the image of islands "forgotten like a coin" to the lived reality of postwar Martinique, where the overseas department was marginalized by the central administration, and the devaluation of the franc served to depress even further the already low standard of living.

In his seminal essay "Poetry and Knowledge" ("Poésie et Connaissance"), which he first delivered as a speech at an international philosophical conference held during his sojourn in Haiti in 1945, Césaire insists on positing a stark opposition between scientific knowledge and the kind of intuition of the truth that clairvoyant poets are alleged to possess. As he puts it uncompromisingly in the essay: "Physics classifies and

explains, but the essence of things eludes it. The natural
sciences classify, but the *quid proprium* of things eludes them. As
for mathematics, what eludes its abstract and logical activity
is the real. In sum, scientific knowledge numbers, measures,
classifies and kills."[14] In keeping with a major surrealist
dichotomy and its implied hierarchy, the non-rational is here
valorized in relation to the rational. The place where the poet
situates himself in alignment with the magician-prophet is
therefore clearly "beyond the pale of null science." By its
polemical tone, then, no less than its title, the prominently
placed poem "Magique" signals Césaire's determination to
vindicate the purely mystical side of the poetic charge
(compare the "magical" implications of the earlier title,
"Miracle Weapons"). Like the finale of *Cahier*, the closing line
of "Incantation" conjures up hope of a re-birth. The child of
Mother Africa, the "black god misbegotten of his thunder"
(whether or not one identifies him with the particular West
African divinity, Ogun, who is associated with thunder and
lightning), is metonym for African religious systems, and by
extension, for a whole civilization.

The enforced diaspora of African peoples wrought by the
slave trade and the Middle Passage is mainly responsible, in
Césaire's view, for the cultural predicament of Martinique. In
some poems the sense of vulnerability entailed by the violent
dislocation is a central leitmotif. Whereas in "Incantation" the
hazards of the transplantation are briefly touched on in
the line "soft gliding of summer grains we once were," they
constitute the main subtext of the poem, "Blanc à remplir sur
la carte voyageuse du pollen" ("Blank to fill in on the visa of
pollen"):

> N'y eût-il dans le désert
> qu'une seule goutte d'eau qui rêve tout bas,
> dans le désert n'y eût-il
> qu'une graine volante qui rêve tout haut
> c'est assez
> rouillure des armes, fissure des pierres, vrac des ténèbres
> désert, désert, j'endure ton défi
> blanc à remplir sur la carte voyageuse du pollen

(If there were nothing in the desert but
a single drop of water dreaming far below
in the desert if there were nothing but
a windborne spore dreaming far above
it would suffice
rusting of weapons, splitting of stones, anarchy of darkness
desert, desert, I endure your challenge
blank to fill in on the visa of pollen)

Despite the pathetic fragility conveyed in the trope of the "windborne spore" traveling through the cultural desert of the present, the voice we hear in this text is defiantly optimistic about the possibility of pollination at some future time. Even a single pollen grain would suffice to enable the Promethean poet to endure his suffering in the knowledge that the blank will one day be filled in.

Once the perilous journey to the New World has been completed, the survivors must adapt their music (symbolic of a total cultural tradition) to the conditions of bondage. The theme of cultural adaptation under adverse circumstances is enshrined in the poem "Blues de la pluie" ("Raining Blues"):

Aguacero
beau musicien
au pied d'un arbre dévêtu
parmi les harmonies perdues
près de nos mémoires défaites
parmi nos mains de défaite
et des peuples de force étrange
nous laissions pendre nos yeux
et natale
dénouant la longe d'une douleur
nous pleurions.

(Aguacero
great blues player
at the foot of a denuded tree
amidst lost harmonies
close to our defeated memories
amidst our hands of defeat
and peoples of alien power
we let our eyes hang down

        and loosening the rein
        of our travail
        we wept)

Within its brief compass, this poem from "Sun Cut Throat" is
an elegantly condensed statement of the spiritual predicament
of the colonized ex-slaves of the New World. A well-known
biblical text (Psalm 137) provides a mythic paradigm for its
portrayal of the historical experience of black enslavement and
its cultural sequelae. The first four verses of the psalm (here
cited in the King James version) constitute a thematic point of
reference for the entire poem:

> By the rivers of Babylon, there we sat down, yea, we
>   wept, when we remembered Zion.
> We hanged our harps upon the willows in the midst
>   thereof.
> For there they that carried us away captive required of
>   us a song; and they that wasted us required of us
>   mirth, saying, Sing us one of the songs of Zion.
> How shall we sing the Lord's song in a strange land?

While the exilic composer of the psalm poignantly alludes to
the particular circumstances attendant upon the Babylonian
catastrophe of 587–586 BC, the Caribbean lyrist concentrates
on the universal aspect of that historic event, and transposes
its significance into terms relevant to the black experience. As
the Old Testament Jews in Babylonian captivity were forced to
sing songs in the strange environment of their captors, so the
uprooted blacks in their African-American diaspora must
perform their "blues" in conditions of grief and cultural
alienation. In lines 3–4 the image of the "denuded tree" is an
allusion both to the words of the psalm: "we hanged our harps
upon the willows in the midst thereof" and, simultaneously,
to a central, recurrent Césairean metaphor of the tree as
signifying ancestral stock (here pictured as partially depleted).
In this intertextual cadre, the phrase "lost harmonies" nostal-
gically recalls the African musical heritage.

The highly suggestive analogy between the Jewish and Black
diasporas is one that several West Indian authors have since

utilized to good effect. Edward Brathwaite, for instance, in his major poem *Rights of Passage*, prefaces the first movement, "Worksongs and Blues," with a quotation from Exodus (16.1) which speaks of the journey of the Israelites from the land of Egypt.[15] Black popular culture in the New World has always drawn heavily on biblical passages as a source for prestigious myths on which to ground an historical identity. An apposite example is the use of scripture in the rhetoric of the contemporary Rastafarian movement in Jamaica. A classic Jamaican "reggae" song of sixties vintage partly paraphrases a portion of Psalm 137 into the Rastafarian idiom:

> By the rivers of Babylon
> there we sat down
> and there we waited
> when we remember Zion.
> But the wicked carry us away [to] captivity,
>   require from us a song.
> How can we sing King Alpha's song in a strange land?

In the Rastafarian idiolect of the anglophone Caribbean that originated in Jamaica, "Babylon" has come to signify the oppressive modern state in which the dispossessed ex-slaves are constrained to make their living.

To return to the plain but deeply resonant text of "Raining Blues," the trope featured in the title is also elaborated in the poem, for the name "Aguacero" in the initial line is Spanish for a heavy downpour of rain. Thus the term "beau musicien" ("great blues player," in my rendition), which is placed in syntactic apposition to "Aguacero," re-formulates the opening equation of blues with rain. By electing to close his blues-poem with the words "we wept" ("nous pleurions"), the francophone lyrist has subtly appropriated (and revitalized) a well-known cliché of French postromantic poetry, as exemplified most famously in Paul Verlaine's "it weeps in my heart / as it rains on the town" ("il pleure dans mon coeur / comme il pleut sur la ville") into a powerful metaphor that conveys the pathos of an exiled people. In this regard it is noteworthy that the tone of the poem's postromantic cadence diverges in one crucial respect from the final modulation of the psalm to which it primarily alludes; for while the psalmist had ended his lament on a note of bitter anger ("O daughter of Babylon, who art to be destroyed; happy shall he be, that rewardeth thee as thou hast served us. / Happy shall he be, that taketh and dasheth thy little ones against the stones"), Césaire eschews the escalation into vengeful imprecation, preferring to sustain instead the primary mood of grief which is, of course, the very signature of the "blues."

Through its intertextual links with the biblical Babylon, "Raining Blues" strikes a predominantly plangent tone. Less passive in its stance vis-à-vis the threat of cultural submersion is the voice that enunciates the lines of "Quelconque" ("Commonplace"), where there is a mood of expansive optimism about imminent social transformation:

> Quelconque le gâteau de la nuit décoré de petites
>   bougies faites de lucioles
> quelconque une rangée de palmiers à éventer mes
>   pensées les mieux tues
> quelconque le plat du ciel servi par des mages en drap de
>   piment rouge
> quelconque la jeune main verte du poinsettia se crispant
>   hors de ses gants à massacre
> Espoir Espoir
> lorsque la vague déroule son paquet de lianes de toute
>   odeur
> et toutes les lance au cou de chevaux bigles
> lorsque l'anse développe sa crinière de sel goudronnée
> au plus rare amidon d'algues et de poissons
> Espoir plane Grand Duc
> danse Espoir et piétine et crie parmi les attentions
>   charmantes des remoras et le beuglement neuf
>   qu'émet le caïman à l'imminence d'un tremblement
>   de terre
>
> (Commonplace the cake of night decorated with tiny
>   firefly candles
> commonplace a row of palms to fan my most subdued
>   thoughts
> commonplace the dish of heaven served up by magi
>   decked in red pepper

> commonplace the green young poinsettia hand curled
>   up outside of its pogrom gloves
> Hope O Hope
> when the wave unrolls its bundle of lianas to let out its
>   repertoire of smells
> and tosses them all at the necks of squinting horses
> when the bay lets grow its dread salt locks all plaited
> with the rarest mucilage of fish and algae
> Hope soar majestic Eagle-owl
> dance, Hope, and stomp and cry among the shark-
>   suckers' seductive spells, and the strange bellowing
>   that caymans make before an impending
>   earthquake.)

The tripartite organization of this poem is reminiscent of "Incantation." In the first segment the string of noun-phrases conveys a cumulative impression of torpor and stasis, under-scored by the anaphora of the adjective "commonplace." At the pivotal midpoint, marked by the address to Hope, the temporal conjunction *lorsque* (when) marks an abrupt transformation: there ensues a dynamic flurry in which emblems of empower-ment hold center-stage. In the third and closing segment Hope is called upon to lead a triumphal celebration ("dance, stomp, cry") that embodies a mood of aggressive optimism. The imagery of empowerment in the middle (transitional) segment is remarkably consistent with the poet's lyric repertory. In this particular case, the natural agents that come into play immediately after the invocation of Hope are drawn from the marine end of the spectrum: the wave (which comes equipped with a very earthy "bundle of lianas") and the bay (*l'anse*), which utilizes its reserves of algae and fish. In the poem's ominous and stentorian closure, it is the shark-sucker (*remora*) and the cayman (*caïman*) that register the impending "earth-quake" of revolutionary change.

The reiteration of the epithet "commonplace" at the start of the first four lines underscores the notion of a banal state of affairs that is destined to prove deceptive. Within this general category of the banal we are shown a number of items that function as superimposed descriptions of colonizer/colonized relations at their most inert (cake of night; row of palms; dish

of heaven; poinsettia hand). With regard to the image of the
poinsettia, I have chosen the expression "pogrom gloves" in my
translation of the phrase "gants à massacre" so as to convey the
underlying idea of the "banality of evil" (to adopt the famous
phrase of Hannah Arendt in her controversial book on
the Eichmann trial).[16] Just when we begin to think that the
spiritual inertia described is insurmountable we are jolted by
the apostrophe to Hope – the figure that comes triumphantly
to the fore in the finale.

As with several of the poems in "Cadaster," the text of
"Commonplace" as we have reproduced it above reflects
significant departures from the first version that appeared in
"Sun Cut Throat." Departures in Césaire's published works
more often than not take the form of simple excisions – the
deletion of words and whole lines. The chief consequence of
this mode of revision (subtraction rather than addition) is
generally to make the poem's "argument" more economical. In
their less redundant and diffuse form, the trimmed texts of
the later collection sit more comfortably beside those of
"Ferrements," most of which were composed, according to
Hale, in the decade 1950–1960.[17] The metamorphosis of
"Commonplace," however, represents an extreme case of such
pruning activity. Can one still think in terms of a pruning
metaphor when the original text has been so drastically cut
back as to retain less than one third of its former growth? All
that remains of this poem after the subtractions is basically
the first ten, consecutively printed lines of the "K" edition,
augmented by a few lines that framed the climax of the poem's
opening sequence. That framing climax, which began with the
line "Hope soar majestic Eagle-owl," is shorn of:

> Espoir troupeau d'éléphants lance une forêt tardive à
>   l'engrais des étoiles
>
> (Hope, herd of elephants, toss a forest of late growth at
>   the stars' thick pasture)

The more egregious alteration, however, lies in the disproportionate size of the main excision – the entire remainder
of the "K" text, in which the speaker continues to apostrophize

Hope in a series (one is tempted to speak of a "forest") of exuberant arabesques. Without conducting an autopsy of the severed trees, we may note that the drastic reduction seems to answer to the poet's desire to refine and consolidate the lyric style he had invented in "Miracle Weapons." For lack of a better term, we may label the more economical style "post-surrealist," with the reservation that the poet never truly abandons the fundamental surrealist principles he enunciated in "Poetry and Knowledge."

As we have indicated in our brief outline of Césaire's meteoric political career in the years leading up to *Cadastre*, there were as many occasions for disillusionment as there were for exultant Hopes dancing to the cry of the caymans. There was, on the one hand, the egregious failure of the Communist movement (as Césaire described it in his resignation letter of 1956); on the other, there was a new sense of solidarity among emerging black nations. A setback of a deeper, more intractable kind was the persistence of racism – a theme that recurs throughout his lyric and one that is intimately tied to his political experience. The poem "Mot" ("Word") is an apt point of departure for a short discussion of this major theme.

Approaching the poem from the outside in, we take due cognizance of its prominent place in the corpus: it opens the small but important volume *Corps perdu*, which first saw publication in a deluxe, limited edition, with black and white illustrations by Pablo Picasso. The drawing adorning the cover of that famous edition – the "Tête de nègre" ("Negro head") – was also re-cycled for the poster advertising the First Congress of Negro Writers and Artists. It is, of course, germane to this collaborative publishing event that the painter was at one stage in his brilliant career regarded as a member of the surrealist camp. Beyond the surrealist fraternity, however, there exists at least one other significant point of convergence between Picasso and Césaire: their shared attraction to African art. As we saw in the case of Apollinaire's love affair with primitive "fetishes," however, Césaire's re-invention of "Africa" was a crucial step in his construction of a mature identity.

Though the Picasso drawings interspersed in *Corps perdu* are a landmark episode in the poet's canonization, it is worth recalling that it is the Afro-Cuban painter Wifredo Lam who has the distinction of having been the first to illustrate a Césaire volume (*Cahier*, see above p. 79). Moreover, in the interval between the Lam and the Picasso illustrations the well-known German avant-garde artist, Hans Hartung, had produced an engraving to accompany the deluxe K edition of "Sun Cut Throat" (1948). These Césaire-inspired visual compositions attest vividly to his remarkable double reception: he is seen in Europe as a key participant in the shaping of a modernist aesthetic; at the same time he has had a major influence on the way colonized francophone blacks have sought to define their selfhood.

As we have earlier remarked, the title *Corps perdu* carries a veiled wordplay that seems to have largely gone unnoticed in the secondary literature. In the poem that shares a title with the whole collection, "Corps perdu," the sense of "breakneck speed" or "headlong precipitation" (French "*à* corps perdu") is pronounced at the very outset:

> Moi qui Krakatoa
> moi qui tout mieux que mousson
> moi qui poitrine ouverte
> moi qui laïlape
> moi qui bêle mieux que cloaque
> moi qui hors de gamme
> moi qui Zambèze ou frénétique ou rhombe ou cannibale
>
> (I who Krakatoa
> I who far better than monsoon
> I who chest bared
> I who storming Laelaps
> I who bleat better than cesspool
> I who off pitch
> I who Zambezi or frenzied or bullroarer or cannibal)

In this explosive outburst nouns tumble out with the force of verbs (the volcano Krakatoa; the speedy hound Laelaps of Greek myth whose name signifies "storm-wind"; the bullroarer – the Greek *rhombos* – used in the ancient Mediterranean mystery cults). The body of the speaker is not so much lost as propelled, like the speedy Laelaps, into the chase of an elusive monster.

Turning now to the text of "Word," let us try to recreate in English something of the reverberations of its first two strophes:

> Parmi moi
> de moi-même
> à moi-même
> hors toute constellation
> en mes mains serré seulement
> le rare hoquet d'un ultime spasme délirant
> vibre mot
>   j'aurai chance hors du labyrinthe
> plus long plus large vibre
> en ondes de plus en plus serrées
> en lasso où me prendre
> en corde où me pendre
> et que me clouent toutes les flèches
> et leur curare le plus amer
> au beau poteau-mitan des très fraîches étoiles

>   (Among me
> from myself
> to myself
> outside every constellation
> in my hands only grasped
> uncommon hiccup in a final delirious convulsion
> vibrate word
>   my luck will change outside the labyrinth
> vibrate more amply, vibrate more broadly
> in waves more thick and fast
> in lasso wherein to snare me
> in loop wherein to hang me
> that I may be pinned by all the arrows
> with their most bitter curare
> to the radiant center-pole of very recent stars)

The "word" that Césaire causes to reverberate throughout the text is identified later in its progress as *nègre*. Although the French word *nègre* has a wider and less abusive connotative range than the American derogatory term "nigger," the latter

expression best conveys the emotional "vibrations" that
Césaire seeks to amplify in the lyric. In its unrelenting focus
on the ethnic stigma exfoliating from a charged word, "Mot"
recalls the technique of the poem "Barbare" (from "Sun
Cut Throat"), which similarly appropriates a negative term
and transforms it into a sonorous cry of defiance. "Nigger" and
"Barbarian" both elicit vociferous indictments of racism on the
part of the stigmatized. The word *nègre* resonates in the unique
sound-chamber of the speaker's self ("parmi moi": "among
me"). Césaire here deliberately "bends" the French language
by making the preposition *parmi* (among) govern the singular
pronoun, *moi* (me). A powerful effect of the distortion is that
the pronoun *moi*, as often in the corpus, is made to subsume a
plurality of identities of the black subject. This multiple self
is the presumptive subject of the second strophe – a subject
who proceeds to suture, with marvellous dexterity, Ancient
Greek and Afro-Caribbean mythological and ritual allusions.
Without becoming too pedantic and heavy where Césaire is
rhapsodic and subtle, we may point to the phrase "outside the
labyrinth," which, like the expression "apart from every
constellation," conjures up the well-known Greek saga of
Theseus and Ariadne (after the latter's abandonment by
Theseus her rescuer, Bacchus, transformed her marriage
crown into the constellation Corona Borealis). The poet here
uses a canonic Western myth to isolate the plight of the
modern black whose "luck" will depend on his extricating
himself from the labyrinth of racism. The heroic persona
assumed by the speaker is, from a cultural perspective, multi-
form: the analogy with the Christian St. Sebastian is manifest
in the image of arrows that fasten the crucified *nègre*, though
their tips contain the poisonous venom curare (a loan-word
taken over into Spanish and Portuguese from the Carib
language). The Caribbean tie-in next receives an African,
in addition to an Amerindian, knot, for in Haitian vodun
ceremonies the *poteau-mitan* (center-post) is the potent central
emblem in the sacred enclosure (known as the "hounfort"). In
the belief system, no less than the rites, of Vodun there is
often elaborate syncretism between Christian and neo-African

elements; hence the "nailing" of the poet-saint to the cult post where the spirits are thought to descend is bold, though not truly iconoclastic, in the Caribbean context.

The remaining two strophes pull no punches in their disclosure of the suffering, physical as well as mental, that racism causes to the victim:

> vibre
> vibre essence même de l'ombre
> en aile en gosier c'est à force de périr
> le mot nègre
> sorti tout armé du hurlement
> d'une fleur vénéneuse
> le mot nègre
> tout pouacre de parasites
> le mot nègre
> tout plein de brigands qui rôdent
> des mères qui crient
> d'enfants qui pleurent
> le mot nègre
> un grésillement de chairs qui brûlent
> âcre et de corne
> le mot nègre
> comme le soleil qui saigne de la griffe
> sur le trottoir des nuages
> le mot nègre
> comme le dernier rire vêlé de l'innocence
> entre les crocs du tigre
> et comme le mot soleil est un claquement de balles
> et comme le mot nuit un taffetas qu'on déchire
> le mot nègre
>   dru savez-vous
> du tonnerre d'un été
>   que s'arrogent
>   des libertés incrédules
>
> (vibrate
> vibrate: quintessence of darkness
> in wing, in throat, by dint of dying
> the word nigger
> sprung fully armed from the howl
> of a poisonous blossom
> the word nigger

all infested with parasites
the word nigger
all packed with roving brigands
with mothers crying
with infants weeping
the word nigger
sizzling sound of flesh burning
acrid, of horn
the word nigger
like the sun bleeding from the claw
on the sidewalk of the clouds
the word nigger
like the last calved laugh of innocence
between the teeth of the tiger
and as the word sun is a crackle of bullets
and as the word night a chiffon to be ripped
the word nigger
    charged you understand
with the thunder of a summer
  taken over by
    disbelieving freedoms)

It would be singularly inappropriate to provide detailed glosses on so searingly explicit a text. If we limit our observations to Césaire's cultural bricolage in constructing his verbal account of racism, it is apposite to remind the reader (apropos of the image in the third strophe: "the word nigger / sprung fully armed from the howl / of a poisonous blossom") that in the well-known Greek myths of Cadmus and of Jason we find the motif of Spartoi ("Sown Men") who arise fully armed from the earth and immediately engage in fratricidal strife. Having shown, by this mythic paradigm, the divisiveness engendered by the "hurling" of racial slurs, Césaire plunges us at once into the gruesome horrors of their logical outcome: the resort to violence, here epitomized in the lynching of blacks in the American south. As in the short poem, "Lynch" (from "Sun Cut Throat"), he does not gloss over the macabre details of the practice that continued well into the early half of this century. He closes his account, however, by annexing the vibrant "word" in the service of liberation, which will be marked by "the thunder of a summer" – a combination of images that recalls the redemptive final verses of "Incantation." The last words of "Break Neck" are "disbelieving freedoms" ("libertés incrédules"). The plural form of the noun suggests, among other things, that the re-possession of the pejorative "nigger" has opened the way to the liberation of the self on several fronts. The unblinkered depiction of racism has not led to an insurmountable despondency on the speaker's part: the way out is always, for Césaire, visible on the horizon, even if dimly seen in the looking-glass of language.

This faith in an eventual transcendence of social evil is apparent in many other Césaire poems that portray the speaker as a witness to racial hatred. Among the most elegantly concise of these is the poem "Spirales" (the fourth poem of "Irons"), which we here reproduce *in toto*:

> nous montons
> mattes de pendus des canéfices
> (le bourreau aura oublié de faire leur dernière toilette)
> nous montons
> belles mains qui pendent des fougères et agitent des
>   adieux que nul n'entend
> nous montons
> les balisiers se déchirent le cœur sur le moment précis
> où le phénix renaît de la plus haute flamme qui le
>   consume
> nous montons
> nous descendons
> les cécropies cachent leur visage
> et leurs songes dans le squelette de leurs mains
> phosphorescentes
> les cercles de l'entonnoir se referment de plus en plus
>   vite
> c'est le bout de l'enfer
> nous rampons nous flottons
> nous enroulons de plus en plus serrés les gouffres de la
>   terre
> les rancunes des hommes
> la rancœur des races
>   et les ressacs abyssaux nous ramènent
>   dans un paquet de lianes
>   d'étoiles et de frissons

(we ascend
dreadlocks of cassias hung
(the executioner having forgotten to administer their
        last hair-do)
we ascend
elegant hands hanging ferns and waving farewells
        inaudible to all
we ascend
cannas tear their hearts out precisely at the point
where the phoenix is reborn from the peak of its
        consuming flame
we ascend
we descend
imbaubas conceal their faces
and their dreams in their skeletal
phosphorescent hands
the circles of the funnel narrow down more and more
        rapidly
we reach the bottom of hell
we crawl we float
in denser and denser crowds we roll in the gulfs of the
        earth
human hate
racial hatred
        and the undertows of the abyss lead us back
        in a bundle of lianas
        stars and shivers.)

In a very flexible but crucial sense, Dante's *Inferno* constitutes an intertext for the movement of thought and feeling in
this short masterpiece. Césaire's profound knowledge of
Dante's text in the original has been attested by Senghor.[18]
Like the circles of hell through which the Italian poet and
Vergil make their exemplary journey, "spirals" suggest a
partly circular movement within a total context of progress.
If we set aside the theological dimension of the trope, spiral
revolutions, which encompass upward as well as downward
movements, are conceptually at home in both surrealist and
Marxist thought (i.e. in philosophical systems that admit
the reconciliation or synthesis of opposites). The poet's
pilgrimage, which, as the inclusive "we" indicates, is imagined

as representative of the fate of his ethnic community, here mediates between the spiritual and emotional antitheses: up/down, depresssion/elation, hell/redemption. In this respect, "Spirales" represents, in miniature, an imitation of the complex upward movement of *Cahier*. In the first ten lines of the poem the upward trajectory takes the voyagers through a montane landscape whose flora comes close to being allegorical of various aspects of Martinican society (e.g. the ferns [*fougères*] recall the "free ferns among cut-throat rocks" of "Incantation"; the foliage of cassias [*canéfices*] are described in another poem ("Elégie") as "the lovely black curls of cassias that are mulatto women / haughty women whose necks tremble a little under the guillotine"; and the red centers of the balisier-plant, which Césaire adopted as the symbol of his political party, remind him, as he has stated in a newspaper interview, of human hearts. Thus the first half loop of the ascending spiral is envisaged as taking place on land and reaching its apex in fire, which is a locus of both death and re-birth ("cannas tear their hearts out precisely at the point where the phoenix is reborn from the peak of its consuming flame").

The downward turn, which occurs at the exact midpoint of the poem, is a precipitous plunge into the watery depths, signifying, *inter alia*, the unconscious (for Césaire, a kind of collective psyche). The floral allegory is continued in the mention of tropical plants I have rendered as "imbaubas" (*cécropies*), for which the poet himself has elsewhere supplied an interesting gloss: "cecropias have the form of silvery hands, yes, like the palm of a black person."[19] As the voyagers descend even further, the circles of hell contract in Dantesque fashion as the bottom approaches ("the circles of the funnel narrow down more and more rapidly / we reach bottom of hell"). Thanks to the "undertows" (sometimes a redemptive symbol in Césaire's œuvre), the poet manages to escape from the infernal abyss where he might have kept on rolling in the gulf of racial rancor. At this crucial juncture, the spiral begins to re-ascend. As the upward motion returns, so does the mountainous flora of the poem's beginning, for the narrator is conveyed to his destination by a redeeming bundle of lianas, which are tropical vines that grow typically on the tree-covered slopes comprising the last vestiges of rain-forest in the Antilles. The sinewy lianas succeed in leading the poet (and others on the journey) to a mythical place where stars, as at the end of "Incantation," define a utopian vision of a transfigured world free from human rancor.

The kind of allusive framework the lyrist employs in "Spirals" to articulate his ordeal is also manifest in several other texts exploring racial oppression and related themes. On the strength of our working premiss that "programmatic" texts yield useful insights for a general survey of a poet's work, let us now turn to the opening poem of the volume *Ferrements* ("Irons") which foregrounds the ex-slave heritage:

> Le périple ligote emporte tous les chemins
> seule la brume garde ses bras ramène la ville au port en
>   palanquin
>
> et toi c'est une vague qui à mes pieds t'apporte
> ce bateau-là au fait dans le demi-jour d'un demi-sommeil
> toujours je le connus
> tiens-moi bien fort aux épaules aux reins
>
>   esclaves
>
> c'est son hennissement tiède l'écume
> l'eau des criques boueuse et cette douleur puis rien
> où nous deux dans le flanc de la nuit gluante aujourd'hui
> comme jadis
> esclaves arrimés de cœurs lourds
> tout de même ma chère tout de même nous cinglons
> à peine un peu moins écœurés aux tangages
>
>
> (the voyage constricts, carries off all passages
> only the mist keeps its hands free to lead the town back
>   to port in a litter
>
> and you it's a wave that brings you before my feet
> the very same boat, without fail, in the half-light of a
>   half-slumber
> I knew it all along
> hold me tight round my shoulders round my loins

                    slaves

hear that whinnying lukewarm foam
muddy creekwater, this grief then nothing
where you and I in the thighs of night sticky now as ever
    before
slaves stashed away with heavy hearts
all the same my love all the same we press on
slightly less heartsick in our pitching vessel.)

In the poem's French title, "Ferrements," there may well be an
intended wordplay with the near homonym "Ferments," as is
evident from the fact that the latter reappears as the title of
a poem in the same collection.[20] While the secondary connotation of "ferment" is subtly developed in the erotic imagery
pervading the latter half of the poem, the primary denotation,
"irons," is clearly appropriate to a group of poems that
deal *in extenso* with the psycho-social effects of slavery and
colonialism.

   The relatively rare Greek word Césaire employs to desig-
nate the voyage ("périple," literally "circumnavigation")
conjures up a circularity in the ship's movement. This circularity corresponds, on the historical plane, to the course
of slave-ships on the notorious Middle Passage in which
European vessels conveyed blacks from Africa to the Caribbean,
then returned to Europe with an exchange of cargo. The
identity of the ship is postponed until the mid-course of the
poem, where the word "slaves" (isolated in a line of verse)
conspicuously names its occupants.

   The vessel and its grim cargo stand for the historic subju-
gation of blacks. As this imagery unfolds the socio-political
sphere coalesces in a subtle way with the erotic. The speaker,
we learn, desires to unite in a strong embrace with the slaves,
and the final lines of the poem utilize tropes for sexual consummation (the word "foam," for instance, evokes ejaculated
semen). The metaphor of coitus suggests intimate communication between poet and audience, from which a poetry of
liberation is begotten. In a later poem in the collection, "Dit
d'Errance" ("Lay of the Wanderer"), Césaire apostrophizes
the island of Martinique in the appellation "foam-begotten"

(*écume-né*) – a clear allusion to the Greek myth of the birth of Aphrodite from the foam (*aphros*) that, in the Hesiodic account, is generated in the ocean when it receives the severed genitalia of the sky-god. The poem's imagery of coitus is intertwined with that of equine rapture, which, for Césaire, is often connected with the state of ritual possession in the Afro-Caribbean Vodun cult. Thus "whinnying" (*hennissement*) is a prime recurrent metaphor for the black Caribbean experience in its intermittent manifestations of a suppressed vigor.[21] The void (*rien*) that is a sequel to grief ("this grief then nothing") is also, paradoxically, the matrix in which is engendered the consolatory hope of the poet-lover. From this deep cultural reserve (a re-enacted mating with the African past), the speaker derives the will to endure the rigors of the spiritual and historical voyage, regardless of pitching (*tangages*) and turbulent seas. The assertion of the poet's perseverance on board ship conveys his renewed confidence derived from engagement with his constituency. That engagement unfolds in the text as a move from differentiation to coalescence in the portrayal of the relation between speaker and audience. Thus at first appearance the slave-ship and its occupants are presented as approaching the speaker in a crepuscular dream-light, whereas in the final lines slaves and speaker unite, physically and spiritually, on board the pitching vessel ("slaves stashed away with heavy hearts"). In the culminating lines the engaged speaker joins forces with the human cargo in distress ("with heavy hearts"), and the performance of the poem becomes a redemptive act that enables the embattled voyagers to pursue their passage with renewed resolve:

> all the same my love all the same we press on
> slightly less heartsick in our pitching vessel.

The poem "Irons" is illuminating on the subject of the writer's relationship with his community, and its stance of Odyssean resolve, so to speak, has many parallels in the sequel. Like all ostensibly "programmatic" texts, however, it does not pretend to represent all the major rhetorical roles the poet adopts in the course of the reader's voyage through the collection. "Irons" includes, for example, several poems in an explicitly eulogistic vein. As we have observed in the case of verses honoring other poets and artists (e.g. Lam, Breton, Péret), the art of encomium is a crucial aspect of Césairean poetics. Like all great encomiasts, European and non-European, ancient and modern, Césaire has always been keenly aware of the power of the written word to retrieve deeds, events and persons from oblivion, and he deliberately composes lyric memorials to unsung heroes with this objective in mind. Thus in the course of a magnificent, lengthy tribute of 106 lines to a Guadeloupian ex-slave rebel and warrior ("In Memoriam: Louis Delgrès"), he loudly affirms this basic function of praise in a manner reminiscent of the ancient Greek encomiast Pindar:

> Louis Delgrès je te nomme
>
> et soulevant hors silence le socle de ce nom
> je heurte la précise épaisseur de la nuit
> d'un rucher extasié de lucioles . . .
>
> (Louis Delgrès, I pronounce your name
>
> and raising up from oblivion the pedestal of this name
> I counter the precise thickness of night
> with a swarm of transported fireflies . . .)

The pronunciation of the name is, of course, a central "speech act" of the praise poem, and Césaire reiterates it at several fulcral points in the "Memorial." In one such reiteration he subtly evokes the Greco-Roman encomiastic tradition as foil to his own discourse of praise, which utilizes tropes from the sphere of sugar cultivation:

> Delgrès point n'ont devant toi chanté
> les triomphales
> flûtes ni rechigné ton ombre les citernes
> séchées ni l'insecte vorace n'a pâturé ton site
> O Briseur Déconcerteur Violent
>   je chante la main qui dédaigna d'écumer
>   de la longue cuillère des jours
>   le bouillonnement de vesou de la grande cuve du temps

(Delgrès: there have not sounded in your procession
triumphal
flutes, nor have the dry cisterns caused your shade to sulk
nor has the voracious insect grazed on your site
O Breaker of Bonds, Violent Confounder
  I sing the hand that scorned to skim
  with the days' long spoon
  the boiling cane juice in the vat of time)

The memorial to Delgrès ends with a grandiloquent flourish that seals, once and for all, the self-fulfilling function of encomium:

Or

constructeur du cœur dans la chair molle des mangliers
aujourd'hui Delgrès
  au creux de chemins qui se croisent
ramassant ce nom hors maremmes
  je te clame et à tout vent futur
toi buccinateur d'une lointaine vendange.

(Now

demiurge of soul in the mangroves' soft flesh
today Delgrès
  in the interstice of crossing paths
gathering your name outside the marshes
  I trumpet you and to all future wind
you proud herald of a distant vintage.)

A striking feature of Césaire's praise poetry is the cultural and racial diversity of the honorands. The same poet who lavishes panegyric on the (hitherto obscure) black "defender of freedom" Louis Delgrès is also magnanimous in celebrating the achievements of the journalist and amateur ethnologist Lafcadio Hearn, or the French surrealist poet Paul Eluard. Other poems celebrate significant events in the anti-colonial struggle, such as the historic decision of Guinea (under the leadership of Sekou Touré) to cut the umbilical cord with France and opt for full and complete independence. Praise poetry is, of course, a universal "speech genre" (to use Bakhtin's term), and Césaire is demonstrably aware of

African, no less than European, traditions when he composes his encomia on various subjects.

The poetry of "Irons" is, on the whole, more lucid in texture than that of earlier volumes. In this respect, it may be said to continue and refine a tendency that was already manifest in the pages of *Cadastre*: the drive towards concision and economy, and a radical pruning of luxuriant imagery. A splendid example of the new voice is the brief poem "Non-vicious Circle ("Cercle non vicieux"), whose plain re-affirmation of the poet's social and political engagement is an appropriate note on which to conclude this chapter:

> Penser est trop bruyant
> à trop de mains pousse trop de hannetons
> Du reste je ne me suis jamais trompé
> les hommes ne m'ont jamais déçu ils ont des regards qui
> les débordent
> La nature n'est pas compliquée
> Toutes mes suppositions sont justes
> Toutes mes implications fructueuses
> Aucun cercle n'est vicieux
> Creux
> Il n'y a que mes genoux de noueux et qui s'enfoncent
> pierreux
> dans le travail
> des autres et leur sommeil
>
> (Thinking is too loud
> has too many hands produces too many bugs
> Besides I have never been mistaken
> people have never deceived me: they have expressions
> that go beyond them
> Nature is not complicated
> All my premises are sound
> All my inferences fruitful
> No circle is vicious
> Hollow
> It's only my knees all entangled and sinking like stone
> into the toil
> of others and their slumber)

CHAPTER 5

The turn to poetic drama

What is the history of the entire New World if not a chronicle of magic reality?

Alejo Carpentier[1]

The struggle of Toussaint L'Ouverture was this struggle for the transformation of a juridic right into a real right, the struggle for the *recognition* of man, and that is why it both inscribes itself and inscribes [*il s'inscrit et inscrit*] the revolt of the black slaves of Saint Domingue in the history of world civilization.

Aimé Césaire

Césaire's path to maturation, both as verbal artist and as elected politician, reached a critical dividing fork in 1956. As we have seen in regard to our earlier discussion of his famous "Letter to Maurice Thorez," the now more experienced and self-confident deputy mayor made the crucial decision in that year to sever his formal ties with the French Communist Party and to found his own organization in his native island (the "Martinican Progressive Party"). This rupture with the central metropolitan bureaucracy converged, in the sphere of his literary production, with a turn from lyric poetry to what might be called lyric drama. It is easy to explain this shift in literary genre as motivated by the sincere desire on his part to narrow the gap in communication between avant-garde writer and provincial audience, and Césaire himself has avowed as much in published interviews. The particular form that his dramaturgy took, however, belies such a clear-cut explanation; for his very first experiment in the new genre, "And the Dogs Kept Quiet" (Et les chiens se taisaient) is composed in a style only marginally less grandiloquent and "surreal" than that of his lyric poetry up to that juncture. The most apt description of its exuberant style is internal to the text: it is pronounced by the main character, the Rebel, who, in an impassioned apostrophe early in the first Act, calls upon personified death to "sow your rapeseed made of lavish verse."[2] In addition to its "lavish verse," the play's formal organization manifestly owes much to avant-garde currents in contemporary Parisian theater, among which we may mention the vogue of the "existentialist" theater of Camus and Sartre, and the earlier, but still influential, experiments of Alfred Jarry (which had entered the surrealist canon).

Chiens received its first textual embodiment not as a theatrical piece, but rather as the long poem that concludes the volume "Miracle Weapons," some overall aspects of which we schematically explored in chapter 3. Césaire has himself bestowed the designation "lyric oratorio" on this dramatic poem – a designation whose resonance it is worth the trouble to unpack briefly. The title "Oratorio" draws attention to the palpably sacral, at times quasi-liturgical, quality of the dialogue, as well as to its contrapuntal musical texture. The familiar term "dialogue" may actually be misleading in this regard, since the many voices that succeed each other diachronically in the text often give the impression of engaging in parallel, even antiphonal, interplay, rather than in mutual conversation. Césaire's transmutation of his "lyric oratorio" into drama is an experiment that is profoundly "modernist" in its demotion of verisimilitude at the level of plot.[3]

Ten years after its birth as a multivocal poem, Césaire transformed *Chiens* into what he called a "theatrical arrangement" ("arrangement théâtral"), reorganizing it into a play of three acts, allocating voices to a configuration of dramatis personae and, in the process, making significant alterations to the text itself.[4] The result, not surprisingly, was a species of poetic drama that retained a great deal of its lyric (hence somewhat static) modality. From a literary-generic point of view, then, it constituted a perfect transition between the earlier poetry and the plays that were to dominate the 1960s. Re-arranged for

the theater, the former "lyric oratorio" unfolds before the
audience not so much as a connected sequence of events – an
Aristotelian "action" – as a series of musically orchestrated
tableaux. To be sure, there is a skeletal plot (Aristotle's
mythos), enacted on stage, in which the chief protagonist, the
Rebel, meets a bloody, violent death at the hands of his jailors.
We learn about the larger action that confers a narrative
context on the Rebel's execution through intermittent
fragments in the course of the vocal interchanges. This story
involves a general slave uprising (prior to the framed events
taking place on stage) that has been triggered by the Rebel's
assassination of his white slave-master. None of the characters
in this lyric drama is designated by an individual proper name.
Instead they all bear general appellations that point to their
roles (e.g. "Lover," "Rebel," "Narrator"). Thus denuded of
particularity, they are meant to represent types which, in the
playwright's conception, are essentially universal. The type of
the Rebel, around whose pathos the play revolves, is the
antecedent, in embryo, of a dynamic breed of defiant, ambitious
black leaders who come to occupy center stage in the Césairean
dramas to follow: Henri Christophe (*The Tragedy of King
Christophe*), Patrice Lumumba (*A Season in the Congo*) and Caliban
(*A Tempest*). In the case of *Chiens*, as we have indicated, the type
is portrayed on a mythic, even cosmic, scale that transcends the
boundaries of a strictly racial identity, even though the socio-
historical context of the rebellion is sketched as a struggle
between black Antillean slaves and their white masters.

Like the *Prometheus Bound* of Aeschylus – a play widely
acknowledged by several critics to have been an important
model for Césaire – *Chiens* depicts a rebellious, titanic protagonist who is imprisoned by an omnipotent oppressor and
visited, at the site of his imprisonment, by a succession of
characters, friendly as well as hostile, who variously attempt to
dissuade him from his set course or comment favorably, if
anxiously, upon it. In Aeschylus' play personified abstractions
called "Force" (*Kratos*) and "Might" (*Bia*) figure among
the emissaries of the (still) tyrannical Zeus, along with the
messenger-god Hermes. In Césaire's postcolonial drama set in

an unspecified West Indian plantation, these intermediary roles are performed, in part, by stern "Jailors," and the punitive decrees of the European tyrant (called "the Architect") are transmitted to the black Rebel by officials with names like "the Administrator." Of the friendly, as opposed to antagonistic, characters who come to the prison to talk to the Rebel, there are two prominent female figures who are closely affiliated with him, the "Lover" (*L'Amante*) and the "Mother" (*La Mère*). As the critic Pestre de Almeida has pointed out,[5] the former interlocutor is assigned a complex, ambivalent role, in that she is potentially an obstacle to the Rebel's ambitious projects, while eventually becoming a supportive co-founder of the powerful myth that the dead hero will leave behind for posterity. Besides these prominent female character-types who engage the hero in a more direct and challenging dialogue, there is a parade of minor voices and interlocutors that perform various self-explanatory metatheatrical functions (e.g. "Echo," who utters the prologue; "Narrator," who is gender-marked in the French and split into "Récitant" and "Récitante"; "Chorus" and "Semi-chorus").

The Aeschylean flavor of *Chiens* is by no means limited to salient elements of its plot such as we have alluded to above. As an extraordinarily percipient reader of the European literary canon (and a former student and teacher of Classical texts) Césaire also understood at first hand that elusive aspect of the Greek tragedian's poetics that is eloquently summed up in the following quotation from the study by the eminent Classicist John Herington:[6]

It may have become clear by now that in many ways Aeschylus' work has the quality not so much of logically organized narrative as of dream – of nightmare. It may display the superficial incoherence or even the impossibility of dreams, their liberation from the order of time and space, their rapid succession of frightful visions, one melting into the other. Yet, by virtue of that very freedom from the limitations that are imposed on the ordinary waking mind, these dramas also possess the compulsive force of dreams.

This unconventional and insightful characterization of Aeschylean stagecraft as dream-like may be transferred

without anachronism to the dramaturgical quality that
Césaire sought to infuse into his "theatrical arrangement" of
Chiens. His reading of archaic and Classical Greek drama, we
may infer, bears a predictable (though, if Herington is right, by
no means distorted) resemblance to a proto-surrealist mode
of representation, in which a nightmarish sequence of
apparitions as well as phantasmagoric "events" are combined
to produce "the compulsive force of dreams."

   At the core of the play's *mythos* is the death of the Rebel,
which is announced at the very opening line by Echo – a line
delivered, according to the stage directions, "as the curtain
slowly rises":

> Bien sûr qu'il va mourir le Rebelle.
>
> (He will surely die, the Rebel)

This brusque prediction dispenses at a stroke with any notion
of suspense surrounding the action, and is the functional
equivalent of the foreknowledge of the myths that an audience
at an ancient Greek theater would bring to a tragic performance. In Jean Cocteau's modernist re-working of the Oedipus
myth, *La Machine infernale*,[7] a disembodied character called
"the Voice" ("La Voix") is assigned an opening function
homologous with that of Césaire's Echo: it is heard announcing
the Delphic oracle: "He will kill his father. He will marry his
mother" ("il tuera son père; il épousera sa mère"). In the
ensuing scenes of *Chiens* what is chiefly played out on stage is
the acute suffering or "Passion" (in the original Latin sense of
the word, corresponding to the Greek *pathos*) of a hero who
incarnates the high aspirations of his people, the enslaved
African blacks, for a genuine liberation from spiritual, no less
than purely physical, bondage. True to its sacral, ritualistic
dimension, the spectacle of the dying protagonist's *pathos*
prepares the audience for his future vindication and figurative
resurrection. Césaire's drama thus echoes, in the main lines of
its underlying myth, an archetypal pattern that is clearly
derived from, and transparently alludes to, ancient Near
Eastern and Mediterranean sources.[8] Above all, as A. J. Arnold

was surely correct in emphasizing, the ancient Egyptian variant of the "dying god" motif – the death and restoration of the murdered Osiris – is arguably the preponderant model in Césaire's eclectic mythography, if only because Egyptian civilization was regarded by the négritude writers as "black"; and elsewhere in his poetry divinities like the mother-goddess Isis and her dismembered son are featured as emblematic of the African historical experience.[9] Those critics who stress the passion of Christ as the major archetype for the Rebel come close to misconstruing the broader significance of Césaire's ornamental use of Christian mythology and ritual; for the Martinican poet had come to adopt a universalist perspective that interpreted Christ's death and resurrection as a younger variant of a much older pattern. Césaire's fundamentally pagan Christ-figure is only superficially connected with Catholic liturgy; or to be more precise, the Rebel's "passion" (death, to be canceled by resurrection) camouflages a deeper, pre-Christian substratum of myth that aligns him with the cycle of male vegetation gods (of the order of the Greek Adonis and Dionysus and the Egyptian Osiris-Horus).

It is precisely this ancient Egyptian mythographic subtext that we must call on to gloss the canine leitmotif in the play's imagery, which is emblazoned in its very title. As signifiers, dogs have two distinct (and contradictory) referents in Césaire's poetry: on the one hand, they are associated with the cruelty of the slave-master who, like the notorious French general in Saint Domingue, Rochambeau, utilized them against rebellious slaves; on the other hand, they become a positive emblem of regeneration throughout most of *Chiens*, where they are closely linked with the Egyptian Anubis, a dog- (or jackal-) headed deity who presided over cemeteries as well as various aspects of mortuary ritual and eschatological destiny. The barking of the dogs, invoked by the Rebel at the play's threnodic close, marks the end of the "silence" imposed on, and internalized by, the oppressed slaves ("And the dogs kept quiet"). This barking signals both a coming liberation and a resuscitation, an access of power and a denial of death, and the Rebel's apostrophe to these protective, canine divinities is important to the thematic crescendo as the play approaches its oratorical end:

> Accoudé à la rampe de feu
> les cris des nuages ne me suffisaient pas
> Aboyez tams-tams
> Aboyez chiens-gardiens du haut portail
> chiens du néant
> aboyez de guerre lasse
> aboyez cœur de serpent
> aboyez scandale d'étuve et de gris-gris
> aboyez furie des lymphes
> concile des peurs vieilles
> aboyez épaves démâtées
> jusqu'à la démission des siècles et des étoiles.
>
> LE RECITANT
> Mort, il est mort
> LA RECITANTE
> Mort dans un taillis de clérodendres parfumés.
> LE RECITANT
> Mort en pleine poussée de sisal
> LA RECITANTE
> Mort en pleine pulpe de calebassier
> LE RECITANT
> Mort en plein vol de torches, en pleine fécondation
>   de vanilliers . . .
>
>
> (with my elbow on the balustrade of fire
> the shrieking of clouds did not suffice
> Bark, O tom-toms
> Bark, guard-dogs of the tall portal
> hounds of the void
> bark, war-weary
> bark, serpent heart
> bark, scandal of incubator, of ju-ju
> bark, fury of saps
> conclave of inveterate dreads
> bark, dismasted wrecks
> until the centuries and the stars give out.
>
> MALE NARRATOR
> Dead, he is dead

FEMALE NARRATOR
  Dead in a grove of perfumed clerodendrons
MALE NARRATOR
  Dead at the acme of sisal growth
FEMALE NARRATOR
  Dead at the acme of calabash pulp
MALE NARRATOR
  Dead at the acme of soaring torches, of vanilla-
    bearing inseminations ...)

Through the profuse vegetal imagery (sisal, sap, calabash, vanilla) the death of the Rebel is revealed to be simultaneously the enactment of a new life. Prior to this osmotic exchange, in which death is transmuted to life, a subterranean chorus has offered a hand to the protagonist who, in response, performs, by a kind of speech-act, his own revivification:

LE CHŒUR *(souterrain)*
  voici ma main, voici ma main
  ma main fraîche, ma main de jet d'eau de sang
  ma main de varech et d'iode
  ma main de lumière et de vengeance ...
LE REBELLE
  Dieux d'en bas, dieux bons
  j'emporte dans ma gueule délabrée
  le bourdonnement d'une chair vivante
  me voici ...

CHORUS (subterranean)
  (Here is my hand, here is my hand
  my cool hand, my hand: a spurt of water, of blood
  my hand of seaweed and of iodine
  my hand of light, of retribution ...
THE REBEL
  Gods below, kind-hearted gods
  I am bearing in my decrepit mug
  the whirr of living flesh
  here I am ...)

In constructing his peculiar version of the myth of "the dying god," Césaire figuratively equates the destiny of the Rebel with that of his own poetic creation. Thus we find the following self-referential turn of phrase ascribed to the "male narrator" in the final act of the drama:

> dépecé, éparpillé
> dans les terrains dans les halliers
> poème éventré

> (dismembered, scattered
> in the soil, in the delta thickets
> eviscerated poem)

The imagery of violent dismemberment is yet another transparent allusion to the fate of Osiris, who suffered this gruesome treatment at the hands of Seth, only to be restored to life by his diligent and nurturing sister-lover, the mother-goddess Isis.[10] At the same time, the expression "eviscerated poem," as a trope for the prostrate Rebel, conveys the subtle suggestion that poem and protagonist have an underlying similarity. Is Césaire playing here on the famous locution of Horace in the *Ars poetica*, "scattered limbs of the poet" ("disiecta membra poetae") as well as on the derivation of "poem" from the Greek "poiema" (= "a thing made")? In any event, evisceration becomes by association a potent symbol, not only for a lyric poem that has been adapted for the stage, but also for a "Promethean" hero who suffers for his philanthropic deeds in order to redeem his community (Prometheus, in the Greek myth, is periodically "eviscerated" by the eagle, sent by a punitive Zeus to gnaw at his immortal liver).

We have so far sketched the major themes of the play as embodied primarily in the archetypal destiny of the protagonist. Several of its minor, related motifs look back to the thematic preoccupations of *Cahier*. For example, both texts enjoin the victim of racism not to succumb to a counter-hatred of the oppressor's race. In *Cahier*, we may recall, the speaker prays at one stage that he be preserved from the kind of hatred that infests his bigoted white oppressor. At a similarly introspective, self-correcting moment in *Chiens* (Act 2) we find the Rebel at pains to disavow blind hatred of the white racist as a trap that merely serves to prolong a kind of psychic dependency. Thus in response to the cry heard from offstage, "Death to the whites!" he reflects:

Ressentiment? non; je ressens l'injustice, mais je ne voudrais pour rien au monde troquer ma place contre celle du bourreau [. . .]

Rancune ? Non. Haïr c'est encore dépendre. Qu'est-ce que la haine, sinon la bonne pièce de bois attachée au cou de l'esclave et qui l'empêtre [. . .]?

(*Resentment?* No; I resent injustice, but I would not want to trade places with the executioner at any price whatsoever [. . .]

Rancor? No. To hate is to prolong dependency. What is hatred if not the firm wooden collar that is placed around the slave's neck to constrain him [. . .])

The Rebel then goes on to adumbrate a utopian vision of a world exorcized of all racism. In his rising rhapsody he deploys the metaphor of the human race as a forest of diverse trees, and his words read like an uncanny manifesto, *avant la lettre*, for what in our time has come to be called "multiculturalism":

Je suppose que le monde soit une forêt. Bon!
Il y a des baobabs, du chêne vif, des sapins noirs, du noyer
    blanc;
je veux qu'ils poussent tous, bien fermes et drus
différents de bois, de port, de couleur,
mais pareillement pleins de sève et sans que l'un empiète
    sur l'autre,
différents à leur base
mais oh!
                              (*Extatique.*)
que leur tête se rejoigne oui tres haut dans l'éther égal à
    ne former pour tous
qu'un seul toit

(I imagine the world to be a forest. Very well!
In it there are baobabs, live oaks, black firs, white walnut
    trees;
I want them all to grow, robust and sturdy,
diverse in wood, deportment, tincture,
but equally full of sap and without encroaching one upon
    the other,
diverse at their base
but O!
                             (*Transported.*)

May they join heads together at the top, yes, very high up
  in the levelling ether so as to form for all
a single roof)

The fact that the character who is made to express this multi-
cultural fantasy is shortly to be punished for the crime of
having assassinated his master rescues the sentiment from any
trace of saccharine banality. A violent act of retribution,
Césaire appears to be obliquely suggesting, does not necessarily compromise the perpetrator, provided s/he is able to
direct it against the individual evil-doer, rather than indiscriminately against any member of that person's race. The
question of legitimate crime in the context of revolutionary
agendas was, of course, very topical in an intellectual milieu
that included among its leading currents the existentialist
philosophy of Jean-Paul Sartre and, to some extent, of Albert
Camus. The latter, in particular, had devoted not only a
discursive volume, but also a dramatic piece, *Les Justes*,[11] to the
moral problematic of revolutionary justice, and to exploring
the vulnerability of humanist values to purist ideologies of
total revolution.

    The poet's turn to the genre of drama (prefigured, as we
have seen, in the stage adaptation of *Chiens*) was decisive and,
as it transpired, relatively sustained. During most of the 1960s
his creative energy was intensely, if not exclusively, focussed on
the theater, for which he composed three major dramas.[12] The
first of these typically protean texts, *La Tragédie du roi Christophe*,
went through a by no means trivial process of re-fashioning
prompted by the playwright's constructive interaction both
with actors and with the dynamic avant-garde director Jean-
Marie Serreau, who master-minded the premier production at
the Salzburg festival and subsequently took it to the Théâtre
de l'Odéon in Paris. The French metropolitan production ran
into bureaucratic obstacles, but the legal difficulties involved
were circumvented by a critical support group, the "Association des Amis du roi Christophe" ("Association of the friends
of King Christophe"), founded by Michel Leiris and counting
among its members such illustrious figures as Pablo Picasso

and Alejo Carpentier. The play proved to be a spectacular success on three continents, including North America and Africa (it was memorably performed in Dakar, Senegal, on the occasion of the Festival of Negro Arts in 1966). A revival at the Comédie-Française in June 1991 under the Mitterrand government was a graphic testament to its latter-day re-canonization. In terms of its spectacular international reception, then, the play has attained an exalted position within the Césairean theatrical corpus, comparable to that of *Cahier* for the lyric œuvre.

The dramatic plot is based on the career of a giant personality in the history of Haitian independence and its aftermath: Henri Christophe, a military leader in the wars against the French who, upon the demise of Dessalines, went on to establish monarchical rule in the northern region of the island of Saint Domingue, as it was then known, in the years 1807–1820. The play concentrates on the later career of the legendary leader, though it also alludes frequently to earlier episodes in his biography, such as his stint as a chef at the "Auberge de la Couronne" in the northern city of Cap François (later renamed Cap Haitien). It dramatizes the monarch's grandiose building projects (whose fabulous ruins still survive), his increasingly despotic rule, and his eventual suicide in the wake of a popular uprising.

Christophe's larger-than-life personality and extravagant accomplishments have inspired many works of fiction, not the least of which is the masterful short novel *El reino de este mundo* (*The Kingdom of this World*) by Alejo Carpentier – the novel that can claim to have ushered in the New World narrative aesthetic that goes by the name of "magic realism." It is worth digressing briefly to recapitulate the artistic premises of this important movement for the light it obliquely sheds on Césaire's analogous approach to the representation of New World historical material.

It is not fortuitous that Carpentier, as we mentioned above, was drawn into the circle of fervent metropolitan admirers of Césaire's dramatization of the life of the Haitian king: he himself had forcefully articulated his notion of the "maravilloso" as inherent in the American reality in what has become a *locus classicus*: the prologue to the original 1949 Mexico City edition of *El reino*. In this spare but seminal text, the Cuban writer professes to have derived his conception of "magic realism ("lo real maravilloso")" from a pilgrimage to Haiti:

After experiencing the authentic sorcery of the Haitian landscape, after having found magical portents in the red roads of the Central Plain, and after having heard the [Vodun] drums of Petro and Rada, I was moved to compare the marvelous reality I had recently lived with the tiresome claim to provoke the marvelous that has characterized certain European literary works of the past thirty years.[13]

On the basis of this claim to an exclusively local, American privilege, Carpentier proceeds not only to devalue European surrealism as inauthentic, but also to promote his own, supplementary project, whose rationale he sums up in a final rhetorical question: "And yet what is the history of the entire New World if not a chronicle of magic reality?"

When we turn from this famous manifesto to Césaire's dramatic representation of subjects from Haitian history, we are struck by the postsurrealist conviction that the authentically magical is immanent in the New World reality. Césaire, too, had made the crucial pilgrimage to the land of Vodun in 1944. The visit, though initially undertaken as part of an official lecture itinerary, had been no less a turning-point for the Martinican poet in his quest to recuperate an African cultural legacy than it was for the Cuban novelist who was attracted to the Afro-Cuban element present in his own society. Césaire's lyric drama set in Haiti is interfused with references to Vodun ritual and belief (the marvelous), while remaining faithful to the historical record enshrining the king's monumental exploits (the real). While respecting the basic historical framework, he shows some concern to dramatize events documented in writing and in oral tradition,[14] but he does not strive to construct the kind of meticulous illusion of verisimilitude that we find in *El reino de este mundo*, and his dialogue sporadically takes flight from the mundane world into the ether of lyric effusion.

Before embarking on his theatrical composition, however,

Césaire immersed himself profoundly in the archival records of the Haitian revolution. The fruit of these scholarly soundings is his robust monograph, *Toussaint Louverture: La Révolution française et le problème colonial. Etude historique*. This excursion into historiography occupies a cardinal position in Césaire's intellectual evolution that has often been overlooked. To re-situate it in the context of his own self-examination and growth, we can do no better than cite his own words:

> a book that I regard with a special fondness is my study on Toussaint Louverture [...]. I wrote it with extreme humility, almost for myself. I needed to understand the history of the French Revolution in the Caribbean, for I was lost in a jumble of events and contradictory realities. This book helped me to see my way through clearly. After that all was settled in my mind.[15]

Césaire is, of course, far from being alone among outstanding Caribbean intellectuals in his compelling need to understand, and come to terms with, the phenomenon of the Haitian Revolution – the only successful slave revolt in recorded history and a unique chapter in the annals of master–slave relations in both hemispheres. The late C. L. R. James, the distinguished Trinidadian man of letters, composed his brilliant and vivid narrative, *The Black Jacobins*, partly out of a desire to explain the seeming paradox of a revolution that defied socialist orthodoxy concerning the crucial role of an industrial proletariat and a vanguard party.[16] Somewhat closer to home, the Haitian writer Jean Price-Mars published a collection of essays under the *imprimatur* of Présence Africaine, three years prior to the appearance of *Christophe*, that included revealing "silhouettes" of the three "fathers" of his country's nationhood, Toussaint, Dessalines and Christophe.[17] In short, the violent transformation that engulfed Saint Domingue (as the French portion of the island was then known) in the early nineteenth century and culminated in independence for the colony is a paradigmatic event that has engaged the minds of all educated West Indians seeking to make sense of their legacy of plantation slavery.

What sense did Césaire, in particular, make of the remarkable career of Toussaint, the strategic genius behind the

military successes that secured the gains of the slave insurrection by humiliating Napoleon's armies, and the Precursor (as
he is known in Haiti) of the Emperor Dessalines and the
ex-general and king, Henri Christophe? Recent critical discussion has drawn attention to Césaire's interpretation of
a fatal episode in Toussaint's life: his decision to attend a
conference with the enemy commander without adequate
protection.[18] In Césaire's reading of the "fatal rendezvous,"
Toussaint is presented as having had a premonition (or even
actual intelligence) of French duplicity, but nonetheless
choosing martyrdom as a means of unleashing the mass
uprising that would be its inevitable outcome. In assessing the
deeper significance of Toussaint's "Sacrifice" (as the relevant
chapter of his monograph is designated) Césaire comes, by his
own admission, very close to asserting that the general was
motivated by a quasi-mystical fatalism, though he opts for the
priority of the political over the mystic in his reading of
the enigmatic gesture:

Toussaint was stuck. Why not then disappear, so as to unite, disappear so as to reunite [the people]? [...]
  This role of martyr Toussaint accepted, better yet, preempted,
because he regarded it as in effect indispensable.
  I will not go so far as to say that the surrender of Toussaint was a
kind of ancient Roman *devotio* : the sacrifice of a life, his own, that of
a leader, in an act of faith, for the salvation of his people.
  I see in it something more than a mystical gesture: [I see it as] a
political gesture.[19]

It is precisely the underlying political significance of the
leader's voluntary sacrifice, as he understood it, that spoke
most profoundly to Césaire's own situation as elected
representative of a pre-independence colony striving for liberation. In his analysis of the Haitian martyr's reluctance to take
the plunge into independence we may discern, by hindsight,
the writer's own political dilemma and self-doubt. In his own
controversial political praxis Césaire has chosen to perform,
albeit on a less grand scale and for much smaller stakes, the
role of Intercessor that he ascribes to Toussaint. What could
be a more accurate description, *mutatis mutandis*, of the

Martinican deputy's self-ordained intermediary role than the following account of Toussaint's that comes at the conclusion of the treatise?

> The struggle of Toussaint Louverture was this struggle for the transformation of a juridic right into a real right, the struggle for the *recognition* of man, and that is why it both inscribes itself and inscribes [*il s'inscrit et inscrit*] the revolt of the black slaves of Saint Domingue in the history of world civilization.

Césaire's own preordained struggle in the role of deputy, as he came to see it, involved a constantly reiterated appeal to the moral conscience of the French authorities to implement equality in the overseas departments, not merely *de jure* but *de facto*, and beyond that, to practice fully in the peripheral ex-colonies what France's own revolutionary tradition had preached at the center. In this fundamental sense, then, the re-examination of Antillean historical exemplars such as the Precursor, Toussaint, and his successor Christophe, was a product of his own on-going self-exploration.

The play *Christophe* is focussed on the later career of the legendary black ruler: it begins with the confrontation between the rival generals, Christophe and Pétion, that led to the bisection of the new nation into a northern monarchy and a southern republic, and it ends with the suicide of the king in the royal palace in the wake of an uprising of his subjects. Our brief dissection of the major themes of the drama will take the opening scene of the play as its point of departure.

The Prologue takes the form of a cockfight, in which Christophe, on one side, and Pétion, on the other, play the parts of fighting cocks, urged on by their partisans among the spectators, the divided Haitian people. The deployment of the cockfight as defining metaphor is meant to register, at the outset, the playwright's views regarding the nature of the relationship between the leader and his following, "the hero" and the "crowd," in postcolonial West Indian societies.[20] Since the cockfight is a popular form of recreation in Haiti that mimics certain features of theater, this "spectacle within the spectacle" obliquely conveys the notion of a general attitude that regards politics as but another form of entertainment. Though it may be an exaggeration to decode Césaire's metaphor as carrying the kind of dense symbolic load that Clifford Geertz famously imputed to the Balinese cockfight,[21] it is appropriate to take the prologic function of the scene seriously in so far as it foreshadows a main preoccupation of the drama: the state of political consciousness of a people in an unstable post-independence order. The cockfight receives its complement in a verbal showdown in Act I, Sc. I – a kind of *agon*, or formal contest, that pits the two leaders against each other. At the close of the exchange Christophe repudiates the limitation on his power proposed, disingenuously, by the new parliament in Port-au-Prince and decides to establish a separate sphere of control in northern Haiti. The confrontation, like the cockfight, succinctly displays some of the socio-economic and cultural polarities that have hamstrung the nation to this day: mulatto versus black "ethnoclasses," elite versus masses, large-scale cultivation versus small peasant landholdings, etc. The stage direction that accompanies the text of the verbal duel is "style parodique" ("in the manner of a parody"), so the reader is left in no doubt concerning the stereo-typing of the characters.

As the Shakespearean cast of its title is meant to evoke, Césaire's play is nominally a "tragedy," though it clearly incorporates elements of the comic. The interplay between gravity and caricature is patent in the complementary roles of two prominent characters who are close to the king: Baron Vastey, his secretary and counselor, and Hugonin, described in the list of *dramatis personae* as "a mixture of parasite, fool [*bouffon*] and political agent." Let us defer analysis of the latter until we consider the main motifs of the play's closure. As for the intriguing figure of Vastey, it is based on an actual personage by that name, who as the regime's official historian wrote an account, which is still extant, of his sovereign's stewardship. At several junctures in the first two acts he is portrayed as interpreter of Christophe's policies and thoughts to different members of the bourgeoisie. Among his many pedagogic pronouncements is a very lucid articulation of the deeper motives behind his monarch's ambitious programs. The occasion is the ceremony in which titular nobilities, as conferred not only by medieval European kings but also by no less a personage than Napoleon, are bestowed on certain deserving citizens. Vastey waxes exuberant when he is warned that the French regard such mimicry as ludicrous (Act i, Sc. 3):

> Le rire des Français ne me gêne pas! Marmelade, pourquoi pas? Pourquoi pas Limonade? Ce sont des noms à vous remplir la bouche! Gastronomiques à souhait! Après tout les Français ont bien le duc de Foix et le duc de Bouillon! Est-ce plus ragoûtant? Il y a des précédents, vous voyez! Quant à vous Magny, parlons sérieusement. Avez-vous remarqué qui l'Europe nous a envoyé quand nous avons sollicité l'aide de l'Assistance technique internationale? Pas un ingénieur. Pas un soldat. Pas un professeur. Un maître de cérémonies! La forme, c'est ça, mon cher, la civilisation! la mise en forme de l'homme! Pensez-y, pensez-y! La forme, la matrice d'où montent l'être, la substance, l'homme même. Enfin tout. [...]

MAGNY Que signifie ce galimatias?

VASTEY Il y en a un qui le comprend d'instinct: c'est Christophe. Avec ses formidables mains de potier, pétrissant l'argile haïtienne, lui du moins, je ne sais s'il sait, mais mieux, il sent, la flairant, la ligne qui serpente de l'avenir, la forme quoi! C'est quelque chose, croyez-moi dans un pays comme le nôtre!

> (The mockery of the French doesn't bother me! Why not "Duke of Marmelade," why not "Lemonade"? These are names to sate the appetite. As gastronomic as you would wish! After all, the French too have their "Duke of Pâté" [? Duc de Foix], their "Duke of Bouillon" and the like. Is that really any more agreeable to the taste? They are clearly precedents for all this! But come, Magny, let's talk seriously. Did you notice the type of personnel that Europe sent us when we requested international technical aid? Not a single engineer. Not a soldier. Not a professor. Instead: a Master of Ceremonies! Form, my friend, is the essence of civilization! The forming of man! Think about it! Form, the matrix that engenders being, substance, man himself. In short, everything [...]."

MAGNY What does all this pompous fluff amount to?

VASTEY There is one man who grasps this point instinctively: it's Christophe. With his awesome potter's hands molding the Haitian clay, he, at any rate – he may not know it, but better yet,

he feels it – he noses the scent, the coiling trail of the future:
in a word, the Form. And that is something, believe me, in a
country like our own.)

Vastey here enunciates a philosophical rationale for the
multiple, interrelated projects of Christophe: the creation of
grandiose monuments and of social hierarchies, the re-making
of the human substance, the total mobilization of the population. The ultimate fantasy of re-fashioning man, which is
shared by all extreme revolutionaries (one thinks of the "new
man" of various socialist utopias), is later echoed by the king
himself, who also deploys the trope of the leader as artisan
(Act I, Sc. 6):[22]

> Voyez-vous, Vastey, le matériau humain lui-même est à
> refondre. Comment? Je ne sais. Nous essaierons dans notre
> coin! Dans notre petit atelier! Le plus petit canton de l'univers
> est immense, si la main est vaste, et le vouloir non las! En avant,
> route!

> (You see, Vastey, the human material itself has to be
> remodeled. How? I can't say. We will try out best in our corner!
> In our little studio! The smallest canton in the globe becomes
> immense, if the hand is huge and the will unflagging! Forward,
> march!)

The psychological underpinning of Christophe's grandiose
project may usefully be compared to Albert Camus's notion of
"metaphysical revolt" that we mentioned above in relation
to the Rebel's ambitions in *Chiens*. This species of megalo-
maniacal rebellion entails a rejection of the limits imposed on
the human condition, and as a corollary, the illusion that a
strong individual, a Nietzschean superman, can re-mold
human nature "closer to the heart's desire." Metaphysical
revolt is, by definition, doomed to failure, and this sense of
inevitability is at the core of the dramatist's neo-Greek conception of tragic discourse. The very scope of Christophe's
rebellion necessitates a vain attempt to construct a "substitute
world" (Camus's "univers de remplacement"), for he comes
to regard the existing Haitian polity as fundamentally
inadequate to the measure of his grandiose dreams. The basic

metaphors that the dramatist employs to describe the nature of the project are mutually re-inforcing. With admirable economy of means Césaire draws upon the professions that the historical Christophe is known to have exercised (cook, mason). These recurrent culinary and building metaphors endow his tragic protagonist with the attributes of a demiurge, a maker, but one who discovers too late that the "material" he has chosen to model in pursuit of an ideal is not as pliable as he had imagined.

So metaphysical a desire veils a fundamental element of solipsism; and it is not surprising that many readers of the play have remarked on Christophe's isolation, which seems to increase as the play progresses, eventually reaching its logical conclusion in the act of suicide and the immuring of his corpse in the walls of the Citadel. In terms of dramaturgy the king's self-absorption is highly structured: at a number of well-orchestrated moments in the drama – most commonly at the closure of Acts as well as of important scenes – Christophe is made to deliver virtual monologues in which he appears to be giving utterance to his most deeply held wishes and over-weening ambitions. By way of illustration, let us consider the final scene of Act I, in which the king is allowed to project his vision of a spectacular monument. Ostensibly he is addressing, at least initially, the prelate Corneille Bresse, who has expressed amazement at the audacity of the project:

> Regardez cette poitrine gonflée de la terre, la terre qui se concentre et s'étire, se déprenant de son sommeil, le premier pas hors chaos, la première marche du ciel!
> MARTIAL BESSE Majesté, à bâtir, ce sont d'effroyables pentes!
> CHRISTOPHE Précisément, ce peuple doit se procurer, vouloir, réussir quelque chose d'impossible! Contre le Sort, contre l'Histoire, contre la Nature [. . .]

> (Look at this earth's puffed-up chest: earth that is bending and stretching, shaking off its slumber. It's the first step beyond chaos, the first step on the path to heaven.)
> BESSE To build here, Your Majesty? Why, these slopes are horrendously steep.
> CHRISTOPHE Precisely the point. The people must look out for itself,

have the will-power, succeed in accomplishing the impossible!
Against Destiny, against History, against Nature [. . .].

Thereafter the king's pronouncements become more and more
rhapsodic as he spells out the emblematic meaning of the
future Citadel:

> Pas un palais. Pas un château fort pour protéger mon bien-
> tenant. Je dis la Citadelle, la liberté de tout un peuple. Bâtie par
> le peuple tout entier, hommes et femmes, enfants et vieillards,
> bâtie pour le peuple tout entier! Voyez, sa tête est dans les
> nuages, ses pieds creusent l'abîme [. . .]

> (Not a palace. Not a stronghold to safeguard my property. I
> mean "Citadel": the Liberty of an entire people; built by the
> entire people, men and women, young and old; built for
> the entire people. See, its head is in the clouds, its feet dig down
> into the chasm [. . .])

As he waxes more eloquent he envisions the Citadel in his
mind's eye as already built:

> A ce peuple qu'on voulut à genoux, il fallait un monument qui le
> mît debout. Le voici! Surgie! Vigie!
>
> *(Halluciné.)*
> Regardez . . . Mais regardez donc! Il vit. Il corne dans le
> brouillard. Il s'allume dans la nuit. Annulation du négrier! La
> formidable chevauchée! Mes amis, l'âcre sel bu et le vin noir
> du sable, moi, nous, les culbutés de la grosse houle, j'ai vu
> l'énigmatique étrave, écume et sang aux naseaux, défoncer la
> vague de la honte! Que mon peuple, mon peuple noir, salue
> l'odeur de marée de l'avenir.

> (This people they wanted to be on its knees needed a monu-
> ment to make it stand up. There it is! Standing up. A lookout
> station.
>
> *(Entranced)*
> Look. Take a good look! It is a living thing. It sounds the horn in
> the fog. It lights up in the night. The slaveship is annulled.
> What an awesome charge it makes! My friends, the bitter salt
> consumed, the black wine of the sand: I, we, the castaways of
> the mighty surf, I have seen the enigmatic prow, foaming blood
> through its nostrils, cleaving to its depths the gulf of disgrace.
> Let my people, my black people, hail the future in the odor of
> the tide.)

The spectators are drawn, via the stage directions, into participation in the hallucination, as the curtain falls with the image of the Citadel projected onto the backdrop. As this closure to Act I makes plain, the monarch is here totally self-absorbed, oblivious of his interlocutors, and alone in the "substitute world" that he is about to reify for posterity.

The complex figure of Christophe receives a very subtle form of articulation by the use of a technique that Césaire borrowed from Shakespeare, whereby a presumed psychic whole is split between two or more characters in a drama. Such is the case, for instance, with King Lear and the enigmatic Fool, who, though given to expressing himself in a riddling manner that conflates the serious and the comic, is nevertheless a kind of alter ego of the aged monarch, and eventually his sole companion in his abject, reduced condition on the bleak heath. This shared identity, as transposed to the configuration of King Christophe and the buffoon Hugonin, Césaire has astutely described as "binomial." Hugonin, then, is the "fool," who paradoxically turns out to be wise, but, at a deeper level, speaks for the king's repressed self; as such, he utters the unspeakable and transgresses taboos in a form that Christophe is able to tolerate, even cherish.

The role of Hugonin, however, goes beyond the Shakespearean "binome" in one very important respect: he moves to a higher plane of existence when he is transfigured, at the play's end, into a powerful Vodun divinity. The metamorphosis, which is at the same time a kind of dénouement, is replete with multiple significance for our understanding of the plot, for it signals the vindication of Afro-American religion, which Christophe had vainly and unwisely attempted to suppress. At the intra-psychic level, Vodun, in the symbolism of the play, represents that repressed component in the protagonist that has been partially foreshadowed in Hugonin, only to reappear fully, and with a vengeance, in the latter's final transfiguration. The changed Hugonin, in the guise of the Vodun god Ogoun Badagri (or is it the other way around, with the god having impersonated the Fool?) approximates what, in Freudian theory, is referred to as "the return of the repressed." A premonition of this fateful return occurs already in the second scene of Act 3, in which Christophe suffers a paralyzing stroke. In the course of a Roman Catholic mass held in the Limonade cathedral at the Feast of the Assumption the king suddenly experiences an hallucination, along with his stroke, in which he has a vision of the prelate Brelle, whose grim death he had previously ordered, and who now reappears to haunt him, like the ghost of Banquo in Shakespeare's *Macbeth*. The crisis of Christophe, which is both psychogenetic and biological, is brilliantly conveyed in Césaire's short scene. At a certain point in the liturgy the king suddenly finds himself pronouncing the names of Vodun spirits in antiphonal response to the priest's Latin litany:

> CHRISTOPHE, *geignant.*
> Loko, Petro, Brisé-Pimba
> toutes divinités de la foudre et du feu
>
> (CHRISTOPHE, *moaning*
> Loko, Petro, Brisé Pimba
> all gods of thunder and lightning)

When he recognizes the ghost in the Cathedral as that of the murdered Brelle, he cries out in agony that he has been the victim of malevolent sorcery. The brusque intrusion of magical belief, as well as Vodun religion, into his subconscious foreshadows the entrance of Hugonin at the play's closure, where the latter is revealed, in nothing less than an epiphany, to be the Haitian funerary deity Baron Samedi, who is associated with cemeteries and the transition to another life. This apotheosis of the Fool compels the spectator to revise his/her preconceptions about the wisdom or folly of Christophe's entire project and to question the efficacy of any grand policy that ignores or devalues the African foundation of Haitian culture. To this extent, at least, the play is a vindication of Césairean négritude.

There is one minor character in *Christophe* whose appearance, though brief, nonetheless resonates with the ongoing dialogue in Césaire's work concerning the fragility of idealist values in a revolutionary, anti-colonialist context. The figure of the rebellious soldier, Metellus, whose name is actually attested in the historical archives,[23] is embellished by the poet into the type of the "pure" revolutionary fighter, who eventually breaks with the supreme leader and chooses execution rather than compromise on his altruistic values. Prior to his death on stage (Act 1, Sc. 5) he launches into a highly lyric effusion in Césaire's own grandiloquent style, which recalls the manner and content of the Rebel's sacrifice in *Chiens*. After recounting his glorious campaigns under Toussaint and the pristine days of the revolution Metellus ends with a litany of disillusionment and condemnation of the postrevolutionary leadership:

> nous allions fonder un pays
>   tous entre soi!
> Pas seulement le cadastre de cette île!
> Ouvert sur toutes les îles!
> A tous les nègres! Les nègres du monde entier!
> Mais sont venus les procurateurs
> divisant la maison
> portant la main sur notre mère
> aux yeux du monde la défigurant
> trivial pantin piteux!
> Christophe! Pétion!
> je renvoie dos à dos la double tyrannie
> celle de la brute
> celle du sceptique hautain
> et on ne sait de quel côté plus est la malfaisance!

> (We were going to found an island nation
>   our very own all by ourselves!
> Not merely to make a survey of this island!
> A nation open to all the islands!
> To all black people! blacks the world over!
> But in came the power brokers
> dividing the house
> laying their hands on our mother
> disfiguring her before the eyes of the world
> into a base pathetic pappy-show!
> Christophe! Pétion!
> I repudiate equally both forms of tyranny:
> the brute,

> the arrogant sceptic –
> hard to tell which is the greater evil.)

It is noteworthy that the metaphor of a land survey ("le cadastre de cette ile") recurs in the title of one of Césaire's poetic collections (*Cadastre*), where the idea of a political and spiritual wasteland is also a haunting presence. The poet-deputy's own recorded comments on the figure of Metellus are especially pertinent in this regard:

In essence, it's the stance of the committed poet, the purist, who has made the revolution, who sees that it must now be maintained, but doesn't know how. His destiny is also a journey towards deception, disarray, solitude and death.[24]

As "maker" (the original meaning of the word "poet"), Metellus has constructed a utopian vision of absolute liberation founded on a community of the faithful. In this sacrificial persona is registered something of the Martinican poet's own passionate commitment to an elusive ideal. The pure dream of the committed poet/maker, Metellus, invites comparison with the grandiose schemes of Christophe, which also led, by a divergent but related path, to disillusionment, disarray, solitude and voluntary death.

Not more than three years separated the publication of *Christophe* from that of Césaire's next play, *Une Saison au Congo* (*A Season in the Congo*). Since the subject of the latter was highly topical – the former Belgian Congo had recently undergone a traumatic re-baptism as Zaire – the Brusssels site of its premiere was both apt and provocative. Faced with a play that candidly exposed the dynamic of decolonization and featured the martyrdom of the charismatic Patrice Lumumba, the Belgian authorities contrived to stymy its production. In a partial replay of the contretemps surrounding the Serreau production of *Christophe*, the poet's influential friends and supporters among the Parisian intelligentsia rallied once again to the cause and succeeded in circumventing the obstacles.[25] Ironically, the topicality of the play caused waves in more than one direction – waves that rippled over the colonized as well as the colonizer; for it also provoked unease in certain sectors of the educated Zairean population after it was re-staged in Paris at the Théâtre de L'Est under Serreau's direction. Césaire's unflattering portrayal of the Machiavellian colonel "Mokutu" (a thinly disguised pseudonym for the infamous Mobutu) has since been vindicated by history, but at the time it struck patriotic younger Zaireans as prematurely negative. In accordance with his normal practice, the author went on to re-model the published text of *Saison* more than once; in this case, the second version (1967) incorporated a new scene in which Mokutu/Mobutu, who is generally suspected to have been complicit in the assassination of Lumumba, appears somewhat contrite about the event and actually decrees a public monument in honor of the victim. The vicissitudes of the text, no less than its mixed reception, illustrate the well-known hazards, artistic and political, of addressing contemporary issues in the theater. Topicality is, by its very nature, not only hazardous but ephemeral. Césaire's play has survived, despite its topicality, by reason of its encapsulation of enduring insights concerning the centrifugal forces at work in the forging of a national identity in the wake of colonial exploitation.

Though the title of the play consciously alludes to a famous poem of Rimbaud that had considerable cachet with the surrealists ("Une saison en enfer," "A season in hell"), the text is far more down to earth, in terms of diction, than either the ethereal *Chiens* or the sometimes grandiloquent *Christophe*. Stylistic differences aside, however, *Saison* is not devoid of lyric tangents, often assigned to the quixotic Lumumba, but also to the cryptic "Sanza Player," a bard/commentator who reappears throughout the play like a one-person chorus. On the whole Césaire's version of the inferno precipitated by the disintegration of the Belgian colony (if the subliminal equation of "hell" and "Congo" is to be read into the Rimbaldian allusion) succeeds in creating yet another vivid portrait of a black anti-colonial leader whose dreams and grandiose visions of an African resurgence are framed by violence and ultimate self-sacrifice.

The action of the play is based on the historical imbroglio that accompanied, even defined, the transition of the Belgian Congo from colony to independent nation. Its protagonist is the leader Patrice Lumumba, who, though chosen to be his country's first head of state, is outmaneuvered by his unscrupulous political opponents and eventually assassinated in a cold-blooded execution. These opponents include not only the Belgian government and their business allies but also rival Congolese leaders, such as "Kala Lubu" (pseudonym of the historical Kasavubu), "Mokutu" (Mobutu), and the cynical "Tzumbi" (Moise Tshombe), who is a leader of the secessionist movement centered in the mineral-rich province of Katanga. The cast of characters extends to the intriguing historical personage Dag Hammerskjöld, then Secretary-General of the United Nations. Depicted as a deeply pious man with a naive faith in the ideal of "neutrality," the earnest bureaucrat adopts a position that is ultimately revealed to be untenable in the context of a convulsive internecine conflict. High-minded neutrality becomes, in this account, tantamount to acquiescence in the status quo, and Césaire's Hammerskjöld himself comes to a belated awareness of this predicament. The voice of the Congolese people is represented on stage by the utterances of the Sanza Player, whose cryptic ditties and pointed remarks enliven and punctuate the drama. Among the other minor characters who interact with the protagonist at critical junctures in the play are Lumumba's wife, Pauline, and Mama Makosi, the patron of a popular dive in Elizabethville frequented by none other than Lumumba himself. The play's personae and plot, then, unabashedly incorporate actual historical events, though these are, of course, telescoped and re-ordered in the interests of dramaturgical economy.

The centerpiece of the whole constellation is the figure – part historical, part legendary – of Patrice Lumumba. He is given an heroic profile that manifests intriguing parallels with that of Henri Christophe. The playwright himself has trenchantly articulated the links in terms that elucidate his conception of both characters:

Both of them were poets cut off from the main body of the flock [...], visionaries who were far ahead of their time. Neither was more of a politician than the other. In their pursuit of a noble ideal they lost contact with a reality that is unforgiving [...] Lumumba, Christophe – these are stalwarts who stand erect when everything is falling to pieces around them.[26]

What is especially salient in this analytical capsule provided by the author himself is the august label of "poet" that he applies to the martyred political leaders as he dramatized them. This label is no casual metaphor in Césaire's lexicon, as can readily be seen, for instance, in his essay "Poetry and Knowledge," in which the figure of the poet is assimilated to a puissant demiurge endowed with clairvoyance and uncommon perspicacity. The poet, then, like Rimbaud's "seer" (*voyant*), is fundamentally a visionary who resolutely, even passionately, pursues his private dream of re-creating the world through the power of the imagination. When transposed to the sphere of statecraft, such a utopian project is foredoomed to failure, since its success would hinge on its being shared with the mass of the people – a most improbable convergence in view of the poet's idiosyncratic powers of vision. In *Saison* what collapses in the wake of Lumumba's personal catastrophe is the elusive dream of a united, decolonized Africa. Like Christophe, the Congolese leader is obsessed with a sense of urgency that pushes him to accelerate his country's journey to full autonomy, and in that very forced march he leaves the common man far behind. The imperative of finding a shortcut to political restoration leads the Haitian king to impose what may be called a "black man's burden" on his subjects that caricatures, even as it matches, the "white man's burden" which was previously inflicted on those same subjects.

In the contemporary example of Lumumba, the vanguard leader's loss of contact with his people on the accelerated march to freedom is particularly poignant, because he is consistently cast as a genuine folk hero who fraternizes with humble people, even as Prime Minister. In the play, as apparently also in real life, he is shown frequenting popular bars and nightclubs (Lumumba in a bar is in fact a recurrent scene throughout), and he is so beloved by the masses that he is at one point liberated by them from prison (Act 3, Sc. 1).

The dramatic incident that best captures the protagonist's increasing distance, spiritually speaking, from the Congolese masses occurs in Act 3, Sc. 2, when, in the euphoria following his liberation from prison, the crowd presses him to don the traditional emblems of monarchy: the leopard skin and the stole. Lumumba's refusal of the proffered elevation is historically accurate; at the same time it has intertextual resonance with Shakespeare's *Julius Caesar*, who famously resisted similar honors from the Roman people. In its African version, however, the leader's gesture of refusal takes on special meaning in a culture that, unlike that of the ancient Roman republic, does not have a national identity born in the overthrow of kingship. For Césaire's African poet-prophet the leader's refusal of the leopard skin and the stole creates an opportunity for a lesson on the inscription of a new kind of hero on the world stage. Thus we have the following peroration from him in the speech in which he explains why he has rejected the symbolic coronation:

Mais ce n'est pas seulement Dieu, que les blancs ont confisqué à leur profit, et ce n'est pas seulement Dieu, que les blancs ont thésaurisé! Et ce n'est pas seulement de Dieu que l'Afrique est frustrée, c'est d'elle, d'elle-même, que l'Afrique est volée! C'est d'elle, d'elle-même, que l'Afrique a faim. C'est pourquoi je ne me veux ni messie ni mahdi. Je n'ai pour arme que ma parole, je parle, et j'éveille, je ne suis pas un redresseur de torts, pas un faiseur de miracles, je suis un redresseur de vie, je parle, et je rends l'Afrique à elle-même! Je parle, et je rends l'Afrique au monde! Je parle, et, attaquant à leur base oppression et servitude, je rends possible, pour la première fois possible, la fraternité!

(But it is not only God that the whites have appropriated to their advantage; not only God they have hoarded! And it is not only God that they have denied Africa. Africa has been robbed of its very self, of its very identity. Africa is hungry for itself, its very self. That's why I don't wish to be either a messiah or a mahdi. My only weapon is my word. I speak and I open men's eyes. I am not here to redress evils, to perform miracles. I am here to breathe new life. I speak and I restore Africa to itself; I speak and I restore Africa to the world! I speak, and by attacking the root causes of oppression and servitude, I make possible – for the first time actually possible – true brotherhood.)

Even as he declines the trappings of supreme authority, the new brand of black hero reveals a no less grandiose desire to transform the world through oratory and persuasion.

Césaire's Lumumba, then, approximates the figure of the poet, in so far as he has a disproportionate faith in the sheer power of words. "I speak and I restore Africa to itself" is, on the face of it, a preposterous claim that reflects, not so much vanity or arrogance as naive trust in the magical efficacy of the word. In short, the pronouncements of the poet-as-leader are, in intention at least, tantamount to speech acts. This view of speech as intrinsically performative is at the other extreme from the unblinkered outlook expressed most tersely by the poet W. H. Auden in the lines:

> For poetry makes nothing happen: it survives
> In the valley of its saying where executives
> would never want to tamper . . .

The Césairean bard, like the leader whose mask he assumes in *Christophe* and *Saison*, does indeed make things happen, or rather, he nurtures the illusion that he is enacting the major transformations he envisions and desires by daring to put them into words. Ironically, however, the poet-leader does not, empirically any more than in the plays' action, succeed in changing the world through incantation, but is defeated by the inertia of neo-colonialism with its crushing combination of internecine strife and cynical capitalism. Lumumba's powerful opponents, both internal and external, eventually puncture the illusion of verbal puissance by the exercise of naked force. At their hands the hero, like the Rebel of *Chiens*, dies a gruesome, sacrificial death by execution on stage. The radical divergence between two types of leader, one visionary and idealistic (and ineffectual), the other pragmatic and narrow (and ascendant) receives thematic prominence in the closing scene of Act 2, where the unscrupulous Mokutu bluntly dismisses the poetic flights of imagery projected by an ecstatic Lumumba:

LUMUMBA Mokutu, sais-tu ce que tu t'apprêtes à faire? Le petit carré
de lumière au haut de la cellule du prisonnier, tu tires là-dessus
le rideau d'ombre! Le grand oiseau arc-en-ciel, qui visite le
plafond de cent cinquante millions d'hommes, le double
serpent, qui de part et d'autre de l'horizon se dresse et s'obstine
pour conjoindre une promesse de vie, une attestation de vie et
de ciel, tu l'abats d'un seul coup de bâton et vois, sur le
continent tout entier, tomber les lourds plis écailleux des
maléfiques ténèbres!

MOKUTU Je ne te suivrai pas dans ton apocalypse! Je n'ai pas à
répondre de l'Afrique, mais du Congo! Et j'entends y faire
régner l'ordre, comprends-tu? l'ordre!

(LUMUMBA Mokutu, do you know what it is you are about to do? The
tiny square of light near the roof of the prisoner's cell – you are
closing the curtain of darkness on it! The great rainbow of a bird
that visits the roof of a hundred and fifty million men, the
serpent that undoubles from one end of the horizon to
the other and persists in subtending a promise of life, a sign of
life and of heaven – you are beating it down with a single blow
and, you see, over the entire continent, the heavy, scaly coils of
malignant darkness descend.

MOKUTU I will not follow you into your apocalypse! I don't have to
answer for Africa, only for the Congo! And I intend to maintain
order there! You understand? Order!)

The stage directions that follow this polarized exchange are
sinister: "The soldiers have entered in silence and occupy the
whole stage." The preponderance of the military presence
– here the soldiers of Mobutu, the future leader of Zaire –
ominously foreshadows the coups that have bedeviled Africa in
the postcolonial period.

In an often-quoted metaphor Césaire has referred to his
next play, *Une Tempête* (*A Tempest*) as the third "panel" (*volet*) in
a larger "triptych," of which the other two components are
Christophe and *Saison*. Apparently he conceived these three
plays, at least initially, as reflecting major sectors of the black
world (Africa, the Caribbean and the USA).[27] This neat
triangular articulation is nonetheless misleading, for the
actual play *A Tempest*, which is purportedly representative of
black America, exhibits elements of all three major theaters

of the African homeland and diaspora. To be sure, the marks of
the Black Power movement in the continental USA of the 1960s
are prominent in the drama in the form of slogans (such as
"Freedom now" or "Uhuru"); but the action of the play takes
place on an island that distinctly recalls the Caribbean, and
Africa is vividly evoked in Caliban's appeals to deities such
as Shango and Eshu. In sum, the central paradigm of the
colonizer/colonized relation, as it is constructed in *A Tempest,*
embraces the totality of the black experience in the New
World.

When Césaire made a fictional Caribbean island the presumptive setting for his adaptation of *The Tempest,* he was by
no means inventing a geographical connection. Shakespeare
scholars have long since pointed out that certain features of his
plot have their documentary source in contemporary history.
Perhaps the most salient of these is the report of an actual
shipwreck off the Bermudas in the early seventeenth century
– an event that indirectly involved several of the bard's influential friends and patrons, such as the Earl of Pembroke and
Southampton, who had a stake in the Virginia Company.[28] The
very appellation "Caliban" is derived from the reality of
Amerindian resistance in the New World context, since it has
been shown to be an anagram of "Cannibal" (the latter being
itself derived, by a process of corruption, from "Carib" –
the name of a prominent Amerindian tribe that occupied the
archipelago at the time of the first European explorations).
The larger issue of the European enslavement of native
populations, whether in the African or the New World context,
was of course very topical in Elizabethan England, in view of
the participation of prominent English seamen, such as John
Hawkins and Walter Raleigh, in the highly profitable slave-
trade.

In addition to the strictly historical referentiality of
Shakespeare's drama, the use of the Prospero–Caliban configuration as a trope for relations between colonizer and
colonized, European master and African slave, has been
quite extensive among both metropolitan intellectuals
and Caribbean writers.[29] One way of reading Césaire's

"adaptation," therefore, is to regard it as an act of re-inscribing this critical psychological paradigm as a drama of rebellion. Let us give a brief account of the modern playwright's re-creation by focussing on the main roles he assigns to Prospero, Caliban and Ariel.

Césaire's Prospero is first and foremost a master whose manipulation of his two principal "slaves," Caliban and Ariel, is deeply problematic. No longer the innocent, slightly naive, egghead ruler who is the victim of a nefarious brother, he is presented as driven, in the first instance, by an anterior "will-to-power." This aspect of his character as reconceptualized by Césaire is indicated at the very inception of the play in the opening prologue pronounced by the Master of Ceremonies:

Atmosphère de psychodrame. Les acteurs entrent les uns après les autres et chacun choisit un masque à sa convenance
LE MENEUR DE JEU Allons, Messieurs, servez-vous . . . A chacun son personnage et à chaque personnage son masque. Toi, Prospero? Pourquoi pas? Il y a des volontés de puissance qui s'ignorent!

Psychodrama atmosphere. The actors enter one after the other, and each choses a mask that is suitable for him.
(MASTER OF CEREMONIES Very well, Gentlemen, help yourselves . . . To each his role and to each role its mask. You, Prospero? Why not? Sometimes the will to power is unconscious.)

The last line evokes the well-known Nietzschean concept of the "will-to-power." By ascribing an inner, unacknowledged desire for power so conspicuously to Prospero in this prelude, the playwright makes it clear that he is about to present a "demythified" figure (to use his own expression).

This Prospero, then, behaves and thinks like a prototypical colonizer. The very source of his authority – his claim to rule over the island and its inhabitants – is fundamentally spurious. Like so many European settlers, not to mention discoverers and conquistadors, he simply takes possession of alien territory by the exercise of superior force. In this respect, Caliban's rival claim of prior possession through inheritance from his mother is at least as valid as Prospero's, if not more so. But it is above all his attitude of gross condescension towards his subjects that betrays the colonial mentality in pristine form. Césaire makes him deliver the old cliché about his having brought the blessings of civilization to primitive natives:

Puisque tu manies si bien l'invective, tu pourrais au moins me bénir de t'avoir appris à parler. Un barbare! Une bête brute que j'ai éduquée, formée, que j'ai tirée de l'animalité qui l'engangue encore de toute part!

(Since you are so clever at abuse, you could at least bless me for having taught you speech. Barbarian! A brute beast that I educated, brought up, hauled out of the pit of a savage state that still clings to you all over.)

Caliban is quick to repudiate this declaration of a "white man's burden:"

D'abord ce n'est pas vrai. Tu ne m'as rien appris du tout. Sauf, bien sûr à baragouiner ton langage pour comprendre tes ordres

(First of all, that's not true. You've taught me nothing at all. Except, of course, how to mangle your language enough to understand your orders . . .)

In this "demythified" account, Prospero's famous magical power offers no room for the equation of magician and verbal artist as occurs in the conventional reading of the Shakespeare play in which, for example, the speech beginning "Our revels now are ended" is taken as the bard's own valedictory to the theater. Instead, the exercise of magic appears to stand in *A Tempest* for absolute power, or more precisely, the protagonist's desire for absolute power. As the play progresses it becomes clear that total control is something of a fantasy on Prospero's part, for the limits to control are made glaringly manifest in more than one scene. To single out only the most salient, Césaire's revision of the masque that Prospero stages for the entertainment of his marriage guests is undermined by an interloper in the form of the West African trickster-god, Eshu, who makes an unsolicited appearance (Act 3, Sc. 3). The latter brusquely intrudes upon an anemic evocation of pagan goddesses (Juno, Ceres, Iris), and Prospero's conjuring skills are powerless to constrain him in any way. Once on stage he proclaims his identity and attributes as a god who delights in carnavalesque inversion and sexual badinage (Act 3, Sc. 3). Eshu's anarchic subversion of Prospero's spectacle parallels, in some measure, the author's re-fashioning of the Shakespeare text. At the same time, the playwright seems to be confirming the insight that all "magic" is, at bottom, relative, despite the totalizing claims made by its practitioners. In the particular context of Eshu, it is crucial that the trickster deity who accomplishes the subversion is of African origin. The function of the Vodun spirits and gods in *Christophe* invites comparison: an avatar of the repressed (African) culture returns, in both cases, to haunt and confound the despotic ruler (whether he be European or African). In *A Tempest* the irrepressible African Eshu serves to debunk the would-be omnipotent European magician. The realization that his magic is limited, if not deeply flawed, is accorded to Prospero in an aside in which he confesses his failure (Act 3, Sc. 5):

> j'ai déraciné le chêne, soulevé la mer,
> ébranlé la montagne, et bombant
> ma poitrine contre le sort contraire,
> j'ai repondu à Jupiter foudre pour foudre.
> Mieux! De la brute, du monstre, j'ai fait l'homme!
> Mais oh!
> D'avoir échoué à trouver le chemin
> du cœur de l'homme, si du moins c'est là l'homme.

> (I have uprooted the oak-tree, caused the ocean
> to rise, shaken up the mountain. Bulging out my chest
> against an adverse fate, I have reacted in kind
> to Jove, thunderbolt for thunderbolt.
> What's more, I have made a man out of a savage brute.
> But oh!
> To have failed to find the route
> to the heart of man – if that's where man is to be found.)

In Caliban we have yet another Césairean portrait of a rebel, this time articulated with a foil in the person of Ariel. The two subordinates represent contrasting approaches to the goal of attaining liberty. For Ariel, who, like the Pétion of *Christophe*, is cast as a mulatto, the road to emancipation is by way of dialogue with the master and repeated appeals to his moral conscience; whereas Caliban categorically rejects the evolutionary model in favor of violent action. Césaire does not seek to disguise the topical aspect of this classic ideological polarity. Through well-paced allusions to the contemporary Afro-American scene, Caliban's position is associated with that adopted by many militant black leaders of the 1960s (e.g. Malcom X; the Black Panthers), while Ariel is obviously comfortable with the moderate stance and outlook espoused most memorably by the Reverend Martin Luther King. In the play, Caliban and Ariel actually engage in a debate about which is the more effective means of achieving liberation (Act 2, Sc. 1). In pursuing his own chosen path of militancy, Caliban continues to defy the master, even after suffering the humiliation of a failed rebellion. The play ends, in fact, with the voice of an alienated Caliban shouting offstage in the distance the word "freedom" ("la liberté") within earshot of an increasingly bemused Prospero. The unresolved, "open" ending points to a postcolonial limbo in which ex-master and ex-slave are living by mutually incompatible principles and aspirations.

One of the more intriguing innovations that Césaire brings to his adaptation is a surprise dénouement in which Prospero, instead of returning to Europe, decides to remain on the island indefinitely. His decision, announced in the final scene, is based on an inner conviction of his civilizing mission. His paternalism colors his vision of the future in which he and Caliban (whom he now calls "my boy," "mon garçon") will share the island under his benign governance. Césaire exposes the self-delusion inherent in this vision at the conclusion of the play, when, after a chronological leap in the dramatic action, he displays an aged, debilitated and lonely Prospero who is struggling against the encroachment of the jungle and desperately, but unsuccessfully, trying to keep his subaltern in check.

In Césaire's re-fashioning of the Shakespearean plot, then, the figure of Caliban is no longer a caricature of the savage, noble or ignoble; rather it incarnates the irrepressible will of the colonized to be his own master. This will-to-freedom (captured in the Kenyan insurrectionary slogan "Uhuru", "Freedom," that Caliban defiantly proclaims) entails the rejection of an image of the self imposed by the colonizer. In an important summary speech in the final scene of the drama, Caliban is made to enact this rejection as well as to affirm its corollary – the acquisition of self-knowledge:

> Prospero, tu es un grand illusionniste:
> le mensonge, ça te connaît.
> Et tu m'as tellement menti,
> menti sur le monde, menti sur moi-même,
> que tu as fini par m'imposer
> une image de moi-même:
> Un sous-développé, comme tu dis, un sous-capable,
> voilà comment tu m'as obligé à me voir,
> et cette image, je la hais! Et elle est fausse!
> Mais maintenant, je te connais, vieux cancer,
> et je me connais aussi!
>
> (Prospero, you are master of illusion.
> Lying is your trademark.
> And you have lied so much to me
> (lied about the world, lied about me)
> that you have ended by imposing on me
> an image of myself.
> "underdeveloped," you brand me, "inferior,"
> That's the way you have forced me to see myself
> I detest that image! What's more, it's a lie!
> But now I know you, you old cancer,
> and I know myself as well.)

In Caliban's strenuous repudiation of the image of himself imposed by the colonizer we recognize the same urge to reconstruct the self, to salvage the self from the ruses of the other, that constituted the thematic backbone of "Journal of a Homecoming." The play is the third and last in a series in which Césaire transposed into the genre of drama the funda-mental motifs that surfaced in his first lyric poem.

CHAPTER 6

The return to lyric: "me, laminaria..."

Poetry is the only means I have found of learning to know
myself. I have never known very well who I was, and poetry
has been a perpetual conquest of myself by myself.

Aimé Césaire[1]

The play, *A Tempest* marks the end of Césaire's concentrated
exploration of the genre of poetic drama. After the creative
storm that left the triptych in its wake, there followed a
relatively extended interlude of silence, or at least, non-
publication, on the literary scene. The interlude was only
definitively terminated with the publication of a new collection
of poems, *moi, laminaire...* ("me, laminaria...") in 1982. To be
sure, the silence had been broken at midpoint by the appearance of an ambitious edition of the author's complete works
(*Œuvres complètes*) in 1976 – an edition that included as a
pendant (under the rubric *Noria*) a group of poems most of
which had previously appeared in journals, notably *Présence
Africaine*. If we exclude the lyrics of *Noria*, we are left with a
picture of virtual inactivity on Césaire's part in the domain of
literary composition for a period of just over a decade (1971 to
1982).

By contrast with this relative artistic quiescence, the 1970s
were far from calm as far as the arena of politics is concerned.
To some extent Martinique, like the rest of the New World,
was experiencing the repercussions of the previous decade
of turmoil – the social agitation of the 1960s, which saw the
proliferation of radical student movements in the United
States, Europe and the Third World. By the early 1970s many of

these intellectual and political currents (such as Black Power) had sent ripples from metropolitan centers in North America into the francophone and anglophone Caribbean and were posing sharp challenges to the authority of such venerable institutions as "departmentalization" and such ageing ideologies as "négritude."

Chief among these new challenges was the fervid advocacy of independence on the part of a younger generation of French West Indians who had witnessed (and celebrated) the emergence of many new African nations. The often brutal methods of repression used by the French gendarmerie to stifle student movements in the Caribbean overseas departments (especially in Guadeloupe) only exacerbated the malaise among the young intelligentsia.[2] The response of Césaire and his party to the new radical temper in Antillean politics during the 1960s and 1970s was complex, if not ambivalent: on the one hand, they spoke out unequivocally against the violent repressive measures employed by the metropolitan authorities; on the other, they balked at the idea of embracing independence as a viable route for Martinique. Thus Césaire, who had himself been a key player in the establishment of the overseas departments, came to admit openly that "départementalisation" – a word that he may himself have coined[3] – had outlived its usefulness; but he continued nevertheless to endorse successive policies, such as "autonomy," that evoked visions of decentralization without acceding to the siren call of complete independence. Remaining squarely within the framework of electoral politics (and thereby siding with Ariel rather than Caliban in his approach to change), Césaire consistently demurred at all radical alternatives that would have cut the umbilical ties with France. At the end of the decade he was welcoming the election to the presidency of the socialist François Mitterrand, and resting his hopes on economic, rather than political, amelioration.[4] Eventually the pressures of an overheated electoral arena began to take their toll on the poet-deputy. Above all, the tension between his own exalted vision of decolonization and the irreducible reality of the island's continued dependence on the "mother country" in the economic sphere had become so pronounced that it was increasingly difficult for him not to succumb to sporadic feelings of disillusionment and self-doubt. The emotional scars from these internal and external conflicts account, in part, for both the prolonged artistic silence itself and the sometimes melancholy tone that creeps into some of the pages of "me, laminaria . . . "

This volume, which marked his return to lyric composition, is arranged in three separately labeled sections: (a) *moi, laminaire . . .* ; (b) *Quand Miguel Angel Asturias disparut*; and (c) *Wifredo Lam*. There is a striking asymmetry, however, in the disposition of the texts in this tripartite scheme, for by far the largest of these sections is the first, which shares its title with that of the collection as a whole and contains 53 poems out of the overall total of 67. By contrast, the middle section consists of a single poem, part encomium, part dirge, on the writer Miguel Angel Asturias; while the final portion, celebrating the Afro-Cuban poet, Wifredo Lam, contains ten poems that had previously appeared in *Noria*.[5]

Both the form and the meanings of the enigmatic title *moi, laminaire . . .* are revealing about the major themes and rhetorical stances of the ensemble. The central question of an artistic and social identity – the very question that permeates the entire Césairean corpus from its very beginning in *Cahier* – here re-surfaces with a vengeance and receives expository prominence in the resounding *moi*. This self-proclamation of the speaking subject (pronounced despite the use of lower-case letters) is separated by a crucial comma from the appositional noun *laminaire*, which is richly polysemous.[6] Its multiple layers of meaning, its potential to exfoliate, are in turn formally underscored by the trailing punctuation (. . .). Since Césaire is normally very parsimonious in his use of punctuation marks, the comma that precedes, no less than the dots that follow, the word *laminaire* are something of a flag for a reader who has become familiar with the earlier lyric. Whereas the comma suggests an apposition (hence a virtual identity) between *moi* and *laminaire*, the dots complicate and extend that identity. The non-closure signified in the dots (. . .) evokes what appears, at least on the surface, to be a boundless sea of connotations. Since we cannot hope to explore this bewildering amplitude in anything approaching completeness, we shall single out a few of the main referents of the locution *laminaire* for a brief elucidation.

The sense of indeterminacy in the title's form and meaning is reinforced by the brief avant-propos that prefaces the first section:

Le non-temps impose au temps la tyrannie de sa spatialité: dans toute vie il y a un nord et un sud, et l'orient et l'occident. Au plus extrême, ou, pour le moins, au carrefour, c'est au fil des saisons survolées, l'inégale lutte de la vie et de la mort, de la ferveur et de la lucidité, fût-ce celle du désespoir et de la retombée, la force aussi toujours de regarder demain. Ainsi va toute vie. Ainsi va ce livre, entre soleil et ombre, entre montagne et mangrove, entre chien et loup, claudiquant et binaire. Le temps aussi de régler leur compte à quelques fantasmes et à quelques fantômes.

(Non-time imposes on time the tyranny of its spatiality: In every life there is a north and a south, an east and a west. At the very extreme, or to say the least, at the crossroads, we find, where one encounters in flight the suite of the seasons, the unequal struggle between life and death, between fervor and lucidity, even where it derives from despair and relapse, the constant strength as well to face tomorrow. Every life follows this pathway, as does this book, poised between sun and shadow, between mountain and mangrove, between day and nightfall, limping and bipedal. Time also to come to terms with certain phantoms and phantasms.)

This pregnant preface, with its string of bipolar opposites, foregrounds the speaker's situation of "liminality" in various aspects of his existence (the French word *liminaire*, "liminal" resonates like an overtone with *laminaire*). On the temporal axis the lyric voice oscillates between the states of elation and despair, optimism and pessimism, fervor and lucidity. On balance, however, there is a larger number of poems in the collection that lean towards the pole of lugubriousness, as opposed to optimistic expansion.[7]

A primary connotation of *laminaire* is, of course, "sea-weed." More technically, it refers, as a proper name in plant biology, to a family of marine algae (the Laminaria). Part of the ludic

ingenuity manifest in the choice of title derives from the fact
that this primary vegetal meaning expresses the very idea of
exfoliation in a fluid medium – a trope, therefore, for the style
and organization of the poetic texts to follow. The poem
that most conspicuously foregrounds the trope is called, not
surprisingly, *Algues* (22) and it is structured by a "taxonomic
series," or strings of parallel noun phrases, of the kind we
recognize as a stylistic trait of Césaire's poetics:

> la relance ici se fait
> par le vent qui d'Afrique vient
> par la poussière d'alizé
> par la vertu de l'écume
> et la force de la terre
>
> nu
> l'essentiel est de sentir nu
> de penser nu
> > la poussière d'alizé
> > la vertu de l'écume
> > et la force de la terre
> la relance ici se fait par l'influx
> plus encore que par l'afflux
> > la relance
> > > se fait
> > > > algue laminaire

> (The re-launch is made from here
> by the gust that comes from Africa
> by the dust from the tradewinds
> by the prowess in the foam
> and in the force of earth
>
> bare
> the essential is to feel bare
> to think bare thoughts
> > the dust from the tradewinds
> > the prowess in the foam
> > and the force of earth
> the re-launch is made from here by the influx
> even more than by the afflux
> > the re-launch
> > > is made
> > > > seaweed laminaria)

The poem culminates in a redundant phrase that juxtaposes the more common word for seaweed (*algue*) with the *laminaire* of the title, thereby re-inscribing the primary reference of the latter. The impersonal subject is here poised for a grand effort of re-dedication to the struggle (the "re-launch"), which will take place from his marginal site in the marine swamp. Like the algae that regenerate and exfoliate in their ecological niche, this subject is neither defeatist nor dispirited; rather he draws on powerful inner and outer resources (wind, foam, earth) to renew his assault on surrounding inertia. In short, by virtue of its mood of self-confidence and a determined re-grouping of forces, the text of *Algues* stands out, along with the almost ecstatic *mot-macumba* that follows it (23), as a luminous contrast to that other dark pole of lugubriousness that the volume also encompasses.

That other polar modality is perhaps best illustrated from the opening strophe of the inaugural poem, "calendrier lagunaire" ("Lagoon almanac"), which, as is the case in other Césaire volumes, is consciously programmatic:

> j'habite une blessure sacrée
> j'habite des ancêtres imaginaires
> j'habite un vouloir obscur
> j'habite un long silence
> j'habite une soif irrémédiable
> j'habite un voyage de mille ans
> j'habite une guerre de trois cents ans
> j'habite un culte désaffecté entre bulbe et caïeu
> j'habite l'espace inexploité
> j'habite du basalte non une coulée
> mais de la lave le mascaret
> qui remonte la valleuse à toute allure
> et brûle toutes les mosquées
> je m'accommode de mon mieux de cet avatar
> d'une version du paradis absurdement ratée
> – c'est bien pire qu'un enfer–
> j'habite de temps en temps une de mes plaies
> chaque minute je change d'appartement
> et toute paix m'effraie

(I live in a sacred wound
I live among fictional ancestors
I live in an obscure desire
I live in a prolonged silence
I live in an unquenchable thirst
I live in a voyage of a thousand years
I live in a war of three hundred years
I live in a disaffected creed between bulb and clove
I live in the unused space
I live in basalt: not where the lava flow erupts
but at the very source of its efflux
where it follows the creekbed upward at every turn
and burns down all the mosques
I adapt as best I can to this avatar
an absurdly failed version of paradise
　　– it is far worse than a hell –
I live from time to time in one of my sores
　　I change apartments by the minute
and every calm terrifies me)

From the point of view of style and form the poem could not be
more representative of Césaire's mature lyric compositions. A
great many poems from all periods of his output unfold in a
series of paratactic clauses, often marked, as in this instance,
by anaphora (*j'habite*, "I live in" in initial position in successive
lines). In most cases these series have the effect of piling up
or superimposing images and concepts that are both inter-
changeable and mutually reinforcing. What is perhaps new in
the catalogue we are given in *Lagoon almanac* (wound, desire,
silence, thirst, sore etc.) is the way in which the accumulation
of items works to create an unbearable, unrelieved pressure – a
pressure whose only positive outcome, revealed in the final
strophe, is to intensify the verbal charge:

> la pression atmosphérique ou plutôt l'historique
> agrandit démesurément mes maux
> même si elle rend somptueux certains de mes mots

> (the atmospheric, or rather historic pressure
> increases my woes beyond measure
> even though it imparts to some of my words an
> 　　extravagant aura.)

Manifest in the titles as well as the organization of several of
these short lyric poems is a conscious effort of retrospection on
the author's part, as though he set out to guide us back with a
firm hand to the major thematic as well as stylistic continuities
throughout his poetic output (compare the suggestive words
of poem 19: "J'ai guidé du troupeau la longue transhumance",
"I have led the herd through its long migration to a new
pasture"). The poem *annonciades* (2), for example, with its evan-
gelistic fervor, cannot but recall the rhapsodic *Annonciation,*
dedicated to André Breton, from the early surrealist collection
"Miracle Weapons." In fine, the overriding impression the
reader derives from these recurrent patterns and cross-
references is that the poet has indeed "returned," not merely
to the genre of lyric (which he had ostensibly abandoned for
drama), but to the enduring spiritual foundations of his poetic
art.

To illustrate this retrospective dimension, we may compare
the poetic title "Banal" ("Trite") from "me, laminaria . . . "
with that of "Quelconque" ("Commonplace") from the early
collection *Cadastre* (discussed above, pp. 108–110). In addition
to the nodal idea of the mundane that is common to both, the
later text distinctly recalls the earlier in respect both to
content and to form, with the anaphoric repetition *rien que*
(nothing but) taking the place of *quelconque* at the start of the
opening catalogues:

> rien que la masse de manœuvre de la torpeur à
> manœuvrer
> rien que le jour des autres et leur séjour
> rien que ce troupeau de douteux lézards qui reviennent
> plutôt gaiement
> > du pâturage et leurs conciliabules infâmes
> > aux découpages de bayous
> > de mon sang méandre à mumbo-jumbo
>
> (nothing but the main force of torpor
> to maneuver
> nothing but the day of others and their stay
> nothing but this herd of uncertain lizards filing back
> quite cheerfully

from the pasture and their squalid caucuses
in the carved out bayous
of my bloodstream's meaningless meandering)

The text of "Banal" conveys throughout its course a sense of
unremitting monotony, the "meaningless meander" that a
committed public life in the Antilles is perpetually in danger of
becoming. The measured repetition of syllables in the opening
verses serves to augment this undercurrent of monotony (*masse
de manœuvre . . . manœuvrer; jour . . . séjour*). In contrast with the
dialectical progress of "Commonplace," which commences
with images of quotidian inertia only to yield in its finale to a
vision of seismic disruption, the banality presented here does
not recede from view, and the caymans who there portend
revolution are here replaced by slothful reptilian presences.
The subject of "Banal" who contemplates the static scene of
routine commitments does so, it appears, with the resignation
of a weary Sisyphus who must forever recommence his cyclic
task of rolling the stone uphill.

Certain items in this catalogue of trite "maneuvers" hark
back to other key poems from the collection *Cadastre*. To take a
conspicuous example, the diction of the line "nothing but the
day of others and their stay" echoes the closing cadence of
the summational text "Non-vicious circle" (see above, p. 125):

No circle is vicious
Hollow
it's only my knees all entangled and sinking like stone
into the toil
of others and their slumber

The atmosphere of "Banal" comes perilously, perhaps even
deliberately, close to contradicting this earlier formulation, in
so far as the speaker's altruistic endeavors ("the toil of others";
"the day of others") can now be sometimes seen as petering out
into the kind of "vicious circle" whose existence had previously
been excluded. It is evident that the two decades intervening
between "Irons" and "me, laminaria . . . " have somewhat
dampened the poet's anticipation of meaningful political and
cultural transformation.

At the center of the triadically arranged volume "me,
laminaria . . . ", Césaire has placed an eloquent homage to the
great Guatemalan writer and Nobel laureate Miguel Angel
Asturias (1899–1974). The style of the homage also bears the
Césairean stamp of repetition (combined with parataxis and,
of course, frequent anaphora), but with a novel inflection of
tone that is powerfully evocative of a ritual litany. Above all
the poem creates an aura of mythmaking that is marvellously
congruent with an important strain in the Guatemalan's work:
his reclaiming, by way of "translation," of the native Mayan
worldview.[8] By adopting a mythographic mode of discourse
(evident already in the poem's title where the death of the
subject is described as a "disappearance") Césaire is subtly
imitating his subject, for Asturias's muse had been profoundly
shaped by his passionate research into, and recuperation of,
Mayan mythology and folklore.[9] The culminating point of the
Latin American artist's total immersion in archaic Mayan
semiotics is his pioneering work *Men of Maize* (*Hombres de maiz*),
which, despite its reputation for opacity, is now gaining more
widespread recognition as a veritable watershed in the history
of Latin American fiction in our time.[10]

Intertextuality is, of course, an integral part of the standard
repertoire of many eulogies, especially those that honor the
deceased, and the homage to Asturias is clearly no exception.
The poem is strewn with echoes of the novelist's iconic
obsessions. The phrase "Strong Wind" ("Grand Vent"), for
instance, deliberately translates a title of an Asturias novel,
Viento fuerte (originally published in 1949); while the final
regenerative image of a "green mountain" conjoins two
recurrent symbols in the Mayan mythic system. The last four
strophes of the poem, in fact, portray the now mythicized
Asturias as going through a fourfold process of metamorphosis
that is modeled on Mayan cosmogonic ritual:

> Miguel Angel immergea sa peau d'homme
>   et revêtit sa peau de dauphin
>
> Miguel Angel dévêtit sa peau de dauphin
>   et se changea en arc-en-ciel

Miguel Angel rejetant sa peau d'eau bleue
　　revêtit sa peau de volcan

et s'installa montagne toujours verte
　　à l'horizon de tous les hommes

(Miguel Angel submerged his human skin
　　and put on his dolphin skin

Miguel Angel took off his dolphin skin
　　and changed himself into a rainbow

Miguel Angel throwing off his skin of blue water
　　put on his volcano skin

and took his stand: mountain perennially green
　　on the horizon of all mankind)

In view of the many suggestive affinities – artistic, biographical and ideological – between Césaire and Asturias, it is by no means surprising that the encomium to the latter occupies so conspicuous a spot in the collection. These affinities include a fructifying, youthful contact with the Paris surrealist avant-garde, and the revalorization of "primitive" cultural traditions, such as those of pre-Columbian Latin America. The two are, of course, closely intertwined; in Asturias's case, the writer's sensibility was whetted by his intense academic apprenticeship under the expert guidance of the eminent ethnologist George Raynaud, who steered him into research on such key Mayan texts as the Popol Vuh.[11] During his student sojourn in the metropolis in the period immediately following the First World War, the Guatemalan writer was eventually to forge both a cultural identity and a literary persona that reflected his quest for authenticity. The analogy with Césaire's quest, inspired by his friendship with Léopold Senghor, for a lost African cultural ancestry is compelling. A felicitous coincidence made the convergence explicit, rather than merely speculative or intuitive: Asturias is known to have composed a laudatory preface to an Italian edition of selected poems by Senghor.[12] The main point of resemblance between the aesthetic trajectories of the two writers, however, is the transition from Old World surrealism à la Breton to New World magic realism à la

Carpentier. Can it be merely fortuitous that Carpentier's
foundational novel *The Kingdom of this World* , whose prologue is
a defining text for magic realism, should have appeared in
the same year as Asturias's path-breaking *Men of Maize*? The
eminent Chilean writer Ariel Dorfman, who has done so
much with remarkable succinctness to draw attention to the
pioneering nature of Asturias's experimental fiction, regards
the conjunction as far from trivial: "A strange fate has befallen
Miguel Angel Asturias' masterpiece, *Men of Maize*. Along with
Alejo Carpentier's remarkable *The Kingdom of this World*, which
was also published in 1949, it could well be said to inaugurate
the extraordinary renaissance of the contemporary Latin
American novel."[13] In short, Césaire's poem pays tribute to
an important precursor of magic realism – an aesthetic
movement, which, as we have seen at several points in our
account, converges in non-trivial ways with what might be
called "francophone surrealism."

Asturias's later career as a diplomat (he held the post of
Guatemalan ambassador to France for several years) brought
him back to the city that had been the site of his own intellectual illumination and re-discovery of his cultural and artistic
roots. If we pursue the comparison with Césaire without
invidiousness we may well concede that Asturias's assimilation
and repossession of his Mayan "skin" was finally more thorough,
in terms of its intimate textual repercussions, than the
Martinican's move towards recovery of his African self; for
the Guatemalan novelist not only co-authored a translation
of the great Mayan text *Popol Vuh*, but also became a major
re-narrator of indigenous myths in such celebrated works
as *Leyendas de Guatemala* (1957) and the afore-mentioned
masterpiece, *Hombres de Maiz* . When Césaire signals Asturias's
moment of "disappearance" and subsequent transfiguration into a "green mountain," he is, among other things,
applauding the posthumous success of the author of *Men of
Maize* in constructing a mythic persona to which posterity will
subscribe.

Of the many important significations of *laminaire* that come
to the surface in a diachronic reading of the collection as whole,

the association, via soundplay, with the surname Lam is particularly pronounced, since the syllable resonates with the entire culminating third section of the volume in praise of the great Afro-Cuban painter, Wifredo Lam. As we have seen (pp. 78–82 above), Césaire not only deeply admired Lam's art, but also felt a very close kinship with his basic aesthetic stance. Both Martinican poet and Cuban painter had arrived at their distinctive idioms by the fecund route of Parisian avant-garde movements, in particular the surrealist circle of creative writers and artists. Lam indeed had been, to some extent at least, a protégé of Picasso's in the years immediately prior to the Second World War, although he consistently developed his own "visual syntax" independently of the Spanish master.[14] Lam's "discovery" by Picasso has intriguing parallels with Césaire's celebrated "discovery" by André Breton (above, pp. 70–71); hence it is no accident that Lam composed illustrations of poetic volumes by both these poets (*Fata Morgana* by Breton; *Cahier* by Césaire). Furthermore, Afro-Caribbean religious cults, such as Haitian Vodun and its Cuban counterpart, Santería, played a central role in the telluric mythography of Césaire no less than in that of the Cuban painter. In the case of the latter, the cultic bond was far from academic or attenuated, since his view of the world was profoundly shaped by his remarkable and dynamic godmother, Mantonica Wilson, an adept in the Afro-Cuban religion of Santería – a gifted woman whose spiritual powers came to be highly respected in her island home. Césaire confers prominence on her role as cultural transmitter by using, as an epitaph to the third section, a citation from Lam's own appreciation of his godmother, in which he claims that she had placed him under the ritual protection of powerful African divinities:

Mantonica Wilson, my godmother, had the power to conjure up the forces of nature . . . I went to visit her in her home stocked with African idols. She put me under the protection of all these gods.

If further testimony to this crucial dimension of Wifredo Lam's formation is needed, we have Césaire's own account of the impact of the priestess on his friend's maturation as an artist:

When you look at Wifredo Lam's paintings, you can find the jungle, Voodoo, Macumba and Santeria in them. You find in them the fundamental gods, the fundamental paganism of the African. He used to tell me, in the same way Léopold [Senghor] tells me about the village poetess who has influenced his esthetic so much . . . well, Wifredo used to tell me about Mantonica. She is a mambo who influenced him very much, who initiated him. All of Wifredo's work continues his rendering of this primitive initiation.[15]

As we expect from the laudatory epigraph to "me, laminaria . . . ," Césaire pays further direct homage to his fellow-artist's black ancestral roots in the poem, "Conversation avec Mantonica Wilson." Using the device of an imaginary dialogue over which the "mambo" mysteriously presides, the poet apostrophizes a potent male speaker ("diseur"). This unnamed addressee is presumably Lam, who here plays an intermediary role as a transmitter of authentic spiritual values:

> toi diseur
>   qu'y a-t-il à dire
>   qu'y a-t-il à dire
> la vie à transmettre
> la force à repartir
>   et ce fleuve de chenilles
>
> (you who speak to us
>   what is there to say
>   what is there to say
> life to transmit
> force to share
>   and this river of caterpillars)

In this part of his "conversation" with an African avatar the poet effects a symbolic fusion – in the sense of a shared ancestral muse – between his own poetic voice and the visual expression of Lam. If we recall that Césaire himself had a revered female figure of his own in the person of his "African" grandmother (see above, pp. 5–6), his identification with Lam through the medium of Mantonica Wilson may have even more profound psycho-social meaning than is indicated here.

By conspicuously referring to his lyric persona in the overall title of his volume as "*Lam*inarian," then, Césaire pays the

Cuban painter the ultimate compliment that a poet can bestow on another artist: he acknowledges his aesthetic affinity by incorporating the name "Lam" into the very texture of the poetic identity that he has fashioned for himself (the epithet *laminaire*, as we have noted, stands grammatically in apposition to the word for "self," *moi*).

Wifredo Lam died in 1982, the year of publication of *moi, laminaire* . . . With his discrete block of poems consecrated to the recent memory of a major Caribbean artist Césaire publicly acknowledges his profound personal debt to the enduring genius of Lam, while simultaneously recapitulating some of his own deeply held poetic convictions. Despite the retrospective tone of the volume as a whole, however, it would be premature, in the light of the historical record, to regard it as a definitive coda to Césaire's lyric œuvre.

Epilogue

quasi cursores vitai lampada tradunt

(like runners they pass on the torch of life)

Lucretius[1]

Two momentous events in the biography of Aimé Césaire – one literary, the other political – have converged to give the impression of a sense of closure to his dual career. The first was his abdication, so to speak, from electoral politics in Martinique in 1993; the second, the publication of his complete poetry in Paris in the following year.[2] This sequence of events, whether coincidental or not, affords us a convenient vantage point from which to sketch an overview of his reception both locally and internationally.

To begin with the artistic horizon of reception: it is undeniable that, despite the apparent marginality of much post-colonial writing, Césaire's creative corpus places him securely within the central purview of the European poetic canon. Though (or more accurately, precisely because) his work is permeated by an indictment of Western imperialism and colonialism, its formal attributes no less than its subject-matter situate its author in an omnipresent dialogue with past representatives of that canon, such as Aeschylus, Shakespeare, Rousseau and Mallarmé. As we have tried to show in some detail in the preceding chapters, to interpret Césaire's writing is to engage in an intertextual discourse that ranges from Greco-Roman to contemporary literatures. An inescapable consequence of this intertextual awareness is that his poetry is far more accessible to the sophisticated metropolitan French reader that it is to the local Caribbean audience. The exception that proves the rule may be the theatrical works; for the dramatic "triptych" on the black world comes closer than any of the author's other poetic compositions to being communicable to a less educated, popular audience. The varied reception accorded his most internationally known work, *Cahier*, is instructive in this regard. Because of its timing, no less than its patently anti-colonial message, the poem exerted a strong ideological impact on the postwar generation in the former French colonies, particularly in West Africa; whereas its local impact in Antillean francophone societies has been notoriously limited to a small intellectual elite. If this point be conceded in the case of *Cahier*, it is even more manifest with respect to the shorter lyric poems, which are composed in a dense, metaphorically laden style. For these reasons the question of the reception of the poetry may best be illuminated at the level of language. Since this is an issue that has aroused a great deal of controversy over the years, it is worth re-framing it succinctly in its cultural context.

Like the rest of the Caribbean archipelago, the island of Martinique is fundamentally bilingual. Alongside the standard languages of the European colonizers (e.g. English, French, Spanish, Dutch) there exist throughout the region various vernaculars that are now globally referred to as "creoles." Interestingly enough, these creole languages exhibit structural parallels that cut across national boundaries – parallels that probably are to be accounted for by a common base in certain recurrent West African linguistic features. Be that as it may, it is important to emphasize that Martinican creole is not to be dismissed in simplistic terms as a bastardized form of French (though it may have begun life as a so-called "pidgin" tongue), but is, in actual fact, a well-developed language in its own right, with a complex grammar and large lexicon. Though all the mature creoles of the region have by now been scientifically described by anthropological linguists, it remains the case that they are used almost exclusively in oral rather than written form. Since Césaire, however, like the vast majority of all published authors in the Caribbean, writes in the language of the former European master, he has from time to time been taken to task by latter-day champions of creole for devaluing the speech of the masses. Especially in the last decade or so, the French Caribbean movement that advocates "créolité" ("creoleness" – a concept that includes but is not limited to linguistics) has become increasingly strenuous in its denunciations of Césaire's adherence to French as his preferred literary medium. For example, a leading exponent of the "créolité" position, Raphaël Confiant, has recently launched a comprehensive as well as acerbic critique of Césaire's intellectual legacy in which the issue of language figures prominently. Homing in on a imprudent remark of Césaire's in a famous interview with Jacqueline Leiner,[3] concerning the supposed deficiencies of creole as a vehicle for thought, Confiant attacks the father of négritude for what he calls "the creole paradox." To add teeth to his own campaign to confer prestige on the language of the majority of his compatriots he even goes so far as to include, as one of several "annexes" to his book, an ingenious rendition in creole of Césaire's best known work, *Cahier*! Like his chief comrades-in-arms, Patrick Chamoiseau and Jean Bernabé, with whom he has collaborated on the epoch-making book *Eloge de la créolité* ("In Praise of Creole Culture"), Confiant sees the so-called "creole paradox" as merely one in a network of profound paradoxes that vitiate the intellectual legacy of a writer and father-figure whom he both admires and rejects. What is ideologically at stake in this inter-generational confrontation on the issue of French versus creole is by no means straightforward, however; for although Césaire may be faulted for having sounded an uncharacteristically condescending note towards creole in the Leiner interview, it is equally clear that to write in creole is to limit one's audience drastically and, in effect, to forgo the kind of international reception that is guaranteed by the linguistic reach of the French language.

Within the acknowledged constraints of the colonizer's language, Césaire has consciously sought to occupy a linguistic space of his own making which is different from that staked out, at least rhetorically, by today's articulate champions of creole. In the same interview with Jacqueline Leiner alluded to above, he had also asserted his intention to "bend" (*infléchir*) the French language. His claim to have engaged in creative distortion is admittedly not dissimilar from the aesthetic projects pursued by many modernist European writers of the twentieth century who have striven to forge an original idiom of expression. The occasional deformations in syntax and vocabulary to which Césaire has subjected standard French do not, in the aggregate, bear out a strong claim for radical linguistic subversion. In short, his achievements as a poet are, as André Breton famously recognized, basically continuous with a metropolitan tradition of avant-garde writing.

The local reception of Césaire's ideology of racial identity, as summed up in the word *négritude*, has been no less mixed than that accorded to his poetic language. Rather than flogging what is by now a moribund, if not dead, horse, let us briefly re-focus on the one recurrent charge that may have some degree of validity: that of biological essentialism.[4] Confiant and his cohorts have not been the first to object to the notion of the "fundamental black" (*le nègre fondamental*), with its implication of an inherited racial substratum that is overlaid by a European cultural veneer. In seeking to strip away the traces of essentialism in his individual construction of blackness, Césaire has long since insisted that "Africa" is for him a culturally transmitted set of values. This sincere attempt at clarification has not, however, been sufficient to convince his most stringent contemporary critics, who continue to regard the hypostasization of "Africa," in the context of Caribbean cultures, as a nostalgic wish for a lost paradise.

Postnégritude movements in the French Departments have typically striven to transcend the Europe/Africa dichotomy by predicating a *tertium quid* that constitutes a unique inter-cultural synthesis. Thus the distinguished Martinican writer Edouard Glissant has sponsored the counter-term "Antillanité" ("Antilleanness") to describe the amalgam that he sees as definitive for the cultures that emerged in the Antilles.[5] More recently, as we have seen, "créolité" has been the preferred term of the currently prominent crop of creative writers on

the Martinican scene. In response to these new challenges and
re-formulations some of the apologists of the older négritude
have made the claim that "créolité" is merely a modern
re-hash of the thesis of cultural hybridization (*métissage*)
propounded earlier in the century by the Martinican Gilbert
Gratiant. Césaire himself, in his well-known essay, "Culture
and Colonization," had long since registered his rejection of
the notion that a "mixed" culture in a postcolonial context
could be integrated and harmonious rather than disjointed.[6]
Whatever side one may chose to take in the ongoing debate
over how best to describe the enigma of Caribbean culture, it
is a lasting merit of Césaire's outmoded formulation that
it continues to inspire precisely the kind of self-reflection
from generation to generation that has helped to generate the
flowering of letters in the French Antilles.[7]

If the ideological aspect of Césaire's multi-faceted legacy, as
we have depicted it, has led to the insemination of a flourishing
debate about the nature of postcolonial society, the strictly
political aspect has had important ramifications that are all
the more difficult to assess in view of their direct impact on the
social and economic well-being of all Martinicans. I refer, of
course, to Césaire's crucial role as midwife in bringing into
being the constitutional status of the French Antilles as "overseas departments" (see above, pp. 93–96). From its very
inception, "departmentalization" provoked sharp objections
from those activists who contend that nothing short of full
independence can prepare the ground for a thoroughgoing
decolonization. By contrast, Césaire has never advocated an
independence platform, even when it became clear to him that
successive French governments were inclined to drag their feet
on implementing the promise of a complete integration of the
French Antilles into the nation of France. For his deep-seated
reluctance to cut the umbilical cord with the Mother Country
(in this case France rather than Africa) he has been roundly
assailed by many younger critics who have appealed to the
example of the independent countries of the former French
West Africa.[8] As with the question of the validity of the concept
of négritude, however, "the jury is still out," as the saying goes,

on the issue of whether political independence automatically leads to the elimination of economic dependence. If indeed the welfare of the island as a whole be considered the main criterion of the success of departmentalization, it must be admitted that, despite all the inveterate problems of post-colonial integration, it is difficult for the unbiased observer to conclude that the nominally "independent" mini-states of the anglophone Caribbean are better off than the countries that form "tropical France." If Martinique and Guadeloupe are fairly described in economic terms as "ersatz" countries,[9] cannot the same pejorative label be applied just as aptly to such tiny nation-states in the former British West Indies as Barbados, Grenada and Dominica?

When all is said and done, it is not Aimé Césaire the politician whom posterity will come to revere, but rather the extraordinary verbal artist who composed poems of the order of *Cahier* and dramas on the level of *Christophe*. This basic opinion is shared, on a more modest scale, by Césaire himself, who has registered the following trenchant exchange at the start of an interview with a noted American scholar:

ROWELL: In the United States we know you mainly as a poet and a playwright.
CESAIRE: The Americans know my better self.[10]

Aimé Césaire's long-lasting stewardship as a statesman in the French Chamber of Deputies, as well as mayor and party leader, achieved definitive closure with his formal resignation from electoral politics in 1993, just a few months prior to his eightieth birthday. In his resignation speech he playfully alluded to his advanced age and disavowed any desire to head a "gerontocracy."[11] It is typical of his style of oratory that he should have graced his valedictory with a citation from the Roman poet Lucretius:

quasi cursores vitai lampada tradunt[12]

(like runners, they pass on the torch of life)

The citation of a Classical passage is not, however, merely an otiose ornament or a gratuitous display of learning on Césaire's part, as is readily apparent if we pay even cursory attention to the original context. Lucretius' simile occurs in the context of a discussion of the unchanging sum of atoms in the universe, which he describes as analogous to the preservation of life in the aggregate, despite the rise and decline of various species. Human beings receive life and, like athletes in a footrace, pass on the torch to the next generation:

Thus the sum of things is renewed always, and mortal beings are mutually interdependent: some species increase, others decrease, and in a short space of time generations of living creatures are changed, and like runners pass on the torch of life.[13]

The famous comparison of the life process to a relay torch-race acquires a certain poignancy in Césaire's allusion if we grasp the inter-generational aspect of his borrowed analogy. By citing the Lucretian verse he indirectly purveys his own insight into what is required in any serious agenda of political renewal for postcolonial Martinique: the older generation, which he embodies, must ultimately yield the arena to the younger. In his own words, "For fifty years I did my best in the service of others, and it was time to pass the torch to another generation. I left politics the way I entered it, with the same innocence."[14] Whatever judgment posterity may eventually pass on Aimé Césaire's protracted career as an elected politician – a career he has always seen as incidental to his role as a seminal thinker – it is certain that his exquisite poetry has earned him a well deserved place in the canon of major twentieth-century writers.

Notes

PREFACE

1 There is as yet no full-scale, authoritative biography of Césaire. A certain core of basic information about his life may be put together from such disparate (and occasionally contradictory) sources as Kesteloot (1962), Ngal (1975), Delas (1991), Toumson and Henry-Valmore (1993) (hereafter "T-H").

2 My translation. The source of the citation is Césaire's preface to the Italian edition of *Les Armes miraculeuses* (see "Al lettore italiano" in Césaire [1962b]. The Italian original reads, "Ho l'abitudine di dire che non ho biografia. E veramente, leggendo le mie poesie, il lettore saprà di me tutto quello che vale la pena di sapere, e certamente piú di quanto io stesso non sappia."

3 Citations of Hale are also accompanied by the author's catalogue number (e.g. Hale 48/105).

INTRODUCTION

1 Cited in T-H, p. 214.

I FROM ISLAND TO METROPOLIS: THE MAKING OF A POET

1 See T-H, pp. 24–25. I owe many of the details in what follows to their succinct but informative account, which supplements at several points the earlier biographical sketch by Ngal (1975).

2 Cited by T-H, p. 26.

3 An example is the start of the poem *Ode to Guinea* where a sequence of solemn oaths reaches its point of culmination in the nostalgic conjuring up of a telluric maternal presence. See Davis (1984), pp. 96–100.

4 It is plausible to posit such an intra-psychic tension without going to the extreme of Césaire's most polemical critic, the

contemporary Martinican writer Raphael Confiant, who excoriates his spiritual father on what he calls the "assimilationist paradox" (see Confiant [1993], pp. 86–93; 125–129).

5 Mudimbé (1988) *passim*.

6 For a general, and largely sympathetic, appreciation of Frobenius see Jahn (1974). A more sober, professional critique of Frobenius' methods and theories can be found in the review article on his earlier book *Und Afrika sprach* by the eminent American anthropologist Robert Lowie (1913).

7 An enthusiastic insider's account of the impact of the German ethnologist on Césaire's circle of friends is provided by Senghor (1973).

8 Ngal (1975) goes further than all other critics in seeing a textual dependence on Frobenian formulations as pervasive in the diction of *Cahier*. His exaggerations are trenchantly challenged by Delas (1991, p.16) among others.

9 Césaire (1971) [1968], p. 75.

10 *Tropiques* 2 (July 1941). Compare also the remarks of Irele (1994), p. xxiv; Kesteloot (1975), pp. 63–82.

11 All six issues were reprinted by Editions J.-M. Place in 1992. For details on this and other student periodicals, see the fundamental work of Kesteloot (1975), pp. 53–109.

12 The review, which saw only a single issue, borrowed its title from a 1926 surrealist pamphlet by André Breton. An English version of this text ("Legitimate Defence") is included in Breton (1978), pp. 31–42. For a retrospective glance at its significance by one of its original editors, see Menil (1979).

13 For full text, translation and exegesis of this poem, "Dead at Dawn" (*Mort à l'aube*), see Davis (1984), pp. 48–51.

14 On this score see the useful but cryptic accounts of Ngal (1975), pp. 62–64 and T-H, pp. 66–69. Césaire's marked reticence concerning his private life has, for better or worse, kept the full details of its onset in obscurity.

15 Erikson (1968), p. 134. The context of the citation is the subsection "Adolescence" of the chapter "The Life Cycle: Epigenesis of Identity."

16 Originally delivered as a paper at a Philosophy congress held in Haiti, and subsequently published in modified form in the review *Tropiques* 12 (January 1945), pp. 157–170. See further Hale 44/38.

17 This is the terrain mapped out in the pioneering study of Arnold (1981). An extensive exploration of Césaire's poetics in relation to nineteenth- and twentieth-century French poets, in particular, is to be found in Mouralis (1979).

18 Clifford (1988), pp. 117–151.
19 See Goldwater (1967), pp. 9–14; Clifford (1988), pp. 138–141. For an insightful critique of the Western artists' appropriation of the primitive (e.g. Picasso's landmark painting *Les Demoiselles d'Avignon*) see the insightful discussion "The 'Primitive' Unconscious of Modern Art, or White Skin Black Masks" in Foster (1985), pp.181–208.
20 It began life as "Reply to Depestre, Haitian Poet (Elements of an *ars poetica*)" ("Réponse à Depestre poète haitien (éléments d'un art poétique")) in 1955; was re-named "Brazilian Letter" (Lettre brésilienne) in a 1973 version and, finally, "The verb 'to maroon'" ("Le verbe marronner") in the *OC* edition of three years later, which also bore a dedication to René Depestre. On this evolution see Hale 55/206.

2 EXPLORING RACIAL SELVES: "JOURNAL OF A HOMECOMING"

1 See Breton (1971) [1944]. The full text of Breton's glowing tribute ("Un grand poète noir," "A great black poet") is reproduced in the Bordas edition (Paris, 1947).
2 Hale 39/2. See further Hale (1981); Pestre de Almeida (1984); E-S (Introduction).
3 Borges (1992) [1932], p. 1136.
4 A substantial extract from the poem (dedicated to André Breton) appeared in the pages of the journal *Tropiques* in 1942 and was later incorporated, with modifications, into the final text. Since this *Tropiques* segment bore the intriguing title "En guise de manifeste littéraire" ("By way of a literary manifesto") it furnishes a welcome signpost for the interpreter who is interested in clues to that elusive critical grail, the "intention of the author."
5 Throughout this book, all citations of Césaire's lyric poems follow the text of M-C, except in the case of *Cahier*. The problem of the lineation of *Cahier* is a notorious crux that has vexed authors (see Davis [1984], pp. 24–25). My departures from the lineation of M-C conform to that of E-S, who claim to have verified their "corrections" with Césaire himself (see E-S, p. 401).
6 Hale 44/38 documents the transmission of this important text, which may be examined in full in the edition of Kesteloot & Kotchy (1973), pp. 112–126.
7 Matthews (1969), p. 8.
8 Cited in Hale 68/400.
9 Despite the misleading comma in the original, the verb "presage"

functions, in my reading, as a "performative" in the expression "that I presage beautiful" ("que je prophétise, belle").

10 Césaire (1973) [1966], p. 103. Sartre's lucid but controversial analysis (Sartre 1948) views négritude as an antithetical stage in an historical dialectic à la Hegel – to be superseded eventually by a synthesis.

11 On the pseudo-derivation of the neologism *verrition* from the Latin verb *vertere* ("to sweep") see E-S, p. 26. Clifford (1988), pp. 175–177 contains an interesting attempt to contextualize the enigmatic vocable.

12 Césaire (1971) [1968], p. 78. The English translation I cite is by Lloyd King. For the publication history of this interview, see Hale 68/400 and 68/401.

3 INVENTING A LYRIC VOICE: THE FORGING OF "MIRACLE WEAPONS"

1 Césaire (1962).

2 The title *Corps perdu* is literally translated "Lost Body." It may contain a concealed wordplay, however, which I have attempted to suggest in my free translation: the French expression "à corps perdu" signifies "at breakneck speed". The elision of the preposition *à* creates a phantom that is not completely exorcized.

3 Delivered at Yale University a few years after the war: Breton (1948), p. 76.

4 Paz (1986) [1967] p. 75.

5 Breton (1971) [1944] pp. 9–11.

6 Kesteloot (1962) in the series Poètes d'Aujourd'hui.

7 Césaire, Suzanne (1943), pp. 14–18.

8 A recent conspicuous exception to the general neglect is Ronnie Scharfman's imaginative appreciation of Suzanne Césaire's contribution to the circle (Scharfman [1995]).

9 Césaire (1971 [1968]), on which see Hale 68/400 and 68/401d.

10 The prologue – a founding document of magic realism – is available in the original Spanish in Carpentier (1974) [1949]. English translation is reproduced, with slight modification, from Davis (1984), p. 10.

11 Alexis (1956), pp. 245–271. Note, however, the Haitian's strenuous efforts to reconcile magic realism with Marxist-Leninist social realism.

12 Césaire (1971) [1968], p. 77.

13 Excerpted in Hale 44/32.

14 E.g. the poem "Lettre de Bahia-de-tous-les-saints" ("Letter from

Bahia-of-all-saints") published in the collection *Noria* (M-C, pp. 475–476).

15 Space does not permit us to try to present the longer poems in the collection, such as "The Thorough-breds" ("Les purs-sang") or the afore-mentioned "Batouque" (for an interesting analysis of the latter see Kesteloot & Kotchy [1973], pp. 73–95). The lengthy, quasi-dramatic poem "And the Dogs Kept Quiet" ("Et les chiens se taisaient"), which rounds off the volume, is discussed below in ch. 5.

16 On this ephemeral journal see Breton (1978), pp. 84–86.

17 Fouchet (1976), pp. 161–180.

18 Césaire (1945–1946).

19 The poem is from the volume *moi, laminaire . . .* , discussed below (ch. 6).

20 Fouchet (1976), p. 23.

21 Paul Celan's German translation of the poem highlights the possible ambiguity of *marais*: singular or plural? See Celan (1983), p. 757. I owe my acquaintance with this translation to Leonard Olschner of Cornell University.

22 Apollinaire (1965), p. 314.

23 Breton (1972).

24 Copies of this Havana limited edition are extremely rare (only 300 autographed copies were originally made).

25 Apollinaire (1965), p. 32.

4 LYRIC REGISTERS: FROM "SUN CUT THROAT" TO "CADASTER"

1 Césaire (1956c), p. 15.

2 Leiris (1955), p. 189.

3 Condé (1978), p. 16.

4 I am grateful to Abiola Irele for having reminded me of this all-important factor. See Irele (1994), pp. xxxiv–xxxv; T-H, pp. 198–206.

5 Cited in T-H, p. 209.

6 Cited in Hale 46/57. Translation mine.

7 See his foreword to Césaire (1956b). Translation mine.

8 Césaire (1971) [1968], p. 74.

9 Césaire (1956c), p. 15.

10 Césaire (1956c), p. 10.

11 For a retrospective view of *Présence Africaine* and an assessment of its various roles since its founding, see Mudimbé (1992).

12 Césaire (1956a), p. 1367.

13 Césaire (1956b), p. 194.

14 Césaire (1945) [1944], p. 157.
15 Brathwaite (1967).
16 Arendt (1964).
17 Hale 60/280.
18 His testimony is quoted in Nathan (1967) p. 5: "Il aurait pu préparer l'agrégation de lettres, naturellement, mais tout aussi bien l'agrégation de grammaire ou de philosophie, d'histoire et de géographie, d'anglais et d'italien. Je me rappelle, *il lisait Dante dans le texte*." ("He would have been able to undertake the *agrégation* in Literature, naturally, but also in Grammar or Philosophy, History and Geography, English and Italian. I recall, he used to read Dante in the original.") Author's emphases.
19 Césaire (1960).
20 Compare Hale 20/280.
21 The cultural origin of the horse metaphor may perhaps be located in the Haitian Vodun conception of the possessed person as a horse (*cheval*) whom the god "mounts" (consult Métraux [1959], pp. 120–121). For the motif compare the poems "Saison âpre" (M-C, p. 333): "esprit sauvage cheval de la tornade . . . en moi tu henniras cette heure" ("spirit wild horse of the tornado . . . in me you will whinny this moment") and "Les pur-sangs" (M-C, p. 71): "les cent pur sangs hennissant du soleil / parmi la stagnation" ("the hundred thoroughbreds whinnying from the sun / amid the stagnation").

5 THE TURN TO POETIC DRAMA

1 Carpentier (1974) [1949], p. 15.
2 The larger sentence from which I excerpt the phrase contains an untranslatable soundplay on *vers*: "et vers le simple silence lancez votre navette faite de vers somptueux."
3 Césaire's modernist dimension is the central topic of Arnold (1981) *passim*.
4 On the alterations, consult Pestre de Almeida (1979); Hale 46/56.
5 Pestre de Almeida (1979).
6 Herington (1986), p. 94.
7 This re-working of both techniques and themes of ancient Greek drama is, of course, a widespread phenomenon shared by many prominent twentieth-century French playwrights, regardless of ideological orientation (e.g. Anouilh, Giraudoux, Sartre). Césaire's use of Aeschylean motifs may owe something to this tradition.

8 The pattern is demonstrably pre-Greek and has been described most memorably in J. G. Frazer's classic, though now out of date, cross-cultural study, *Adonis, Attis, Osiris* (Frazer [1914]).

9 Consult Davis (1984), pp. 109–112; Arnold (1990), pp. xx–xxii.

10 Compare the poem, "Dit d'errance" ("Lay of the Wanderer"), lines 48–55, (M-C, p. 239).

11 Camus (1951) and (1950).

12 *La Tragédie du roi Christophe* (1963), *Une Saison au Congo* (1966) and *Une Tempête* (1968).

13 Translation mine. The parallels (and divergences) between magic realism and surrealism are discussed in Davis (1984), pp. 9–15.

14 Harris (1973), pp. 113–117.

15 Césaire (1994b), p. 61.

16 James (1963). Singham (1970) contains a penetrating analysis of this work.

17 Price-Mars (1960), pp. 11–84.

18 Compare Delas (1991), pp. 99–100.

19 Césaire (1962a [1960]), pp. 282–283.

20 Singham (1968) uses these terms in his classic monograph on Geary's Grenada.

21 Geertz (1972), pp. 1–37; Antoine (1984), pp. 9–11.

22 For the implications of the trope in its dramatic context see Conteh-Morgan (1983).

23 It is a wry testimony to Césaire's reception in the Antilles that this name, of ancient Roman origin, has been adopted by the contemporary Haitian writer Jean Metellus.

24 Cited in Harris (1973), p. 86.

25 The incident is mentioned in T-H, pp. 194–198.

26 Cited in T-H, p. 196 (with note 68); see also Hale 66/372. With Césaire's portrayal of the Congolese leader compare the perceptive essay by Sartre (1963).

27 See Hale 67/388.

28 For details on the historical shipwreck (and miraculous deliverance), as well as the involvement of Shakespeare's patrons, consult Orgel (1987), p. 32.

29 E.g. Mannoni (1950); Lamming (1992) [1960], pp. 98–117: Rodó 1967 [1900].

6 THE RETURN TO LYRIC: "ME, LAMINARIA . . . "

1 Césaire (1994a), p. 60.
2 See T-H, pp. 179–185.

3 The claim is made by Césaire himself, as related in T-H, p. 210.

4 See T-H, pp. 202–206.

5 Four poems from the *Noria* group were excluded from the new collection. They include *le verbe marroner* discussed above, ch. 1, pp. 15–19.

6 For explorations of this polysemy and its ramifications see Toumson (1984); Arnold (1990).

7 For a general discussion of the significance of the collection, see the interview with Maximin (Césaire [1983]).

8 See Christ (1993) [1975].

9 Richly explored in Prieto (1993).

10 Martin (1993) testifies to this re-valuation: it brings together in one volume an English translation, based on a critical edition, of Asturias's enigmatic *magnum opus Men of Maize* and, as an important pendant, a series of critical essays and appreciations by eminent scholars and creative writers.

11 See Harss/Dohmann (1993), pp. 420–421.

12 Cited in Prieto (1993), p. 30.

13 Cited in Martin, p. xiv. In another famous formulation (made in a 1967 essay), Dorfman stated that he considerered *Men of Maize* to be "the fountainhead and backbone of all that is being written in our continent today."

14 See Sims (1987).

15 Césaire (1989), p. 67. I have reproduced the interviewer's translation with the sole removal of a typographical error in the printing of the name Mantonica.

EPILOGUE

1 *De Rerum Natura* 2.78, cited by Césaire in the Latin original on the occasion of his speech announcing his retirement from politics (see further below, note 12).

2 By the publishing house Editions du Seuil.

3 Césaire (1978).

4 See my discusssion above, pp. 60–61.

5 See Dash (1995), pp. 126–154.

6 Césaire (1956b), pp. 202–203.

7 For an excellent account of the debate between competing ideologies, see Burton (1992).

8 For a balanced yet critical view of Césaire's amibivalent political stances, see Armet (1973).

9 Confiant (1993), pp. 245–304.

10 Césaire (1989), p. 49.

11 My source for information (anecdotal and otherwise) regarding this momentous event is T-H, pp. 213–214.

12 T-H include the Lucretius citation (*De Rerum Natura* 2.79) in their narrative (p. 213), but they inadvertently misquote the Latin text in printing the unmetrical "quasi cursores *lampades vitae* [*sic*] tradunt."

13 The Latin passage (*De Rerum Natura* 2.75–79) reads: "sic rerum summa novatur / semper, et inter se mortales mutua vivunt: / augescunt aliae gentes, aliae minuuntur, / inque brevi spatio mutantur saecla animantum / et quasi cursores vitai lampada tradunt." Lucretius is here cited in the edition of Rouse and Smith (1982).

14 Césaire (1994), p. 61.

Bibliography

This bibliography makes no claim to be exhaustive. In addition to primary texts I have included a selection of basic secondary works (books and articles in French and English) that I have found especially useful in constructing my account of Césaire's artistic and political career.

BIBLIOGRAPHIES

Arnold, A. J. 1984. "Etat présent des écrits sur Aimé Césaire. Bibliographie sélective et raisonnée." In *Césaire 70*. M. a. M. Ngal and M. Steins, eds. Paris: Editions Silex.

Case, Frederick Ivor. 1973. *Aimé Césaire: Bibliographie*. Toronto: Manna.

Delas, Daniel. 1991. "'Bibliographie raisonnée." In *Aimé Césaire*. Paris: Hachette, 203–217.

Hale, Thomas. 1978. *Ecrits d'Aimé Césaire: bibliographie commentée*. Etudes Françaises Vol. 14.3–4. Montreal: Les Presses de l'Université de Montréal.

WORKS BY CESAIRE

EDITIONS OF COLLECTED WORKS

1976. *Œuvres complètes*. Vol. 1 (*Poésie*), Vol. 2 (*Théâtre*), Vol. 3 (*Œuvre historique et politique*). Fort-de-France: Editions Désormeaux.

1983. *Aimé Césaire: The Collected Poetry*. Clayton Eshleman and Annette Smith, trans. Berkeley/Los Angeles/London: University of California Press.

1994. *La Poésie*. Daniel Maximin and Gilles Carpentier, eds. Paris: Seuil.

POETRY

1946. *Les Armes miraculeuses*. Paris: Gallimard.
1948. *Soleil cou coupé*. Paris: Editions K.
1950. *Corps perdu*. Paris: Fragrance.
1956 [1939]. *Cahier d'un retour au pays natal*. Paris: Présence Africaine.
1960. *Ferrements*. Paris: Seuil.
1961. *Cadastre*. Paris: Seuil.
1982. *moi, laminaire . . .* Paris: Seuil.

DRAMA

1956. *Et les chiens se taisaient*. Paris: Présence Africaine.
1969. *Une Tempête*. Paris: Seuil.
1970 [1963]. *La Tragédie du roi Christophe*. Paris: Présence Africaine.
1974 [1966]. *Une Saison au Congo*. Paris: Seuil.

ESSAYS, SPEECHES, MONOGRAPHS

1941. "Introduction à la poésie nègre américaine." *Tropiques* 2, 37–42.
1942a. "Introduction au folklore martiniquais" (co-author René Ménil). *Tropiques* 4, 7–11.
1942b. "Vues sur Mallarmé." *Tropiques* 5, 53–61.
1943a. "Isidore Ducasse Comte de Lautréamont." *Tropiques* 6–7, 10–15.
1943b. "Maintenir la poésie." *Tropiques* 8–9, 7–8.
1944. "Introduction à un conte de Lydia Cabrera." *Tropiques* 10, 11.
1945 [1944]. "Poésie et connaissance." *Tropiques* 12, 157–170.
1945–46. "Wifredo Lam." *Cahiers d'Art* 20–21, 357.
1948. "Victor Schoelcher et l'abolition de l'esclavage." Introduction to *Esclavage et colonisation* by V. Schoelcher. Paris: Presses Universitaires de France.
1951a. Preface to *Végétations de clarté* by René Depestre. Paris: Seghers.
1951b. Preface to *Les Bâtards* by B. Juminer. Paris: Présence Africaine.
1955a [1950]. *Discours sur le colonialisme*. Paris: Présence Africaine.
1955b. "Sur la poésie nationale." *Présence Africaine* 4, 39–41.
1956a. "La mort des colonies." *Les Temps modernes* 123, 1366–1370.
1956b. "Culture et colonisation." *Présence Africaine* 8–10, 190–205.
1956c. *Lettre à Maurice Thorez*. Paris: Présence Africaine.
1959a. "L'homme de culture et ses responsabilités (Deuxième Congrès des Ecrivains et Artistes Noirs)." *Présence Africaine* 24–25, 116–122.
1959b. "La Martinique telle qu'elle est." *French Review* 53.2, 183–189.

1959–60. "La pensée politique de Sékou Touré." *Présence Africaine* 2, 65–73.

1961. "Crise dans les départements d'Outre-Mer ou crise de la départementalisation." *Présence Africaine* 36, 109–111.

1962a [1960]. *Toussaint Louverture: La Révolution Française et le problème colonial*. Paris: Présence Africaine.

1962b. "Al lettore italiano." In *Le armi miracolose*. Anna Vizioli and Franco De Poli, trans. Parma: Guanda.

1963. "Hommages à Jean Amrouche." *Présence Africaine* 4, 187–196.

1969. Preface to *Les Antilles décolonisées* by Daniel Guérin. Paris: Présence Africaine.

1973a [1966]. "Discours sur l'art Africain." *Etudes Littéraires* 6.1, 100–109.

1973b [1972]. "Société et littérature dans les Antilles." *Etudes Littéraires* 6.1, 9–20.

ENGLISH TRANSLATIONS OF CESAIRE'S WORKS

POETRY

Cahier d'un retour au pays natal

Abel, Lionel and Goll, Ivan. 1947. *Memorandum on My Martinique*. New York: Brentano.

Berger, John and Bostock, Anna. 1969. *Return to My Native Land*. Baltimore: Penguin Books.

Snyder, Emile. 1971. *Return to My Native Land*. Paris: Présence Africaine.

Lyric (exclusive of Cahier)

Davis, Gregson. 1984. *Non-Vicious Circle: Twenty Poems of Aimé Césaire*. Translated with Critical Introduction and Notes. Stanford: University Press.

Eshleman, Clayton and Smith, Annette. 1983. *Aimé Césaire: The Collected Poetry*. Berkeley/Los Angeles/London: University of California Press.

1990. *Aimé Césaire: Lyric and Dramatic Poetry: 1946–82*. Berkeley/Los Angeles/London: University of California Press.

Eshleman, Clayton and Kelly, Dennis. 1966. *State of the Union*. (Poems from *Les Armes miraculeuses, Cadastre* and *Ferrements*.) Bloomington: Caterpillar Press.

Snyder, Emile and Upson, Sanford. 1973. *Cadastre*. New York: Third Press.

DRAMA

Manheim, Ralph. 1969. *The Tragedy of King Christophe: A Play by Aimé Césaire*. New York: Grove Press.
1968. *A Season in the Congo: A Play by Aimé Césaire*.
Miller, Richard. 1985. *A Tempest*. New York: Ubu Repertory Theater Publications.

ESSAYS, SPEECHES, MONOGRAPHS

Arnold, James. 1990. "Poetry and Knowledge." In Eshleman and Smith: *Aimé Césaire: Lyric and Dramatic Poetry: 1946–82*.
Pinkham, Joan. 1972. *Discourse on Colonialism*. New York and London: Monthly Review Press.
Letter to Maurice Thorez. 1957. Paris: Présence Africaine.

SELECT INTERVIEWS

1960. "Aimé Césaire et les nègres sauvages." With Jeanine Cahen. *Afrique Action*, Nov. 21, 1960. 23.
1971 [1968]. "Interview with René Depestre." *Savacou* 5, 77–86.
1973. "Entretien avec Aimé Césaire." With Lilyan Kesteloot. In *Aimé Césaire, l'homme et l'œuvre*. Lilyan Kesteloot and Bartélemy Kotchy, eds. Paris: Présence Africaine, 227–243.
1978. "Entretien avec Aimé Césaire." With Jacqueline Leiner. In *Tropiques* 1, v–xxiv. Paris: Editions Jean-Michel Place.
1983. "Aimé Césaire: La poésie, parole essentielle" With Daniel Maximin. *Présence Africaine* 126, 7–23.
1989. "It is through poetry that one copes with solitude: an interview with Aimé Césaire." With Charles. H. Rowell. *Callaloo* 12.1, 47–67.
1994a. "Le long cri d'Aimé Césaire." With Gilles Anquetil. *Le Nouvel Observateur* 17–24 février, 60–62.
1994b. "Un entretien avec Aimé Césaire." With Frédéric Bobin. *Le Monde* 2 avril, 2.

WORKS ABOUT CESAIRE

COLLECTIONS OF ARTICLES

Aimé Césaire. Ed. Lilyan Kesteloot. *Esprit Createur* 32.1. 1991 (Special issue).
Aimé Césaire ou l'athanor d'un alchimiste: Actes du premier colloque

international sur l'œuvre littéraire d'Aimé Césaire. Paris: Editions Caribbéennes. 1987.

Soleil éclaté: Mélanges offerts à Aimé Césaire à l'occasion de son soixante-dixième anniversaire par une équipe internationale de chercheurs. Ed. Jacqueline Leiner. Tübingen: Gunter Narr Verlag. 1984.

Césaire 70. M. a. M. Ngal and M. Steins, eds., Paris: Editions Silex. 1984.

ON CESAIRE'S POETRY

Arnold, A. J. 1981. *Modernism and Negritude: The Poetry and Poetics of Aimé Césaire*. Cambridge, Mass.: Harvard University Press.

1990. Introduction to *Lyric and Dramatic Poetry 1946–82 by Aimé Césaire*. Charlottesville, Virginia: University Press of Virginia.

Breton, André. 1971 [1944]. "Un grand poète noir." Preface to *Cahier d'un retour au pays natal*. Paris: Présence Africaine.

Cailler, Bernadette. 1976. *Proposition poétique: une lecture de l'œuvre d'Aimé Césaire*. Sherbrooke: Editions Naaman.

Combé, Dominique. 1993. *Aimé Césaire: Cahier d'un retour au pays natal*. Etudes Littéraires. Paris: Presses Universitaires de France.

Condé, Maryse. 1978. *Cahier d'un retour au pays natal: analyse critique*. Paris: Hatier.

Davis, Gregson. 1977. "Towards a 'Non-Vicious Circle': The Lyric of Aimé Césaire in English." *Stanford French Review* 1.1, 135–146.

Hale, Thomas. 1981. "Structural Dynamics in a Third World Classic: Aimé Césaire's *Le cahier d'un retour au pays natal*." *Yale French Studies* 53 (1976), 163–174.

1981. "Two Decades, Four Versions: The Evolution of Aimé Césaire's *Cahier d'un retour au pays natal*." In *When the Drumbeat Changes*. Carolyn Parker and Stephen Arnold, eds. Washington: Three Continents.

Hountondji, Victor M. 1993. *Le Cahier d'Aimé Césaire: Evénement littéraire et facteur de révolution: essai*. Paris: L'Harmattan.

Hurley, Anthony. 1992. "Link and Lance: Aspects of Poetic Function in Césaire's *Cadastre* – an Analysis of Five Poems." *L'Esprit Créateur* 32.1, 54–68.

Irele, Abiola. 1967. "Aimé Césaire: An Approach to his Poetry." In *Introduction to African Literature*. Ulli Bayer, ed. London: Longmans, 59–68.

1984. "Les obscures espérances ou l'imagerie de l'œuvre poétique d'Aimé Césaire." In *Soleil éclaté*. Tübingen: Gunter Narr Verlag 187–215.

1987. "Les royaumes de la colère, ou les voies de la révolte dans l'œuvre poétique d'Aimé Césaire." In *Aimé Césaire, ou l'athanor d'un alchimiste*. Paris: Editions Caribbéennes, 63–86.

1994. *Aimé Césaire: Cahier d'un retour au pays natal*. (Critical Introduction, French text, English Commentary). Ibadan, Nigeria: New Horn Press.

Kesteloot, Lilyan and Bartélemy Kotchy. 1973. *Aimé Césaire, L'homme et l'œuvre*. Paris: Présence Africaine.

Kesteloot, Lilyan. 1982. *Comprendre le Cahier d'un Retour au Pays Natal d'Aimé Césaire*. Issy les Moulineaux: Editions Saint Paul.

"Politique, poétique et quête mystique dans la poésie d'Aimé Césaire." *L'Esprit Créateur* 32.1, 7–15.

Marteau, Pierre. 1961. "A propos de *Cadastre* d'Aimé Césaire." *Présence Africaine* 37, 125–135.

Mouralis, Bernard. 1979. "Césaire et la poésie française." *Revue des Sciences Humaines* 48.176 (oct.–dec.), 125–152.

Ngaté, Jonathan. 1977. "*Mauvais Sang* de Rimbaud et *Cahier d'un retour au pays natal* de Césaire: la poésie au service de la révolution." *Cahiers Césairiens* 3 (1977), 25–32.

1992. "Aimé Césaire on Aimé Césaire: A Complementary Reading of 'Crevasses' (from *moi, laminaire . . .*)." *L'Esprit Créateur* 32.1, 41–53.

Pestre de Almeida, Lilian. 1984. "Les versions successives du *Cahier d'un retour au pays natal*." In *Césaire 70*. Paris: Editions Silex.

1993. "Aimé Césaire, ancien marin devenu paysan: lecture des derniers poèmes césairiens dans leur rapport à l'oralité." In *Carrefour de Cultures: Melanges offerts à Jacqueline Leiner*, 503–523. Tübingen: Gunter Narr.

Sartre, Jean-Paul. 1948. "Orphée Noir." In *Anthologie de la nouvelle poésie nègre et malgache de langue française*. Léopold S. Senghor, ed. Paris: Presses Universitaires de France, ix–xliv.

Scharfman, Ronnie Leah. 1980. *Engagement and the Language of the Subject in the poetry of Aimé Césaire*. Gainesville: University Press of Florida.

Songolo, Aliko. 1977. "*Cadastre* et *Ferrements* de Césaire: une nouvelle poétique pour une nouvelle politique." *L'Esprit Créateur* 17.2, 143–158.

1985. *Aimé Césaire, une poétique de la découverte*. Paris: L'Harmattan.

Toumson, Roger. 1984. "Situation de *moi, laminaire . . .* " In *Césaire 70*. Paris: Editions Silex.

Walker, Keith Louis. 1979. *La cohésion poétique de l'œuvre Césairienne*. Tübingen: Gunter Narr Verlag.

ON CESAIRE'S DRAMA

Antoine, Régis, ed. 1984. *La Tragédie du roi Christophe d'Aimé Césaire*. Paris: Bordas.

Arnold, A. James. 1978. "Césaire and Shakespeare: Two Tempests." *Comparative Literature* 30.3, 236–248.

Bailey, Marianne. 1987. "Césaire: père du théâtre africain et fils de la tradition liturgique. Le rôle de l'hiérophant-metteur en scène chez Césaire." In *Aimé Césaire ou l'Athanor d'un alchimiste*. Paris: Editions Caribbéennes. 239–257.

    1993. "Mythopoesis: an Interpretation of *La Tragédie du roi Christophe* by Aimé Césaire and *Death and the King's Horseman* by Wole Soyinka." In *Carrefour de Culture: Melanges offerts à Jacqueline Leiner* (Etudes Littéraires Françaises 55). Ed. Régis Antoine. Tübingen: Gunter Narr, 481–450.

Benamou, Michel. 1975. "Demiurgic Imagery in Césaire's Theatre." *Présence Africaine* 93, 165–177.

Conteh-Morgan, John. 1983. "A Note on the Image of the Builder in Aimé Césaire's *La Tragédie du roi Christophe*." *The French Review* 57.2, 224–230.

    1994. *Theatre and Drama in Francophone Africa: A Critical Introduction*. Cambridge University Press.

Dayan, Joan. 1992. "Playing Caliban: Césaire's *Tempest*." *Arizona Quarterly* 48.4, 124–145.

Hale, Thomas. 1985. "Dramaturge et public: la nature interactive du théâtre d'Aimé Césaire." In *Aimé Césaire, ou l'athanor d'un alchimiste:* Paris: Editions Caribbéennes.

Hamner, Robert. 1992. "Dramatizing the New World's African King: O'Neill, Walcott and Césaire on Christophe." *Journal of West Indian Literature* (Bridgetown, Barbados) 5.1–2, 30–47.

Harris, Rodney E. 1973. *L'Humanisme dans le théâtre d'Aimé Césaire: Etude de trois tragédies*. Ottawa: Editions Naaman.

Irele, Abiola. 1968. "Postcolonial Negritude: The Political Plays of Aimé Césaire." *West Africa* 264.3 (Jan.), 100–101.

Lemarchand, Jacques. 1965. "La Tragédie du Roi Christophe à L'Odéon." *Le Figaro Littéraire*, 23–29 septembre, 12.

Little, Roger. 1994. "Questions of Intertextuality in *La Tragédie du roi Christophe*." *French Studies: A Quarterly Review* 48.4, 439–451.

Mbom, Clément. 1979. *Le Théâtre d'Aimé Césaire ou la primauté de l'universalité humaine*. Paris: Nathan.

    1984. "Aimé Césaire, poète ou dramaturge." In *Soleil éclaté*. Jacqueline Leiner, ed. Tübingen: Gunter Narr Verlag, 261–272.

1987. "La femme dans le théâtre d'Aimé Césaire." In *Aimé Césaire ou l'athanor d'un alchimiste*. Paris: Editions Caribbéennes, 223–237.

Moreau, Alain. 1984. "Eschyle et Césaire: rencontres et influences dans *Et les chiens se taisaient*." In *Soleil éclaté*. Ed. Jacqueline Leiner. Tübingen: Gunter Narr Verlag, 285–302.

Nixon, Rob. 1987. "Caribbean and African Appropriations of *The Tempest*." *Critical Inquiry* 13.3, 557–578.

Ormond, Jacqueline. 1967. "Héros de l'impossible et de l'absolu." *Les Temps Modernes* 23, 1049–1073.

Owusu-Sarpong, Albert. 1987. *Le temps historique dans l'œuvre théâtral d'Aimé Césaire*. Sherbrooke: Naaman.

Pestre de Almeida, Lilian. 1978. "Christophe cuisinier, entre nature et culture." *Présence Africaine* 105–106, 230–249.

1982. "Le comique et le tragique dans le théâtre d'Aimé Césaire." *Présence Africaine* 121–122, 180–192.

Toumson, Roger. 1981. *Trois Calibans*. Havana: Edición Casa de las Américas.

1994. "Aimé Césaire dramaturge: le théâtre comme nécessité." *Cahiers de L'Association Internationale des Etudes Françaises* 46, 213–229.

Williams, Sandra. 1970. "La renaissance de la tragédie dans l'œuvre dramatique d'Aimé Césaire." *Présence Africaine* 76, 63–81.

Wolitz, Seth. 1969. "The Hero of Négritude in the Theater of Aimé Césaire." *Kentucky Romance Quarterly* 16 (1969), 195–208.

PERIODICALS

Cahiers Césairiens 1–4. 1974, 1975, 1977, 1980. Pennsylvania State University.

Legitime Défense. 1932. Reissued 1979: Editions Jean-Michel Place. Paris.

Présence Africaine. 1947– . Paris.

Revue du Monde Noir 1–6. nov. 1931–juin 1932. Re-issued 1971: Kraus Reprint. Nendeln, Liechtenstein.

Tropiques 1–14. 1941–1945. Re-issued 1978: Editions Jean-Michel Place. 2 vols. Paris.

VVV [*Poetry, Plastic Arts, Anthropology, Sociology, Psychology*] 1–4. June 1942–Feb. 1944. New York.

GENERAL

Alexis, Jacques. 1956. "Du réalisme merveilleux des Haïtiens." *Présence Africaine* 8–10 (June–Nov.), 245–271.

Apollinaire, Guillaume. 1965. *Œuvres poétiques*. Marcel Adéma and Michel Décaudin, eds. Paris: Gallimard.

Arendt, Hannah. 1964. *Eichmann in Jerusalem: A Report on the Banality of Evil*. New York: Viking Press.

Armet, Auguste. 1973. "Aimé Césaire, homme politique." *Etudes Littéraires* 6.1, 81–96.

Audoin, Philippe. 1973. *Les Surréalistes*. Paris: Seuil.

Balandier, Georges. 1990. "La Mort de Michel Leiris: La reconnaissance de l'autre." *Le Monde Hebdomadaire* (3 octobre), p. 16.

Bastide, Roger. 1961. "Variations sur la Négritude." *Présence Africaine* 36, 7–17.

Bernabé, J., Confiant, R. and Chamoiseau, P. 1989. *Eloge de la Créolité*. Paris: Editions Gallimard.

Blanchard, Marc, ed. 1992. *On Leiris*. Yale French Studies 81 (Special Issue).

Borges, Jorge Luis. 1992 [1932]. "Las versiones homéricas." *Publications of the Modern Language Association of America* 107.5 (5 Oct. 1992), 1134–1142.

Brathwaite, Edward. 1967. *Rights of Passage*. London: Oxford University Press.

Breton, André. 1948. "The Situation of Surrealism between the Two Wars." *Yale French Studies* 1.2 (Fall–Winter 1948), 67–78.

   1972. *Martinique charmeuse de serpents*. Paris: J.-J. Pauvert.

   1978. *What is Surrealism? Selected Writings*. Franklin Rosemont, ed. New York: Monad Press.

Burton, Richard. 1992. "Towards 1992: Political-Cultural Assimilation and Opposition in Contemporary Martinique." *French Cultural Studies* 3, 61–86.

Camus, Albert. 1951. *L'Homme Révolté*. Paris: Gallimard.

   1950. *Les Justes*. Paris: Gallimard.

Carpentier, Alejo. 1974 [1949]. *El reino de este mundo*. Buenos Aires: América Nueva.

Celan, Paul. 1983. *Gesammelte Werke*. Vol. 4. Frankfurt-am-Main: Suhrkamp Verlag.

Césaire, Suzanne. 1943. "1943: Le Surréalisme et nous." *Tropiques* 8–9 (oct. 1943), 14–18.

Chénieux-Gendron, Jacqueline. 1990 [1984]. *Surrealism*. Vivian Folkenflik, trans. New York: Columbia University Press.

Christ, Ronald. 1993 [1975]. "The Text as Translation." In *Men of Maize*. Gerald Martin, ed. Pittsburgh/London: University of Pittsburgh, 435–444.

Clifford, James. 1988. *The Predicament of Culture: Twentieth Century*

Ethnography, Literature, and Art. Cambridge/London: Harvard University Press.

Condé, Maryse. 1974. "Négritude césairienne, négritude senghorienne." *Revue de littéraire comparée* 3–4, 409–419.

Confiant, Raphaël. 1993. *Aimé Césaire: une traversée paradoxale du siècle.* Paris: Editions Stock.

Coulthard, G. R. 1961. "The French West Indian Background of négritude." *Caribbean Quarterly* 7.3 (December), 128–136.

Dash, J. Michael. 1995. *Edouard Glissant* (Cambridge Studies in African and Caribbean Literature). Cambridge University Press.

Davis, Gregson. 1995. "On Césaire." *Research in African Literatures* 26.2, 174–184.

Delas, Daniel. 1991. *Aimé Césaire.* Paris: Hachette.

Depestre, René. 1980. *Bonjour et adieu à la négritude.* Paris: Seghers.

Erikson, Erik H. 1968. *Identity, Youth and Crisis.* New York: W. W. Norton.

Fanon, Frantz. 1952. *Peau noire, masques blancs.* Paris: Seuil.

Foster, Hal. 1985. *Recordings: Art, Spectacle, Cultural Politics.* Seattle: Bay Press.

Fouchet, Max-Pol. 1976. *Wifredo Lam.* New York: Rizzoli.

Frazer, James. 1914. *Adonis, Attis, Osiris: Studies in the History of Oriental Religion.* 2 vols. London: Macmillan & Co.

Frutkin, Susan. 1973. *Aimé Césaire, Black Between Worlds.* Coral Gables, Florida: Center for Advanced International Studies, University of Miami, xi–66.

Geertz, Clifford. 1972. "Deep Play: Notes on the Balinese Cockfight." *Daedalus* 101 (1972), 1–37.

Gérard, Albert. 1964. "Historical Origins and Literary Destiny of Negritude." *Diogenes* 48, 14–38.

Goldwater, Robert. 1967. *Primitivism in Modern Art.* Rev. edn. New York/Toronto: Vintage Books.

Glissant, Edouard. 1956. "Aimé Césaire et la découverte du monde." *Lettres Nouvelles* 34 (Jan.), 44–54.

1981. *Le Discours antillais.* Paris: Seuil.

Guérin, Daniel. 1956. *Les Antilles décolonisées.* Paris: Présence Africaine.

Harss, Luis and Dohmann, Barbara. 1993. "The Land Where the Flowers Bloom." In *Men of Maize.* Gerald Martin, ed. Pittsburgh/London: University of Pittsburgh Press, 413–423.

Herington, John. 1986. *Aeschylus.* New Haven/London: Yale University Press.

Irele, Abiola. 1990 [1981]. *The African Experience in Literature and Ideology.* Bloomington/London: Indiana University Press.

Jahn, Janheinz. 1961. *Muntu*. London: Faber & Faber.

1974. *Leo Frobenius: The Demonic Child*. Occasional Publications of the African and Afro-American Studies Research Center. Vol. 8. Reinhard Sander, trans. Austin: University of Texas.

James, C. L. R. 1963. *The Black Jacobins: Toussaint L'Ouverture and the San Domingo Revolution*. 2nd edn. New York: Random House.

Juin, Hubert. 1956. *Aimé Césaire, poète noir*. Paris: Présence Africaine.

Kesteloot, Lilyan. 1962. *Aimé Césaire*. Series: Poètes d'Aujourd'hui No. 85. Paris: Seghers.

1975. *Les Ecrivains noirs de langue française: naissance d'une littérature*. 5th edn. Brussels: Editions de l'Université de Bruxelles.

Kunene, Mazisi. 1969. Introduction to *Aimé Césaire: Return to My Native Land*. John Berger and Anna Bostock, trans. Harmondsworth: Penguin.

Lam, Wifredo. 1970. *Wifredo Lam*. Text by Michael Leiris. New York: H. N. Abrams.

Lamming, George. 1992 [1960]. *The Pleasures of Exile*. Ann Arbor: University of Michigan.

Leiner, Jacqueline. 1980. *Imaginaire, Langage, Identité culturelle – Négritude: Afrique – Guyane – Haïti – Maghreb – Martinique*. Etudes Littéraires Françaises 10. Tübingen: Gunter Narr Verlag.

1986. "Africa and the West Indies: Two Négritudes." In *European-Language Writing in Sub-Saharan Africa*. Albert Gérard, ed. Budapest: Akadémiai Kiadó, 135–153.

1993. *Aimé Césaire: le terreau primordial*. Etudes Littéraires Françaises 56. Tübingen: Gunter Narr Verlag.

Leiris, Michel. 1955. *Contact de civilisations en Martinique et en Guadeloupe*. Paris: Gallimard.

1973. "Qui est Aimé Césaire?" In *Aimé Césaire, l'homme et l'œuvre*. Lilyan Kesteloot and Bartélemy Kotchy, eds. Paris: Présence Africaine, 7–16.

Lowie, Robert. 1913. Review of *Und Afrika sprach* by Leo Frobenius. *Current Anthropological Literature* 2, 87–91.

Mannoni, Octave. 1950. *Psychologie de la Colonisation*. Paris: Seuil.

Martin, Gerald, ed. 1993. *Men of Maize*. Pittsburgh/London: University of Pittsburgh Press.

Matthews, J. H. 1969. *Surrealist Poetry in France*. Syracuse, New York: Syracuse University Press.

Memmi, Albert. 1963. *Le Portrait du colonisé*. Montréal: Editions du Bas Canada.

Menil, René. 1979 [1932]. Preface to *Légitime Défense*. Paris: Jean-Michel Place.

Métraux, Alfred. 1959. *Voodoo in Haiti*. Trans. Hugo Charteris. New York: André Deutsch.

Michel, Jean Claude. 1982. *Les Ecrivains noirs et le Surréalisme*. Sherbrooke: Editions Namaan.

Mudimbé, V. Y., ed. 1988. *The Invention of Africa: Gnosis, Philosophy, and the Order of Knowledge*. Bloomington/London: Indiana University Press.

1992. *The Surreptitious Speech: Présence Africaine and the Politics of Otherness 1947–1987*. Chicago/London: University of Chicago Press.

Nathan, F. 1967. *Aimé Césaire, écrivain martiniquais*. Paris: Nathan.

Ngal, M. a. M. 1975. *Aimé Césaire: un homme à la recherche d'une patrie*. Dakar: Nouvelles Editions Africaines.

1971. "Chronologie de la vie d'Aimé Césaire." *Présence Francophone* 3, 163–166.

1984. "Aimé Césaire devant le grand public africain francophone." In *Césaire 70*. Paris: Editions Silex, 163–202.

Orgel, Stephen, ed. 1987. *The Tempest*. Oxford/New York: Oxford University Press.

Paz, Octavio. 1986 [1967]. "André Breton, or the Search for the Beginning." In *On Poets and Others*. Michael Schmidt, trans. New York: Seavey Books, 66–78.

Pallister, Janis. 1991. *Aimé Césaire*. New York: Twayne Publishers.

Price-Mars, Jean. 1960. *Silhouettes de nègres et de négrophiles*. Paris: Présence Africaine.

Prieto, René. 1993. *Miguel Angel Asturias's archaeology of return*. Cambridge University Press.

Rodó, José Enrique. 1967 [1900]. *Ariel*. Gordon Brotherston, ed. Cambridge University Press.

Rouse, W. H. D. and Smith, M. F. 1982. *Lucretius: De Rerum Natura*. 2nd edn. Cambridge, Mass.: Harvard University Press.

Sartre, Jean-Paul. 1956. "Le colonialisme est un système." *Les Temps modernes* 123 (mars–avril), 1371–1381.

1963. Preface to *La pensée politique de Patrice Lumumba*. Ed. Jean van Lierde. Paris: Présence Africaine.

Scharfman, Ronnie. 1995. "De grands poètes noirs: Breton rencontre les Césaire." In *Nouveau monde, autres mondes: Surréalisme & Amériques*. D. Lefort, P. Rivas and J. Chénieux-Gendron, eds. Collection Pleine Marge, 5. Paris: Lachenal & Ritter.

Senghor, Léopold Sédar. 1964. *Liberté 1: négritude et humanisme*. Paris: Seuil.

1973. "The Lessons of Leo Frobenius." In *Leo Frobenius 1873–1973: Eine Anthologie*. Eike Haberland, ed. Wiesbaden: Franz Steiner Verlag.

Sims, Lowery S. 1987. "Wifredo Lam: The Decades of the 1960s and 1970s." In *Repères: Cahiers d'art contemporain*. Paris/Zurich/New York: Galerie Maeght Lelong.

Singham, Archie. 1968. *The Hero and the Crowd in a Colonial Polity*. New Haven/London: Yale University Press.

1970. "C. L. R. James on the Black Jacobin Revolution in San Domingo." *Savacou* 1.1 (June), 82–96.

Toumson, Roger and Henry-Valmore, Simonne. 1993. *Aimé Césaire: Le nègre inconsolé*. Fort-de-France: Vents des îles.

Index

Aeschylus, 128–130, 190n7
Apollinaire, Guillaume, 14, 83–84, 89–91
Asturias, Miguel Angel, 73, 165, 172–174
Arnold, A. James, 67, 130, 186n17
assimilation, cultural, 7–8, 12
Auden, W. H., 65, 155

Bandung Conference, 99–101
Breton, André, 14, 20–21, 67–72, 78, 86, 87, 175

Cabrera, Lydia, 76, 88
Camus, Albert, 127, 136, 144
Caliban, 156–162
Carpentier, Alejo, 73–74, 126, 137–138, 174
Celan, Paul, 189n21
Césaire, Aimé
  life: childhood, 4–7; education, 5–10;
    political career, 2, 3, 62–66, 93–101,
    111, 126, 141, 163–165, 178, 183–184
  drama: 126–156; *Et les chiens se taisaient*,
    126–136; *La Tragédie du roi Christophe*,
    136–150; *Une Tempête*, 156–162; *Une
    Saison au Congo*, 150–156
  poems (volumes): *Les Armes
    miraculeuses*, 62–89; *Cadastre*, 92, 93,
    101–120, 125; *Cahier d'un retour au pays
    natal*, 13, 19, 20–61, 62, 63, 80–81, 92,
    162; *Corps perdu*, 92, 111, 112, 117,
    186n8, 188n2; *Ferrements*, 117–125;
    moi, laminaire..., 11–12, 163–177;
    Noria, 16, 163, 165, 193n5 (ch. 6);
    Soleil cou coupé, 89–91, 93, 101–111
  poems (individual): "Algues," 167–168;
    "Banal," 170–171; "Blanc à remplir
    sur la carte voyageuse du pollen,"
    104–105; "Blues de la pluie,"
    105–108; "Calendrier lagunaire,"
    168–169; "Conversation avec

Mantonica Wilson," 176; "Co
perdu," 112–113; "Ferrements
120–122; "Mémorial de Louis
Delgrès," 123–124; "Le grand
86; "Léon G. Damas: feu son
toujours," 11–12; "Le verbe
marronner," 16–19; "Magiqu
90–91, 101–104; "Mot," 113–11
"N'ayex point pitié," 82–86;
non vicieux," 125; "Quand M
Angel Asturias disparut," 17
"Quelconque," 108–111, 170;
"Spirales," 117–120; "Tam-ta
86–89; "Tam-tam II," 77–81;
"Wifredo Lam...," 81–82
  prose (discursive): "Culture et
    colonisation," 102–103, 182; *i
    sur le colonialisme*, 1, 64; *Lettre
    Maurice Thorez*, 96–98, 126; "
    des colonies," 100–101; "Poé
    connaissance," 14, 24, 103–1(
    *Toussaint Louverture: La Révol
    Française et le problème colonia*
Césaire, Suzanne, 13, 66, 71–72, 1
Clifford, James, 14–15, 188n11
Confiant, Raphaël, 180, 181, 186r
Communist Party, 16, 66, 96–98
Condé, Maryse, 94
Congress of Negro Writers and .
  99, 102–103, 111
creole: language, 179–181; cultu

Damas, Léon, 10–12, 99
Dante, 118–120, 190n18
Delgrès, Louis, 123–125
départements, 66, 93–96, 164, 182–
Depestre, René, 15–19, 72–73; 9;
Diop, Alioune, 97, 99, 100
Dorfman, Ariel, 174

Eluard, Paul, 67, 96, 124
Erikson, Erik, 13
Etiemble, René, 64
L'Etudiant Noir, 10

Fanon, Frantz, 2
Festival of Negro Arts, 137
Frobenius, Leo, 8–9, 85, 186n6, 186n8

Geertz, Clifford, 142
Glissant, Edouard, 2, 181

Haiti, 17, 33, 74–76, 126. *See also* Césaire,
    drama: *La Tragédie du roi Christophe*;
    Toussaint L'Ouverture
Hale, Thomas, 21, 110
Hartung, Hans, 112
Harlem Renaissance, 9
Hearn, Lafcadio, 124

independence, Antillean, 164–165

James, C. L. R., 139

Kesteloot, Lilyan, 70

Lam, Wifredo, 1, 77–82, 89, 165, 174–177
Légitime Défense, 10
Leiner, Jacqueline, 180, 181
Leiris, Michel, 15, 93, 99, 136
Lévi-Strauss, Claude, 87
Lucretius, 178, 183–184, 193n12, 193n13
Lumumba, Patrice, 152–156

Mallarmé, Stéphane, 14, 178
McKay, Claude, *see* Harlem Renaissance
magic realism, 73–74, 111, 174
Menil, René, 63, 70

métissage, 10, 182
Mitterrand, François, 164
Mobutu, 151, 152, 156
multiculturalism, 135–136

négritude, 6, 12–13, 20, 27, 47–51, 53,
    60–61, 148, 164, 181

Odyssey, 22, 40, 43

Parti Progressiste Martiniquais, 98, 126
Paz, Octavio, 69–70, 87
Picasso, Pablo, 1, 67, 77, 90, 111–112, 175
Péret, Benjamin, 14, 67, 78, 86–89, 102
Présence Africaine, 98–99
Price-Mars, Jean, 10, 139

Rastafarians, 107
Rimbaud, Arthur, 14, 151, 153

Sartre, Jean-Paul, 53, 99, 136, 188n10
    (ch. 2)
Sekou-Touré, 124, 127
Senghor, Léopold Sédar, 7–8, 99, 173
Shakespeare, William, 30, 147, 148, 154,
    156–162
surreal, surrealism, 25, 66–76, 84, 86, 88,
    90, 174. *See also* Breton, André;
    Péret, Benjamin; Carpentier, Alejo

Toussaint L'Ouverture, 73, 75, 126,
    139–141, 149
Tropiques, 9, 63–64, 71–72

Vodun, 17, 36–38, 73, 114–115, 122, 138, 147,
    160, 190n21

Wilson, Mantonica, 175–176